WILLIAMS
The business of Grand Prix racing

Alan Henry
Foreword by Nigel Mansell

PSL
Patrick Stephens Limited

First published in 1991
Reprinted in 1991

British Library Cataloguing-in-Publication Data
Henry, Alan
    Williams: The business of Grand Prix racing
    I. Title
    796.7

ISBN 1 85260 369 0

Printed in Great Britain by J.H. Haynes & Co. Ltd.

Patrick Stephens Limited, a member of the Haynes Publishing Group, has published authoritative, quality books for enthusiasts for more than twenty years. During that time the company has established a reputation as one of the world's leading publishers of books on aviation, maritime, military, model-making, motor cycling, motoring, motor racing, railway and railway modelling subjects. Readers or authors with suggestions for books they would like to see published are invited to write to:
The Editorial Director, Patrick Stephens Limited, Sparkford, Nr. Yeovil, Somerset, BA22 7JJ.

CONTENTS

FOREWORD

by Nigel Mansell, OBE

I suppose you could say that the Williams team has become my spiritual Formula 1 home in many ways. Not only did they give me a big chance in 1985, which I like to think I repaid with 13 Grand Prix victories over the three seasons but, in giving me that opportunity, they helped me to mature even further as a professional racing driver. It's true what they say: once you've won your first Grand Prix you gain a certain confidence and subsequent success flows more easily. Frank Williams, Patrick Head and their team certainly helped me on that score.

After four seasons with Williams, I moved to Ferrari from where, in the middle of 1990, I determined to retire from Formula 1. Yet here I am leading the Williams team in 1991, aiming at the World Championship title with more confidence than probably at any time in my career to date. Why?

The answer to that is the dream deal that Frank, Patrick and Sheridan Thynne successfully put together and offered me. It gives me what I regard as the best opportunity of the World Championship, with a superbly competitive car and an environment where I feel totally comfortable, confident and benefiting from 100 per cent support.

Grand Prix racing has evolved into a highly complex and professional international business since I first drove a Formula 1 car in anger during the summer of 1980. And, during that time, Williams have been consistently among the most professional and technically competitive teams in the game.

In this book for the first time the team has disclosed details of the relationship between itself and Honda, the personal chemistry between the team and its drivers, viewed from Frank Williams's perspective, and the depth of the complex infrastructure which underpins a World Championship challenge. In short, the book offers a shrewd insight into what makes the whole business tick.

Nigel Mansell
April 1991

AUTHOR'S PREFACE AND ACKNOWLEDGEMENTS

When the opportunity arose to write a book about Williams Grand Prix Engineering with the full and open collaboration of the company, I knew that I must curb the inclination purely and simply to talk about the racing achievements of the team. Seventeen years' first-hand experience of watching and reporting from the circuits of the world, as Williams grew from a shambles into one of the most consistently competitive and accomplished teams in the pit lane, signalled that this would be an easy route to take.

In avoiding a litany of potted Grand Prix reports, we have aimed to chart a subtly different course. Using Williams Grand Prix Engineering as the medium, our intention has been to project the challenge of Formula 1 racing as an intensive, bruisingly competitive, high technology business. Also to explain the complexities of all the relationships – human, technical and commercial – which go into making it so.

Without the extensive collaboration of Frank Williams and Patrick Head, both of whom have spent considerable time being interviewed and generally bothered with queries over the past year and a half, the book would never have got off the ground. First and foremost I must thank them for their efforts.

Equally, Williams GPE director Sheridan Thynne has been a major co-conspirator, so to speak, in this project. He assisted in unlocking crucial doors, and helped me to cajole Frank and a somewhat hesitant Patrick into taking part, as well as providing a fund of reminiscences about the happy, amateur days of the 1960s when Frank was starting out in the motor racing game.

I also offer my thanks to Nigel Mansell for contributing the foreword, Keke Rosberg, Carlos Reutemann, WGPE factory manager David Williams (no relation), Steve Herrick of CSS Promotions, Charlie

Crichton-Stuart, Jonathan Williams (no relation either), Charles Lucas, Bubbles Horsley, Max Mosley, Peter Windsor, Frank Dernie, Alan Challis, Gary Crumpler, Michael Cane, Colin Cordy and Professor Sid Watkins of the London Hospital, FISA's medical delegate. Also a special word of appreciation is due to Lady Sarah Aspinall who so kindly agreed to share her memories of life with the Williams team when her first husband, the late Piers Courage, was its sole driver.

Alan Henry
Tillingham, Essex
April 1991

PROLOGUE

The squat, two-storey building nestles beneath the protective shadow cast by the giant twin cooling towers of Didcot power station and is unremarkable at first glance. Many such buildings are scattered across England, housing such diverse enterprises as machine tool manufacturers and food processing plants. But this one is different. The unknowing eye would not realise that, of course, particularly during those weekends when the distinctive trio of colourfully sign-written articulated transporters are absent from their customary parking place just inside the main gate.

The factory is one of the biggest single employers in this small staging post on the former Great Western Railway line between London and Bristol. Yet it is not subject to those disciplines and constraints between employer and employee which, all too often, stifle output and compromise efficiency elsewhere.

This is a workplace where men toil if need be until the job is done. Excellence is the aim; achieving that benchmark is only just good enough. It is the home of Williams Grand Prix Engineering, one of Britain's most successful Formula 1 motor racing teams, a rare and heady blend of engineering talent and commercial perspicacity.

Purpose-built for the team over the winter of 1983-4, the Williams team factory in Basil Hill Road was officially opened on 16 June 1984, by Michael Heseltine, MP for South Oxfordshire, and at that time Minister of Defence. The ceremony, also attended by the Lord Lieutenant of Oxfordshire, could hardly have been performed by a more appropriate personality.

Back in 1962, when a penurious Frank Williams was attempting to make his name as a racing driver, Heseltine was handing over the deeds of his house, the keys of his car and everything else he owned to a sympathetic bank manager in an attempt to keep his own fledgeling publishing empire from disappearing beneath the waves. Like Williams, he knew all about hard times and surviving them. Also like Williams, Heseltine and his Haymarket Publishing group eventually prospered. Appropriately, one of his magazines is *Autosport*, the bible of Britain's motor racing fraternity, which has charted the rise and rise of Frank and his team over the past two decades.

It was a great and memorable day for Frank, 23 years after launching himself on the club racing circuits of England at the wheel of a home-brewed Austin A35. His Grand Prix team had made it to the big-time after more than a decade of struggle.

Three weeks after the factory opening, his number one driver Keke Rosberg would drive a car carrying his name, powered by a turbocharged Japanese Honda engine, to a brilliant victory in the Dallas Grand Prix beneath a sweltering Texas sun. It was a success which served to cement what seemed like an open-ended alliance between the specialist English racing car manufacturer and the Japanese motor maker.

Grand Prix motor racing, Frank Williams's business, is the most challenging, competitive and complex of 20th century sports. Unpredictable and volatile, it has evolved almost beyond recognition over the past generation, revolutionized by both the application of high technology engineering and massive world-wide television coverage. From what was perceived as a minority pastime which looked inwards for its sources of finance, the 16-race World Championship now ranks alongside the Olympic Games and the World Cup as a multi-media, televised spectacular, attracting enormous commercial investment from non-motor industry corporations.

Yet it is also a sport brim full of contradictions. On the one hand it requires meticulous long-term planning, both from an engineering and commercial standpoint. Yet it is the underlying need for an instant response to changes in circumstances, be they technical or commercial, which provide the biggest test of a Grand Prix team's real strength. Such a potentially overwhelming challenge was lurking in wait for Williams, three years down the road after that happy factory opening in the summer of 1984.

In July 1987, with some 18 months of its engine contract to the Williams team remaining, Honda managed to bring itself to tell Frank that the company would be terminating its supply of turbocharged engines at the end of that year. Frank's reluctance to make overt, outspoken criticism of Honda is mirrored within the pages of this volume, yet this was a breach of contract by Honda, justification for which was offered with the bland suggestion that the contract's termination was by mutual agreement.

It may be disturbing to those from a Western culture – and indeed may make Honda's senior management extremely embarrassed in retrospect – but the apparent facts of the matter are that the Japanese company could not come to terms with doing business with a quadraplegic. By then, Frank Williams was confined to a wheelchair as the result of a road accident while returning to Nice airport from the Circuit Paul Ricard following the team's final pre-season test session at the beginning of 1986.

It was ironic that, with Frank hospitalized and fighting for his life, the well-ordered management structure at Williams Grand Prix Engineering ensured that the team operated successfully, and to excellent effect, throughout the 1986 season. The joint efforts of drivers Nelson Piquet and Nigel Mansell resulted in the team winning 10 races, clinching the Constructors' World Championship in the process.

Yet, somehow, that was not enough. Williams Grand Prix Engineering may have been getting the right results, but as far as Honda was concerned, they were not getting them for the right reasons. The subtle contradictions implicit in that observation will be examined in greater detail later on in these pages. Suffice to say for the purposes of this introduction, by August 1987, the Williams team was in a potentially parlous situation.

Consider this analogy. Had Honda decided to terminate its collaboration with British Leyland at six months' notice, the consequences for this country's car industry would have been incalculable. Yet here was Williams, a small specialist company, on the face of it being deprived of its life blood with little in the way of advance warning save the intuition of at least one Williams GPE director that something was not quite right with the relationship.

In walking away from its obligation, Honda had demonstrated a decidedly uncompromising side to its corporate nature which was, at first glance, as unpalatable to the world at large as it was unexpected. At Williams Grand Prix Engineering, however, there was no time for self-pity, precious little for post-mortems. It was all hands on deck for a major change of technical direction. In double-quick time.

At the height of an intensive racing season, with the entire workforce committed to winning a world championship, the team was obliged to tackle the major disruption which affected both its short- and long-term prospects. It had to draw on its inherent organisational flexibility to change course mid-stream in a fashion that would induce apoplexy in the managing director of any conventional commercial concern.

Not only did development of the existing Honda-engined car have to continue apace for the rest of the year but, in a matter of weeks, a new source of engine supply had to be arranged. This in itself was complicated by the fact that Formula 1 was undergoing a period of transition as far as engine regulations were concerned, aimed at the outlawing of turbos altogether in favour of a new breed of naturally aspirated engine in 1989.

It would therefore take an inspired gamble to keep Williams in competitive play during 1988. Taking into consideration such diverse technical priorities as all-up weight, potential fuel capacity and possible power output, Williams GPE's Technical Director Patrick Head decided that the team would switch to the brand-new, untried 3.5-litre non-turbo V8 engine which was then (summer 1987) being manufactured by Rugby-based race engine specialist John Judd.

Momentous decisions had to be made. Yet Williams came to terms with its troubles, made the necessary key decisions for the future, initiated an engine deal and formulated an outline of the new car within three weeks of Honda officially breaking the news. Moreover, all this was achieved without disrupting the highly-stressed racing programme. Nelson Piquet and Nigel Mansell clinched the Constructors' World Championship for a second successive year, this time with nine race victories between them out of 16 events contested.

The nature of the challenge facing the Williams team throughout that fraught summer of 1987 highlights the complexity of Grand Prix racing as a business – as well as underlining the fundamental differences which set it aside from any other high-visibility international sports competing for television air time.

Seldom can anything in Formula 1 be taken at face value. When Boris Becker fumbles a serve or Nick Faldo misses a three foot putt, what you see is the reality of the moment. Yet when Riccardo Patrese's Williams-Renault overtook Gerhard Berger's McLaren-Honda to assume the lead of the 1990 San Marino Grand Prix at Imola, it was more than simply one man and his machine exerting an advantage over another. Onlookers were witnessing the final move in a complex game of chess wherein the excellence of the individual is inextricably and fundamentally bound up with the performance of the specialist machinery at his disposal.

Although the driver is out in the front line, performing under the spotlights, paradoxically Grand Prix racing is the most closely-knit team sport imaginable. In football, there may be 11 players working towards the same end, but when Patrese won at Imola his victory was as much the product of Williams GPE's team work as any inspired goal of Gary Lineker's might rely on the adroit footwork of a colleague to ensure that the ball is in the right place at the appropriate milii-second.

The difference is, of course, that if Lineker's team-mate mistimes the pass, all that is lost is a chance to score. If a Williams engineer or mechanic makes a fundamental mistake in his specialist area, a valuable car may be completely destroyed. Worse still, there lurks the ever-present spectre of injury to a driver.

Here is another aspect to consider. Grand Prix motor racing is probably the most expensive professional sport in the world. Only ocean yacht racing can claim to be in the same league when it comes to comparing long-term financial outlay on complex, specialist machinery. When an international golfer or tennis player goes to a tournament at the other end of the world, he just packs a bag and hops on an aeroplane.

It's not like that in Formula 1. Grand Prix single seaters certainly do not travel as personal baggage. In Europe they are moved about in purpose-built articulated transporters, together with all their equipment and spares. But it takes a Boeing 747 freighter, weeks of planning and three full days of loading to ready the Grand Prix circus for races outside Europe. All this involves massive expenditure in terms of investment and sponsorship.

It goes almost without saying that such a financial requirement means that any serious Grand Prix team must be operated as a properly managed business. The very nature of Grand Prix racing requires a considerable specialist workforce for any team to have a hope of attaining significant success. At the time of writing, Williams currently employs around 160 people. This reality is where sport and commerce become inextricably intertwined.

Today's top Grand Prix team must be as adept at boardroom negotiations as pushing forward the frontiers of vehicle technology. It must have a clear and credible view of its own potential, and the ability to push across the global marketing benefits it can offer to a corporation which becomes involved as an investor. And it must convince that investor that Grand Prix racing can offer benefits not available from an association with several other highly visible international sports.

That is the first hurdle to be cleared. Delivering consistently reliable performance on the track, achieving sustained success, is the next. But these two facets of being a successful Grand Prix racing team in the last decade of the twentieth century are absolutely dependent on each other.

This is not just the story of one man setting out to realise a dream, because Frank Williams freely admits he had no specific strategy – other than to become "a racer" – when he first got involved in motor racing 30 years ago. But it is the story of how one man's singlemindedness and commitment helped create a company, a determined group of ambitious colleagues, which has developed into one of the most famous Grand Prix racing teams in the world.

PART ONE

Frank Williams

1

When the world was young

If you walked into Frank Williams's light, airy office situated at the outer extremity of the first floor at the Williams Grand Prix Engineering factory at any time from 1987 onwards, your initial impression would be one of overwhelming normality. Wearing a navy blue, crew-neck sweater, Frank Williams would, as like as not, be sitting behind his desk, grinning broadly.

He would beckon the visitor to be seated. It is a bright and cheerful room, adorned by family photographs, an expensive model of a Lear 35A executive jet, and a selection of motor racing books. But Frank Williams would not rise to welcome you. One disastrous day in March 1986 he broke his back and nearly died. Since that moment he has been confined to a wheelchair, requiring constant medical supervision.

On that fateful Saturday afternoon when his rented Ford Sierra plunged off a secondary road into a field between Le Camp and Brignoles, just inland from Bandol, in southern France, Frank Williams's life changed for ever. Up to that moment he was ultra-fit, lean and alert, like an over-anxious whippet, missing no detail, always ripe for a fresh opportunity.

Poised almost on the balls of his feet, he was a serious runner long before it was athletically fashionable to be so. The day the accident happened he was scheduled to run a half-marathon back home in England. It is with a wry smile he recalls how his friend and colleague, longtime Williams Technical Director Patrick Head, went straight over to comfort his wife Ginny –'and nicked the pasta she was preparing for me!'

David Warren, a keen amateur runner who finished eighth in the 800 metres during the 1980 Moscow Olympics, is quick to confirm that Frank was no mere amateur jogger. The two men met up when Warren was doing promotional work for the Canon office equipment company, one of the Williams sponsors, and well remembers being invited for a run with

Frank on the evening prior to the San Marino Grand Prix at Imola.

'Frank came up and asked me if I fancied "going 10" later that evening,' recalls Warren. 'I naturally assumed he meant 10 kilometres, as we were in Italy and anyway, since we didn't get back to the hotel until about 9.30 in the evening, I figured he would forget all about it and suggest we met up in the bar.

'Not a bit of it. He was down in the lobby, ready to go, in about 10 minutes. And he meant 10 miles. What's more, he was running six minute miles throughout, which, I promise you, is serious stuff. That's not jogging by any means. Believe me, he was superbly fit.'

The accident put paid to all that, of course, yet the prevailing alchemy within Frank's office is laughter, enthusiasm and optimism. He can be congenial company. If self-pity or depression play a part in his personal repertoire, the visitor is not permitted to become aware of them. They are forbidden to intrude above the surface. Even his closest friends from way back admire Frank even more for his outward resilience and stoicism since the accident than they did for his considerable motor racing achievements beforehand.

Once the uninitiated visitor gets used to the fact that Frank can do little more than flap his arms in unco-ordinated gestures, he will probably be surprised how quickly he feels at ease in a situation which might appear fraught with self-consciousness.

In the wake of the accident, Frank's positive approach towards his own disabilities has had the effect of putting even the most unfamiliar visitor at ease. He would briskly describe his own physical shortcomings as he might a hobbled racing car. He perceives his own irreversibly damaged frame with a detached objectivity. Some people found it slightly unnerving, but they soon relaxed.

Frank displays no longing for the past, just a willingness to come to terms with what, as he is quick to explain, are his own self-inflicted injuries. He blames nobody but himself. That in itself may have helped.

Hand-in-hand with this pragmatic view is a relaxed candour when it comes to talking about the accident.

'I never had a problem from the mental standpoint,' he says firmly. 'I was extraordinarily fortunate in that respect. I can't think why it has happened like that. From the moment the car came to rest after the accident, when I couldn't feel anything, it never crossed my mind that I was paralysed. Months later, when nothing seemed to be happening, I just found myself thinking "Well, this is a bit of a thing here . . ."

'There was just too much to think about in the immediate aftermath . . . when I was going to have my next pee, whether I would be able to swallow the food the right way next time . . . there just wasn't time to think "God, am I paralysed . . .?" It was tough because of the pain.

'I was fortunate that I had the business on which to concentrate my mind. It gradually dawned on me that I was in big trouble. Nobody tried to hide anything from me and Professor Watkins told Ginny – rather abruptly I thought – that I was completely screwed. Incontinence, no sex . . . nothing. But I managed to piece all that together for myself. Nobody had to show me a blackboard and say "Right, now pay attention, these are your problems mate" and go through them one by one.'

Frank shrugs aside the notion that he has a brave approach to his affliction. 'It's just a natural response which 99 out of 100 people would come to terms with. You blank the self-pity out of your mind and just get on with it. The mind has a great capacity for dealing with this sort of thing. Human nature, I suppose.

'I'm now pretty organised in my life. When I look back to 1986 and 1987, with no frame to stand up in, not really being organised, that's the period at which I look back and think, "Hell, how on earth did I manage to deal with that . . ." '

He also freely concedes that the accident was his fault. 'I had broken the back of the journey,' he says with unconscious black humour. 'I was on a long left-hander, the car started oversteering. I must have over-corrected because the car went off on the inside of the corner.

'During those months I lay in hospital, I periodically found myself wondering what that corner was really like. I had in my mind's eye the vision of a short, tree-lined straight followed by another left-hander. Later I came to realise that, in the fraction of a second before going off the road, my brain must have picked up and stored the image of the road ahead in my mental memory bank. Only when I went back there in 1987 with Peter Windsor did I realise that the image in my mind was the straight I didn't get to and the corner beyond it.'

Windsor, a respected former Grand Prix journalist, now the Williams team manager, was the sole passenger in the car when Frank had his accident. He dragged his boss from the wrecked car, terrified that leaking fuel might turn it into their funeral pyre.

Windsor's recollections of the accident are meticulous and extremely specific. He vividly remembers the moment at which he realised the car was going off the road. Of immediate concern to him was that it seemed on course to hit, end-on, a low stone wall on his side of the car.

'There was a drop of about six feet from the road into the field,' he explained. 'The car went over and the windscreen pillar on Frank's side took the first impact. Then it went over a couple of times more. I opened my eyes and began to see if I could move and Frank was saying "get me out of here . . ."

'I was totally disorientated. Seat belts seemed to be tangled everywhere. I suppose it took me about 30 seconds to find the ignition key and switch everything off. Frank was already saying that his legs felt as though they were flying, and I was trying to think straight, the one thing foremost in my mind was not to touch his neck while I tried to get him out'.

Of course, in purely practical terms, getting Frank out of the wrecked car was hypothetical. As Windsor quickly realised, he was trapped every bit as much as his boss. The doors were locked. The whole place stank of petrol. Mercifully, the pressures of the moment hardly allowed Windsor the luxury of being scared.

Suddenly, Windsor saw some legs walking around outside. He attracted the stranger's attention and beckoned him to smash the Sierra's rear screen. A nearby rock proved just the instrument for such impromptu emergency work. Later, through a chance conversation, they would discover their rescuer to be a mathematics teacher, one of whose pupils was Cora Reutemann, teenage daughter of one-time Williams team driver Carlos.

Gently, they lifted Frank from the wrecked car. A lot of blood was pouring from a gash on his scalp into his eyes and ears. Cradling his employer's head in his arms, Windsor managed to think clearly enough to tell the passer-by to get word to the Williams team members who would still be at the Paul Ricard circuit. For 45 minutes Frank waited, calmly observing that the feeling was draining from his body. He asked for the last rites.

Nelson Piquet and Nigel Mansell arrived on the scene. Small, irrelevant details seem to lodge in the mind at such times of great stress. Windsor remembers that Mansell had changed into 'civvies', but Piquet still wore his overalls. By then a small Citroën ambulance had come from Toulon. It took 45 minutes to reach the hospital.

More wide-ranging medical support had also swung into action. Windsor put through a call to Arrows team boss Jack Oliver back in England. He in turn contacted Formula One Constructors' Association President Bernie Ecclestone who alerted F1 medical supremo Professor Syd Watkins. Highly respected as the chief of neuro-surgery at the London Hospital, Watkins has high-level medical connections all over the world.

Frank was quickly transferred to the more elaborately equipped Marseilles hospital. Piquet drove Mansell, Windsor and the team aerodynamicist Frank Dernie to see him. 'I hope you don't mind if I'm not driving quickly,' remarked Nelson thoughtfully during the journey. Nobody raised any objections. They were all too immersed in their private reflections.

Initially, the prognosis did not look good at all. Through that Saturday night at the hospital, Mansell and Piquet dozed together on the same bed, unwilling to leave Frank's side.

On Sunday morning Ginny Williams flew out to be with her husband. Within a few days Bernie Ecclestone had furnished his private jet and flown Frank back to Biggin Hill. Prime Minister's son Mark Thatcher, a long-time friend of Frank and his team, organised a police escort to the London Hospital.

The next six weeks were to be a traumatic and toughening time, not only for Frank's family, but also for Peter Windsor who was to grow emotionally much closer to Frank as he spent day after day at his bedside. But that deep-seated streak of independence at the core of Frank's character eventually asserted itself. The slightly distant formality between employer and employee eventually reasserted itself.

'People were saying glibly "Oh, he's better off dead" immediately after the accident,' reflects Windsor. 'But during those early weeks my only motivation was "Please God, let him live". I really thought his personality would change. While he was in hospital back in London he got quite reflective, telling me he wished he'd spent more time on holiday, smelling the flowers, if you like, doing all the things that F1 people always say they will do but never have time for.

'But Frank will always be Frank. He will never let anybody get emotionally too close to him.'

In fact, Windsor had witnessed a behavioural trait with which surgeons are extremely familiar. 'It was a parallel to the situation experienced when a surgeon saves somebody's life with a complicated operation,' explains Professor Watkins. 'Psychologically the patient often becomes distant, feeling somehow embarrassed. Sometimes it's because they feel awkward about feeling indebted to a person who, perhaps, has saved their life. On other occasions it's the fact that they associate that person with an event in their life that they would prefer to forget.'

Later, Windsor would recall Frank giving an interview to Paris Match in which he remembered there being a time while he was in hospital 'when I felt a bit wishy-washy. But now I'm back to normal'.

Whatever the intricacies of their personal friendship, it is quite clear that Williams acknowledges an enormous debt to Peter Windsor and is only glad that he emerged unhurt.

'If I had ruined his life it would have been dreadful,' he muses. 'We were very lucky. The car was upside down, all four doors had self-locked, the whole thing stank of petrol. If it had gone up we would have burnt to death, no question about it. It was about three minutes before anybody came and broke the rear window with a large rock and we went out that way.'

Windsor later expressed anguished concern that he might have exacerbated Frank's injuries by hauling him out of the car in such understandably unceremonious fashion. Indisputably, though, he took the correct course of action. 'The number one priority was to get us out of there at all costs,' Frank agrees emphatically.

On Frank's return to work, almost a year after the accident, you might have expected friends and acquaintances to be unsettled when he joined them for lunch, being spoon-fed like a toddler. Yet such is his overwhelming naturalness that any unease evaporated. It was still Frank in there – energetic, vibrant, mentally on the ball. Granted, his body didn't work properly, but he shrugged that aside as his problem. He could still talk motor racing . . .

Cars – especially racing cars – have been the inspirational force in the life of Francis Owen Garbett Williams ever since his schooldays. Born on 16 April, 1942 in South Shields, on Tyneside, the young lad grew up imbued with a resilience and fighting spirit indigenous to that hard, unyielding, often deprived outpost of England's industrial heartland.

His father, an RAF officer, split up from Frank's mother who brought up her child alone in Jarrow, the bleak township that spawned the hunger march to London by a vast army of unemployed labourers during the great economic depression of the early 1930s.

He talks of his mother in respectful tones, yet with a sense of distant formality. He has met his father only about four times in his life. There was not much to be said between the two of them. Frank's mother made a career out of teaching sub-normal and backward children, but found it difficult to relate to her own son. 'It was as if she didn't allow him too close,' recalls his friend Jonathan Williams, 'almost as if because he was normal he therefore did not need her affection and support.' Jonathan also recalls that when he and other friends visited the Williams home near Nottingham, Frank's mother steadfastly wanted nothing to do with them. Nevertheless, Frank stands up for her stoically: 'She skimped and saved to give me a decent education and I'll always be very grateful for that. In the end, I was the one who left home to follow my own life.'

From an early age Frank was mad about cars. 'If there was nothing else, a ride on the bus provided my excitement. I read *Autocar*, *Motor*, knew all the prices, the cubic capacities, the horsepower and so-on. I could quote you everything. Then, gradually, when I was in my early teens, a competitive element began to surface.'

He was educated at St. Joseph's College, Dumfries. 'Ecurie Ecosse country,' he recalls. In the mid-1950s, the great Edinburgh-based Scottish team was at its zenith, fielding private Jaguar C and D-types at Le Mans, which they won in 1956 and 1957. The parents of a friend were acquainted with David Murray, the Ecurie Ecosse patron. Frank confesses to being 'virtually speechless with excitement' when he was offered a ride in a Jaguar XK150S, one of the most covetable of sports cars in the late 1950s. 'After that, I was in. There was nothing else but motor racing.'

Of course, the prospect of realising his lofty ambitions brought Frank face to face with one crucial tangential consideration. Lack of cash. Breaking into motor racing was no easy task in the early 1960s. Although the costs involved were minuscule by comparison with the outlay involved in the most junior category of racing today, even adjusting figures for inflation, it was far beyond the resources of the average enthusiast.

Sponsorship as we know it today simply did not exist. Club racers might occasionally receive the odd free set of tyres or can of oil, at best some fleeting assistance with the preparation of their car from a friendly local garage. But beyond that you just had to dig deep into your personal resources, a luxury which Frank Williams was ill-equipped to indulge.

Jonathan Williams remembers first meeting Frank at a Mallory Park club meeting in 1962. Sitting atop the bank at Gerards Corner, against which he had firmly parked his own Austin A40, Jonathan was hypnotised by the sight of this 'complete idiot in a grey A40 getting progressively more and more out of shape each time he came through the corner. He looked the part all right . . . straight-armed driving style, Herbert Johnson crash helmet perched on the back of his head a bit like Stirling Moss . . .'

Inevitably, Williams F. joined Williams J. sitting on the bank, surveying their bent motor cars. Frank had a lot of style behind the wheel, Jonathan concedes, 'but he was prone to the odd memory lapse.'

After a couple of seasons' saloon car racing, during which he was attempting to hold down a succession of jobs ranging from Campbells soup salesman to filling station attendant, in 1963 he tossed aside all his inhibitions and moved to London. He was going to be a racer. More precisely, he was going to be Jonathan Williams's mechanic, working on his newly acquired Formula Junior car.

Jonathan was to become a member of a now-legendary *demi-monde* of Formula 3 drivers and hangers-on who helped to make the mid-1960s so rich in variety and fascination. While racing an Austin A40 in 1962, Frank had frequently scrounged space on a sofa in a house in Lower Sloane Street shared by Sheridan Thynne, scion of the Marquess of Bath's family, and brewery heir Piers Courage, known to his pals as 'Porge' or 'Porridge'.

'I also used to go in during the day and kip in one of their beds,' recalls Frank with some pleasure, 'and even borrow one of Porridge's striped shirts . . . that sort of thing.' The glee with which he recounts these minor tactical triumphs almost 30 years later is enhanced by the fact that he often does so in front of Sheridan who is now Commercial Director of Williams Grand Prix Engineering.

In assessing Frank's expertise as a mechanic, Jonathan concedes 'he sometimes stood at the right end of the car'. But he acknowledges a genuine debt to his namesake for looking after him throughout the rest of the European season after he had crashed his Merlyn at Monaco practising for the Formula Junior classic which traditionally supported the Grand Prix.

More specifically, Jonathan recalls that it was quite clear that Frank took life a bit more seriously than his more privileged contemporaries. 'For the rest of us, the main priority was to ensure that the fun times kept happening, but Frank was different,' he says firmly. 'Frank was always going to be somebody. He had ambitions. He was going to make something of his life.'

'I replaced the Merlyn with a Lotus 22,' remembers Jonathan, 'but I drove for the rest of the year suffering with delayed concussion. Frank was more than my mechanic. He was my minder. I kept asking where we were, what race we were supposed to be at the following weekend. It drove him mad, I think.'

On the basis that who you know is more important than what you know, Frank made a crucial breakthrough in late 1963 when he began sleeping on another sofa, this time in what was to become a notorious motor racing flat in Pinner Road, Harrow. Here he expanded his social circle and met such diverse characters as Charlie Crichton-Stuart, grandson of the fifth Marquess of Bute, whose family owned much of Cardiff city centre; Charles Lucas, the son of a wealthy Yorkshire land owner; and wheeler-dealer Anthony Horsley – 'Bubbles' to all and sundry. He also got to know Piers Courage much more closely.

They were lighthearted days dedicated to keeping the good times rolling, where the nicknames – Charlie Stu, Sherry, Luke, Bubbles, Porridge – rolled off the tongue like something from the pages of P.G. Wodehouse. Frank was delighted to gain acceptance within this exclusive and good-humoured motor racing enclave, but was conscious of being the poor kid on the block. He had to live on his wits.

Frank would do anything – anything – for a bet. Charlie Crichton-Stuart wagered him 10 shillings (50p) that he wouldn't run, stark naked, across the road outside the flat on a Sunday morning when the church next door was just decanting its congregation.

'We locked the door by the time he returned,' Charlie recalls with glee. 'But, being Frank, he called our bluff. He went back into the middle of the road and started leaping around like a dervish, banging his fists on his chest, with us hanging out of the window pleading for him to come in again.'

Charlie tends to endorse Jonathan Williams's view about Frank's mechanical aptitude: 'He had none at all, absolutely zero. He also claims the first time he did anything for me was when I asked him to do an oil change on my Cooper. I can't remember whether that's right, but I'm sure it is. I wouldn't have had the faintest idea what an oil union was, anyway. Frank had obviously advanced to the level where he could take a sump plug out, well ahead of my capability!'

The flat quickly developed into a clearing house for motor racing talent, with the likes of Innes Ireland and Jochen Rindt passing through from time to time.

For 1964, Frank teamed up with Bubbles and they embarked on a programme of European F3 races. Horsley was a wheeler-dealer par excellence. Charles Lucas recalls with delight how 'Bubbles was working in a hamburger joint somewhere in Fulham when he overheard a couple of Americans apparently talking about a Formula 1 team. Somehow he managed to strike up a conversation with them and offered his services as their team manager.'

Thus the amiable Bubbles became van driver cum general dogsbody for the Scirocco-Powell F1 team, a short-lived private venture funded by Americans Tony Settember and Hugh Powell. It was based in a small motor racing *demi-monde* in Goldhawk Road, Shepherds Bush, behind a car dealership owned by moustachioed extrovert amateur racer Cliff Davis. It was here, in this nest of fledgeling racing drivers and motorcyclists, that Bubbles first met Frank Williams in the summer of 1962. He was attempting to sell a winter overcoat.

The domestic British motor racing scene of the 1960s is an essential element of the Frank Williams story. It was a time when enthusiasts could scrimp, save, barter and deal, live on a diet of egg and chips, prepare their own cars and go motor racing on a shoestring. Moreover, within the confines of this particular story, the early racing careers of several key players were as firmly intertwined as the aristocracy's blood lines.

There were dozens of Formula Junior (F3 from 1964) races dotted all over Europe in those days in out-of-the-way places, enabling the impecunious enthusiast to earn a living and avoid racing against the better financed young rising stars. It was not necessary to race against the leading lights if you trailed your Volkswagen pick-up truck, containing its old Cooper or Lotus, to Roskilde in Denmark, to Vallelunga in Italy, to Brno in Czechoslovakia or Schleizer-Dreiack in East Germany.

Seldom has the mood, atmosphere and camaraderie of the moment been better captured than by Jonathan Williams. Contributing to a beautiful little private circulation biography of the late Piers Courage in 1971, he explained it thus:

'A meal in Dover, the midnight boat, bacon and eggs in Aachen with the lorry drivers, gaining skill at passing frontiers quickly with race cars and trailers. East Germany on Thursday, laughing at the Communists, but a bit in awe of the guards in their tall towers.

'Another race, another result, getting better, learning how to do it ... moving to Monza, revelling in the unaccustomed heat, the excitable people, different food and new sounds. Refusing to stop when blackflagged in the race, so strong was the desire to do well, to "show them".

'Constantly moving about Europe, Italy, France, Germany and Holland, always laughing with Picko, Bubbles, Charlie Stu and Frank in a great mob after the race, making fun of each other's incidents. Feeling rich with starting money on Monday morning, having splendid breakfasts and then splitting up until the next weekend.' Small wonder that Frank Williams was drawn hypnotically into this Aladdin's cave of enthusiasm and excitement.

For 1963, Bubbles had acquired two cars, an Ausper and a crash-repaired Brabham. The elderly Ausper was driven by its owner, while Frank did a deal to prepare and race the Brabham. Together, they lurched their precarious path round Europe. At Nürburgring, Frank crashed the Brabham almost in front of its owner. Bubbles, furious at his new partner's lapse, lost his cool and crashed the Ausper almost at the next corner.

Charlie Crichton-Stuart was also competing in this particular event: 'Bubbles winded himself and lost his specs. In the process of looking for them he'd somehow managed to step on them. So this is all unfolding as I'm racing. One lap I come round and there's this madly grinning idiot hanging over the edge of the track. That was Frank. Next lap, there's the ambulance attendants trying to load up Bubbles who looked more seriously injured than he actually was.

'They eventually threw him into the ambulance, but the gate to get out of the circuit was locked. While the ambulance driver was arguing with the marshal, Bubbles opened the rear door and hopped out, bumbling around like Mr McGoo, looking for Frank. The ambulance, meanwhile, goes screaming off to the hospital at Adenau where they find nobody in it when they open the doors. Absolutely true. They were last seen looking for a rather overweight racing driver with no glasses . . .'

Bubbles recalls how they existed on a dramatically precarious financial knife-edge. After initially towing the cars round Europe behind an old Morris van, they switched to an equally ancient 1955 Plymouth which Bubbles had acquired during one or other of his nefarious deals. Two episodes particularly stick in Bubble's mind.

'Not only did Frank lose my wallet – the team's wallet – by leaving it on the roof of the Plym when we stopped for a swim, but I also woke up one morning to find that he had eaten the one salami roll we had to last us four days while waiting for the ferry at Reggio Calabria,' he recounts with perfectly timed mock indignation.

'The idea was that we should go down to the F2 race at Syracuse, in Sicily, where they were accepting a few F3 runners to make up the field. It looked like being a bit of a pay day, but Frank had lost the bloody wallet, so we were potless. We couldn't get the ferry. So we spent four days camped out in the AGIP petrol station by the ferry entrance, surviving only because the lad at the pumps kept us supplied with drinkable water. Only when the racers began coming through on their return journeys did we borrow a hundred quid from a fellow racer, Eddie Fletcher, which enabled us to start on the journey home.'

Frank's sheer resourcefulness made a big impact on Charlie Crichton-Stuart: 'On one occasion I was giving him a lift to Nürburgring after he'd lost his passport. He'd got a statement from the British consul in Rome explaining the situation, saying that he was a British subject, and so on, but when we got to the German border they wouldn't let him through.

'The whole exchange got out of hand, to the point where I made some pretty strong remarks to the border guard and the upshot of that was that we were turned back. Obviously this bloke had telephoned along to all the adjacent border posts to watch out for two guys in a Cortina towing a racing car, so we met the same response when we back-tracked about 10km to another border post which was just back over the Rhine.

'Eventually Frank says "Blow this Charlie. You can get in because you've got a passport. Drop me here and I'll swim across'. I said, 'Don't be stupid, the Rhine is about 400 yards wide, it flows very quickly and in April it's bloody cold.' Well, he just did it.'

Charlie also remembers Bubbles being kept in the bath for three days while suffering from chicken pox: 'He had this gigantic Revell plastic kit of a destroyer which he filled up with lighter fuel and set ablaze and said "Look, this ship's burning". When he got out of the bath there was only about two inches of water in it – that's how much he displaced!'

If the relationship between Horsley and Williams became strained during their joint racing careers, it was as nothing compared with the aggravation they caused each other with their business dealings. Bubbles was trading cars, rather looking after this month's debts and not daring to think too much about what might happen next month. It wasn't long before he and Frank were muscling in on each other's deals, notably the occasion when Bubbles got badly outmanoeuvred over a set of Brabham wheels.

'I had a Braby in stock which was en route to a customer in New Zealand,' he remembers, using terminology calculated to flatter the row of lock-up garages where his second-hand racers were stored. 'This was at a time when there was an acute shortage of Brabham wheels. Meanwhile Frank had flogged a similar car to some Swede and couldn't get any wheels because they were on something like eight weeks' delivery.

'The arrangement on these export deals was that you got paid when the shipper took delivery and the shipping papers were raised. At the time I'd gone off for a few days to the Forest Mere health hydro to shed a few pounds, when suddenly the telephone goes. It turns out to be one of Alan Rees's sidekicks at Winkelmann Racing asking me what the hell's going on with this Brabham for New Zealand.

'I said "No problem, just go round and pick it up". He replied "It's sitting on a couple of trestles. It hasn't got any wheels". I thought, "Oh Christ, bloody Frank . . ." It took about one hundredth of a second for the penny to drop. I rang him immediately and asked him what the bloody hell he thought he was doing. "I was desperate," he replied. He really shafted me well and truly on that particular deal!'

Yet Bubbles would get his revenge, with surgical subtlety, many years later. The action moves forward a decade to when Frank was buying the stock of Formula 1 cars sold off when Lord Hesketh closed down his flamboyant Grand Prix operation at the end of 1975. Bubbles had been

Alexander's team manager and, when Frank arrived to take delivery, had the cars all lined up on trestles in the courtyard at Easton Neston, the Hesketh family seat near Towcester. 'And I made the so-and-so pay extra for the wheels,' Bubbles recalled with considerable satisfaction.

Charlie Crichton-Stuart: 'There was also the occasion when Frank and Bubbles sold an old Morris van to a bloke in Eltham, or somewhere. The springs had collapsed on one side, so they jacked it up and jammed a block of wood under one side to make it look straight.

'They sold it to this guy. Next thing, a letter came saying: "Dear Mr Horsley and Mr Williams. I'm an ex-Desert Rat from the Eighth Army and you've stitched me up. I was going round a roundabout and your wooden block fell out, and my van ended up listing at 45 degrees . . .' or words to that effect.

'About the only response they could produce was "What the hell is a Desert Rat?" The letter went straight in the bin. The next thing was that a letter arrived from Earl Alexander of Tunis saying "You've stitched up one of my men". And that got their undivided attention, I can tell you.'

Trawling the pages of old motor racing magazines can be illuminating and instructive in connection with Frank's early career, not to say inadvertently amusing. For 1965, Frank decided to purchase the Formula 2 Cooper belonging to Guildford garage owner John Coombs, which Graham Hill had driven on several occasions the previous year.

He adapted it for what turned out to be a catastrophically disappointing season. Nevertheless, he managed to register his first international result of consequence with a fourth place at Skarpnack, Sweden, on 5 September, behind the Brabhams of Trevor Blokdyk, Picko Troberg and Harry Stiller.

The 15 October, 1965 edition of *Autosport* carried the following item: 'Frank Williams has sold his ex-John Coombs F3 Cooper-Ford T72 to the Swedish driver Ake Lindberg. Williams hopes, finance permitting, to have a Brabham for next season'. No reader could have hoped to comprehend just what a straitened set of circumstances those two words 'finance permitting' glossed over.

Portentously, this news item was hidden away on the same page as a picture captioned: 'Mr Honda chats with BRM's Tony Rudd with the aid of an interpreter', as well as news that Cosworth Engineering were to build a new Ford Grand Prix engine for the forthcoming 3-litre F1. Both companies would reach out and touch Frank Williams in the decades that followed.

For 1966 Frank acquired a Brabham, at the wheel of which it's fair to say that he underwhelmed the opposition in pretty conclusive fashion. He was quick, but judged as incredibly erratic by his colleagues. Asked in the late 1960s what had been the biggest problem he faced as a driver, Frank would reply, 'the corners. The straights were absolutely no problem at all, but the corners . . . they got me every time!'

In the paddock at Vila Real, according to Jonathan, Frank finally reached the conclusion that he was never going to make the grade as a driver. He'd just wrapped his Brabham into a level crossing at the Portuguese track. 'I'm going home to concentrate on my spare parts business,' he confided. In fact, he did a few more races before calling it a day, achieving a major ambition with a minor international win at Knutsdorp, Sweden, on 28 August.

In 1967, Frank duly dropped out of racing in order to build up the dealing side, but he firmly intended to make sufficient money to buy himself a properly competitive car for a return to F3 the following year. But things just didn't work out that way.

'By the end of 1966 the whole thing had become impossible,' be confesses. 'I just couldn't make ends meet. I sold the F3 Brabham which I'd raced very enjoyably, thought I would take a year off and make some real bread. A slight career detour, if you like, for financial expediency.

'In fact, what happened was that I got so thoroughly immersed in the business that I never got back into the cockpit. It was like the old ferry going out. One minute it was a three foot gap to the quay, then four feet, then suddenly 10 feet and I couldn't get back in. It was too late.

'I regretted that a lot. In my heart, I still wanted to be a racer for another 10 years, even into the 1980s. I talked seriously with Patrick Head about racing a touring car to get it out of my system, because I knew I was eventually going to have a big accident on the road and, sure enough, I did just that. It was a fact of life.'

He sold a half share in his new company for £5,000 to Chris Moore, a friend who raced a private F3 Lotus 41. It was to be a tragically short-lived partnership, for Moore developed an inoperable brain tumour and died later that year.

Frank adopted an enterprising, businesslike approach to the challenge of selling racing cars, very ambitious and expansive by the standards of the time. In the 3 March, 1967 issue of *Autosport* he took a full page advertisement. Under a photograph of Frank himself, cornering hard in a Brabham, the text read 'Who is Frank Williams? He sells racing cars . . . and guarantees them. Telephone: Harrow 0460/7854 (Middlesex)'.

This was followed on 10 March with a photograph of some portly soul carrying a large lump of concrete, above the caption 'Frank, I thought you said that chicane was flat'. Finally, on 17th March there appeared a photograph of Frank's fellow racers Picko Troberg, journalist Bill Gavin, Denny Hulme and Peter Arundell, standing naked by a Swedish lake, their modesty saved only by a handful of birch twigs, with the legend: 'This lot got fleeced . . . but not by me!'

I have suggested to Frank that such advertisements might not have stood the test of detailed scrutiny under the Trades Descriptions Act. For example, what did this "guarantee" constitute? 'I guaranteed they would get delivery, that I wouldn't scarper with their money,' he replied with all the seriousness he could muster.

Sheridan Thynne, who stuck his head into the lion's den by actually purchasing a Formula Ford Titan Mk 4 from Frank for his brother-in-law Richard Cardew to drive in 1968, admits it would have been amusing, not to say intriguing, to have attempted lodging a claim under this 'guarantee'. By the time Sherry became a customer, Frank Williams (Racing Cars) Ltd had established itself in premises on Bath Road, Cippenham, Slough, where the boss would find it convenient to live in a flat above the workshops.

2

Learning the ropes together

The most significant turning point for Frank Williams, both professionally and personally, would be his burgeoning friendship and subsequent
partnership with Piers Courage which really kicked off at the end of 1967,
Frank's first non-racing season. This alliance not only brought Frank
into the big time, launching his team down a long, tortuous and difficult
road to Grand Prix stardom, but it also brought him face to face with
personal tragedy when Piers was killed in the Williams team de Tomaso
during the 1970 Dutch Grand Prix at Zandvoort.

Piers Raymond Courage was born into the famous English brewing
dynasty on 27 May, 1942. His father Richard and brother Charles still
farm near Shenfield, in Essex, where Piers grew up in circumstances that
were distinctly privileged as compared with those of Frank Williams.
Piers was educated at Eton, where he met Sheridan Thynne. His parents
intended that he should pursue a career in accountancy before moving
into the brewery business.

However, at the age of 16 somebody lent him a copy of Rex Hayes's
book *The Vanishing Litres.* From that point onwards, scholastic
endeavours took a back seat. Piers' teenage mind was captivated by
images of huge green Bentleys thundering down the Mulsanne straight en
route to victory at Le Mans.

The story of Piers as a teenage motor racing fanatic is the story of
thousands of impressionable youngsters furtively hiding beneath
half-opened desk lids in the fifties and sixties, leafing through copies of
Autosport and *Motor Sport,* two journals which were priority reading for
wide-eyed kids with an interest in cars and motor racing. Piers even
recalled how he went to a Goodwood race meeting in 1958, a tortuous
adventure by train to London's Liverpool Street from his home in rural
Essex, tube to Victoria, train again to Chichester and a bus out to the
track.

While attending a 'crammer' at Notting Hill Gate, arranged in a vain attempt to raise his academic game to the point where he might conceivably scrape into university, Piers paid £5 for his first car. It was an elegant 1934 Triumph Gloria drophead coupé. 'It broke its front axle on the A4 bridge just outside Reading, as I recall,' says Frank Williams with a wicked grin.

The crammer, predictably, was money down the drain. Piers had long since been seduced by the world of cars and motor racing. There was nothing else in his mind. He failed the entrance examinations, took a brief trip to France and then returned to London where, his father believed, he would settle down in a firm of accountants, studying for his professional qualifications. It was a forlorn hope.

On his return Piers moved into the flat with Sheridan Thynne, Jonathan Williams and Mark Fielden – a charming fellow who was tragically later killed in a freak accident in the Silverstone pits – where he met up with the penurious Frank Williams for the first time. The correspondence course in preparation for his accountancy examinations slipped further and further down the list of priorities.

In 1962, Piers was bought a Lotus Seven for his 20th birthday. He and his father built it up from an assemble-yourself kit of parts, a popular means of marketing small specialist sports cars at the time which enabled the customer to avoid the purchase tax charged on the factory gate price of a completed car.

It wasn't long before the Lotus was exchanged for a sports racing car built by Merlyn, the small specialist constructor situated near Colchester only 30 miles or so from the Courage family home. Piers soon realised that he would need somebody to assist in the preparation, so his path led back to Shepherds Bush once again, to that little mews off Goldhawk Road. There he was introduced to Roy Thomas, nicknamed 'Tom the Weld' as a well justified tribute to his talent for straightening bent racing car chassis, not to mention their accurate duplication.

It was through Tom the Weld that Piers met up with Charles Lucas, whose wealthy father ran a pre-cast concrete business. 'Luke' had also somehow managed to get himself saddled with a Merlyn sports car. 'They were touted as Merlyn's answer to the Lotus 23, then the most competitive small sports racer on the English scene,' recalled Luke over 20 years later, 'but all I can remember is that my car handled like a bowl of spaghetti.'

In the winter of 1963–64 Piers was packed off to yet another accountancy college in North Wales where his half-hearted attempts to buckle down to serious study proved no more successful. They were not helped by tempting letters from Jonathan Williams urging Piers to give it all up and join him for a season of F3 racing on the Continent the following year. Eventually, the attraction of such a life proved irresistible. One night, Piers crept out of the college and pointed his Triumph TR3A in the direction of Charles Crichton-Stuart's flat in Harrow.

'That decision didn't exactly switch off the family funds,' recalls Sheridan Thynne dryly, 'but it certainly reduced them from a stream to a trickle. He certainly wasn't very popular at home, so when he wasn't eating and sleeping at Lower Sloane Street he was eating and sleeping with Jonathan Williams's parents in Colchester.'

Undaunted, Piers and Jonathan Williams scraped together sufficient resources to purchase a couple of outdated Lotus 22s which they fielded under the grandiose title of the Anglo Swiss Racing Team, reflecting the fact that they based themselves at Chuck Graemiger's place in Lausanne.

Piers financed this shoestring racing programme with the income from a trust fund which he had inherited on 27 May, 1963, his 21st birthday. By what he described as 'various devious means' the Lotus 22s were acquired through the trade at rock bottom prices, they bought a couple of 1-litre Holbay-modified Ford F3 engines for £250 a time and Piers chipped in another £100 for a spare unit. Having sold his old Jaguar Mk 7 road car to Charles Lucas for £70, he traded up to a four-year-old Ford Zodiac. This cost him £360 on hire purchase and, topped off with a £30 trailer, the Anglo Swiss Racing Team was on the road.

Piers had taken the diplomatic decision to write to his father explaining that he had finally abandoned accountancy in favour of a motor racing career, and Richard Courage soon became completely reconciled with his son. He took his wife to Monaco in May 1963 to watch Piers competing in the F3 race which traditionally supports the Grand Prix through the streets of the Mediterranean principality.

Fortunately, in view of how things transpired, Piers told them not to expect too much. He crashed at the Mirabeau right-hander on the first lap of practice, an accident heard by Frank Williams, although not actually witnessed by his future boss. Above all else, Frank recalled the hoots of laughter from the crowd at Piers's misfortune.

Piers's best international placings that year were third at Reims behind Jackie Stewart's Cooper-BMC and Lucien Bianchi's Alpine-Renault, and a fifth at Caserta, the rugged Italian road circuit. At the end of the season he loaned the much-abused Lotus to Charles Lucas for a race at Brands Hatch which ended when Luke somersaulted the car at Clearways, breaking his leg in the process.

This unfortunate accident produced another delightful exchange that could have come from a Bertie Wooster script. As Luke was loaded into the ambulance, he found time to say 'Sorry about the car, Porge, can't think what I was doing'.

'That's OK, Luke. Not to worry,' replied Piers.

'I suppose I'd better buy it, if you were thinking of selling.'

'Well, it had crossed my mind.'

'How much were you thinking of?'

'Oh, about a thousand'.

Luke was well able to pay his friend. At the end of 1964, he had inherited a sum of money, large by the standards of the time. Jonathan Williams remembers him needing little persuasion that the best possible use for this windfall would be 'to buy a fleet of Formula 3 cars in which his friends could continue enjoying themselves.' Duly encouraged, Luke did just that, in fact acquiring a trio of 1964 Formula 2 Brabham chassis which were then re-worked for the junior formula.

The drivers for this colourful new team would be Luke himself, Piers and Jonathan, with Peter Gethin recruited to drive an older Lotus 22 'because he was a thoroughly good bloke to have around'.

'Looking back, all I wanted to do was knock around with Jonathan and Piers,' smiles Lucas, 'although I suppose I must have wondered what on earth I thought I was doing, providing toys for the boys!'

Luke never believed himself to be much good as a driver, although the evidence available suggests he is being excessively modest. 'I wish in retrospect I'd had more belief in myself at the time, perhaps taken it all more seriously.'

Many years later Gethin would tell the author of his belief that he was asked to join the team only because Luke fancied his girlfriend. Challenged with this allegation in 1990, the former team boss confirmed the story with considerable relish and amusement!

Piers gained a reputation as one of Britain's promising young stars during that 1965 season driving the Lucas Brabham, as a result of which Luke was invited to field the works Formula 3 Lotus 41s the following season. Although the pencil-slim 41 did not gain wide acceptance as the best-handling machine in the business, Piers managed to kick off his Lotus association with a commercially crucial victory in the wet at the 1965 Boxing Day Brands Hatch meeting.

Immediately after that success, Piers flew off to Argentina for the F3 Temporada series, although he never took part in any of the races. Practising an older Charles Lucas Team Lotus 35 for the first event at Buenos Aires, he crashed heavily when the throttle stuck open, and ended up in hospital with a burnt foot, suffering from para-typhoid.

By now Piers was engaged to Lady Sarah Marguerite Curzon, daughter of motor racing pioneer Earl Howe who died at the age of 80 in 1964 when she was barely out of her teens. She had briefly been engaged to Charlie Crichton-Stuart, and Piers first set eyes on her getting out of her Alfa 1750 GTV as he emerged from beneath his Merlyn sports car at Goldhawk Road, covered from head to toe in oil. 'I'm going to marry that girl one day,' he mused to Charles Lucas. Luke was quick to bring him down to earth: 'Take a look at yourself, will you . . . you look as though you've just been dunked in a vat of Castrol R!'

Lady Sarah had grown up in a motor racing environment and attended many races with her father when he was President of the British Racing Drivers Club. Sally, as she was popularly known, had gone off to the United States after breaking off her engagement to Charlie Stu, and when she eventually returned to London it was to find Piers waiting on her staircase.

'He said he wanted to go out with me, but I had a boyfriend coming over to visit me from the States,' she remembers. 'Piers took us both down to Brands Hatch, behaved abominably towards this other guy and spent all the time he wasn't in his car holding my hand. He drove so madly on the way back to London that my friend from America eventually asked to be dropped off at Earls Court tube station, saying "Don't worry, just leave me here." '

Immediately after the Buenos Aires accident, Sally flew out to be with Piers in Argentina. Luke recalls with affectionate delight the sheer incongruity of 'this blonde, mini-skirted motor racing Twiggy' suddenly appearing amidst the ranks of pallid patients at the rather dank, depressing convent in which Piers had been hospitalised. They were married in March that year in London, at Holy Trinity Church, Brompton Road. Charles Lucas was the best man.

Piers could hardly have chosen a more ideal wife. She was born into motor racing, and for all her sophisticated upbringing she got on with the Pinner Road flat brigade like a house on fire. Reflecting in 1990 on those happy times of youth, she mused: 'they all had such tremendous vitality and enthusiasm for what they were doing and I loved them all for it. Those were magical days.'

Throughout 1966 Piers consistently found himself up against Chris Irwin in the Chequered Flag team's Brabham BT15. Most people regarded Irwin as the more stylish driver of the two, but his career ended, tragically and prematurely, after a huge accident at the Nürburgring in 1968 in a Ford F3L sports car. He suffered serious cranial injuries which badly affected his personality and subsequently led to the break-up of his marriage to Charlotte Lucas, Charles's sister.

'Piers was inconsistent,' says Luke. 'Sometimes he drove like a dream, sometimes he flew off into the trees for no apparent reason. To my mind, he wasn't as good as Chris Irwin who thought much harder about what he was doing. It was the same when they were driving for BRM together in 1967; Piers got too twitchy and went over the top.'

In retrospect, an invitation for Piers to join BRM was premature. As a driver, he was still impulsive and erratic. During 1967 he also drove a Formula 2 McLaren M4A for John Coombs, the man who'd sold Frank the ex-Graham Hill Cooper a couple of years earlier. Piers crashed so frequently that Coombs begged him to pack up racing 'or you'll kill yourself. I know you will!'

Frank did not rank among the majority who by now harboured serious doubts as to Piers's ability. Far from it. He thought Courage was a fantastic driver and invited him to take the wheel of the prototype Brabham BT21B Formula 3 car he had entered in the prestigious Brands Hatch Motor Show 200 meeting at the end of 1967.

From the touchlines, this may have looked like a step down in terms of career progress, but it turned out to be absolutely the correct decision. Piers won the first heat by 10 seconds on a rain-drenched track, going some way towards salvaging a reputation badly tarnished when he was dropped from the BRM 'junior squad' as early as the Monaco Grand Prix.

'My desire to have Piers in the team stemmed from trying to help a pal re-establish his career,' explains Frank. 'That Brands Hatch result helped sell a few Brabhams and also gave Piers some confidence to leg it back up the ladder. It was that F3 entrant's deal which opened my mind to the serious possibility of becoming an entrant, but what really precipitated my move up into Formula 2 for 1968 was Piers persuading me to help him.'

From a personal viewpoint, Frank can hardly conceal the fact that he simply adored Piers – as indeed did all his pals.

'As a character, there seriously has not been anybody like him in motor racing since,' he insists. 'He wasn't an aristocrat, but he came from a very privileged family. He went to Eton, lived among a group of friends like Sheridan, who were different to your average geezer that I was accustomed to.'

Warming to his theme, inevitably with Sheridan – 'my resident aristo' – present, he continues: 'You see, they're different to us, the old aristos, and I mean that very charmingly. Piers lived a very social life in London, married to Sally who really did come from an aristocratic background. They moved in a small circle of acquaintances which, in many ways, is much smaller today because there are not so many of them around.'

Frank had become an official Brabham agent over the previous couple of years, selling dozens of the fine-handling, easy-to-maintain Formula 3 racers built by Jack and his practical, down-to-earth confederate Ron Tauranac. He made a few hundred pounds on each sale and was doing pretty well. Then, at the start of 1968 he found himself with an unsold Brabham BT23C Formula 2 car on his hands, the result of a last-minute cancelled order by Rollo Feilding, now the Earl of Denbigh. This was the car that was used for Piers to drive in that season's European F2 Championship.

'To be honest, I never really budgeted it out,' Frank admits, 'because I didn't really know what I'd blundered into. We got some financial assistance from Dunlop, but the team was basically set up on the profits of the previous year's trading, such as they had been, and they didn't amount to much. The car cost £2,500 and the same again for a Cosworth FVA engine, then a bunch of wheels, spare engine and gear ratios. I suppose the whole thing cost about ten grand.'

By the start of the 1968 season Piers had gone some way to restoring his image with a splendidly consistent sequence of outings in the winter Tasman Series, capping off this 'down under' tour with a magnificent victory on the challenging Longford road circuit in Tasmania. Driving the McLaren M4A which he had purchased from John Coombs, Piers never put a foot wrong on a wet track and returned to Europe with a dramatically enhanced reputation. 'By the time he came to me he had a lot more credibility,' acknowledges Frank.

The dark blue Williams Brabham proved consistently competitive throughout the summer of 1968, Piers growing in confidence with every race. He won his heat at Zandvoort, ran a strong second to Jochen Rindt's similar Winkelmann Racing BT23C at Crystal Palace before retiring, and rounded off the season with solid third places in the French races at Reims and Albi. On the F1 front he was welcomed back into the BRM fold, albeit running for the semi-works Tim Parnell-operated second string team and scored his first World Championship point at the wheel of a P126 V12 in the rain-soaked French Grand Prix at Rouen.

During the mid race tyre change, Parnell's staff were assisted by a spectating Sheridan Thynne who vividly recalls his terror as John Surtees's Honda and Pedro Rodriguez's works BRM swept by Piers's stationary car, seemingly inches away on a very narrow road, running neck-and-neck in a huge cloud of spray.

Piers's F1 obligations naturally took precedence over Frank's F2 programme, so with his number one driver committed to the Dutch Grand Prix, Frank invited his old mate Jonathan Williams to drive the BT23C in the Monza Lottery F2 event. In 1966 Jonathan had quit the British F3 scene for the warmer climes of southern Europe, accepting an invitation to join the Rome-based de Sanctis team as their works driver. He quickly became something of a dab hand at the black art of Monza slipstreaming and duly notched up the first F2 victory for Frank Williams Racing Cars, beating Alan Rees's Winkelmann Brabham by a length. His fee, he recalls, was a slap-up dinner at Frank's expense.

By the end of the season a certain momentum was building within the Williams organisation, a sequence of catalysts almost inadvertently steering Frank towards Formula 1 through no fault of his own. The Tasman organisers had been highly impressed with Piers the previous winter and Ron Frost, the man behind the Australasian series, approached Frank to see whether he might be interested in running a car in the 1968-1969 championship.

Six thousand pounds was on offer, so Frank bought an ex-works Brabham BT24 and a couple of 2.5-litre Cosworth DFW V8s to power it. These were short-stroke versions of the full 3-litre DFV Grand Prix engines which could be reconverted to F1 specification with obvious ease. All the signposts were beckoning towards the sport's premier category.

'I remember sitting in my little flat above the garage in Slough one lunchtime, having soup with my secretary Norma Robb, a lovely girl who tragically later died of cancer,' Frank explains. 'We were thinking

"Look, we've got all this equipment, so we really should be thinking about F1." It wasn't a question of "Let's go and see Dunlop", it was a case of "Let's convert those engines to 3-litres. No problem. Let's do it". '

First, a busy winter beckoned. Before Piers jetted off to the Tasman series, there was the Argentine Temporada series of four races to be contested. Frank sent out no fewer than five cars – one for Piers, the others for local drivers Juan-Manuel Bordeu, Carlos Pairetti, Jorge Cupeiro and Eduardo Copello. While in Argentina, Williams would meet a serious-minded Argentinian called Carlos Reutemann for the first time. He was driving a Tecno for the rival Ron Harris F2 team and Jonathan Williams told Frank that Reutemann was terrific. Frank wasn't convinced at the time. Eleven years later, Reutemann would almost win the World Championship in a Williams FW07B.

In Australia, Piers was re-living the bad old days, throwing away his chances with a series of silly incidents. Even so, Frank's F1 programme had now been firmed up.

Frank says: 'We did have problems getting our hands on a suitable car, which I suppose you can now look back and say reflects the haphazard nature of the planning that went into the whole business. Eff all, as usual, in other words. Eventually we tracked down an ex-works Brabham BT26 which had been bought by northern enthusiast Charles Bridges – he'd previously raced Chevron sports cars – who bought it from the works with gearbox, but minus its Repco engine.

'We employed Robin Herd, who would later go on to be one of the founders of March Engineering, to adapt the chassis to take a Cosworth V8, but we had to do the deals quietly and discreetly. Jack Brabham was switching his works team to Cosworth power in 1969 and, since he was contracted to Goodyear, the last thing he wanted was one of his ex-works cars racing against him on Dunlops.'

By the end of 1969, there was no longer a question mark hanging over Piers's ability as a Grand Prix contender. He started nine races in the dark blue Williams Brabham and, although he only registered four finishes, two of those were splendid second places. The first came at Monaco, where he finished runner-up to Graham Hill's works Lotus 49B, the second in the United States Grand Prix at Watkins Glen where he followed Jochen Rindt's Lotus across the line.

His performance at the Glen was tremendous. 'It absolutely knocked me out,' smiles Williams. 'He was running third between the works Brabhams of Jacky Ickx and Jack Brabham himself and the way he kept Jack behind, hurling stones all over the man whose company had built the Williams car in the first place. Ickx retired, so Piers had a clear run to second place in the closing stages of the contest, many observers reporting that this was one of the few occasions they had seen Jack Brabham in a black fury at the end of a race.'

Just to make his point, as he swung the works BT26 out of the pit lane towards the paddock after the race had finished, Jack cut so sharply in front of the Williams Brabham that the works car's right rear wheel sliced off Piers's left front nose wing. To have been beaten by a Dunlop-shod car on Goodyear's home ground was bad enough, but that it was one of his own ex-works cars fielded by a privateer was almost more than the triple World Champion could bear!

Courage also notched up fifth places at Silverstone and Monza, dropping from the leading bunch in the Italian race only when the Williams Brabham developed a slight fuel feed problem and consequent misfire. After the British Grand Prix, Courage castigated Frank for not keeping him sufficiently well informed of Jochen Rindt's recovery and the Lotus slipped by to take fourth on the very last lap. Witnesses say this was the only occasion they can remember Piers and Frank raising their voices at each other in public.

At Monza, however, it was left to Jackie Stewart to pay Piers the ultimate compliment: 'To my mind, that was the day Piers came of age as a Grand Prix driver. Up until that point, I had always been just a little concerned about his unpredictability in close traffic, but he ran with the leading bunch – Rindt, Beltoise, McLaren and me – for many laps and I never had a moment's worry. He was driving immaculately and with total discipline.'

On the Formula 2 front, Piers drove Frank's new Brabham BT30 to victory in the Mediterranean Grand Prix at Enna-Pergusa, a scorching dust bowl of a circuit skirting a snake-infested lake in central Sicily. That same race saw F1 Ferrari driver Jacky Ickx appear at the wheel of a neat little F2 machine produced by the Modena-based de Tomaso company. Frank had made the acquaintance of its designer, Gianpaolo Dallara, and this led to a meeting with company boss Alessandro de Tomaso during the Italian Grand Prix weekend at Monza.

De Tomaso was a dynamic and successful Argentinian whose marriage to wealthy American Isabelle Haskell had spawned an auspicious business partnership. They were already manufacturing his own Ford-engined high performance sports cars in an attempt to challenge Ferrari and Lamborghini, and would later acquire controlling interests in both Maserati and Innocenti.

The energy and enthusiasm radiated by de Tomaso impressed Frank Williams enormously. The Argentinian proposed that his company should build a new Grand Prix machine which Williams would prepare and enter for Piers Courage in 1970. Frank's contribution to the partnership would be furnishing the engine, driver and organisational expertise, a prospect which seemed a whole lot better than paying for everything himself.

The deal was duly done and symbolically cemented a few weeks later when Piers squeezed himself into the cramped cockpit of the F2 de Tomaso for the Rome Grand Prix at Vallelunga, smashing the lap record in practice to start from pole position. He finished third in the first heat and retired with electrical trouble in the second. It seemed promising enough.

In retrospect, Frank recalls it as rather a one-sided deal. 'I wasn't as clever as de Tomaso,' he grins, 'and, of course, you've got to remember that he was giving me something he wanted. I was never that clever, never very streetwise; I just worked hard. He was a very clever operator.'

Piers gave the de Tomaso type 505 his best shot. Turning down a £30,000 offer to join Jacky Ickx at Ferrari, he stayed on with Frank at a nominal £3,000 retainer and made up much of the difference by joining the Alfa Romeo sports car squad which offered another £22,500.

'You must understand, because of Piers's personality as an individual, rather than as a racing driver, that he found the concept of achieving success with Frank enormously appealing,' says Sheridan Thynne. 'It was a case of wanting Frank and Porridge to show Ferrari and Lotus that they could get the job done. Consequently, he was strongly motivated to stay with Frank and have things continue as they had been in the past.'

Sherry also recalls Piers saying constantly that he definitely wanted to stay with Frank because he was a superb organiser. Frank is not so certain this flattery was warranted: 'Sure, we used to polish the cars beautifully. They looked immaculate. Forget the fact that, in 1968 at least, they were sometimes set up with positive camber on one wheel and negative on the other!'

Tragically, 21 June, 1970 was the day the circus left town for that group of bright-eyed young racers who had grown up together since the mid-sixties. Running midfield in the Dutch Grand Prix at Zandvoort the de Tomaso crashed, caught fire and Piers perished in the inferno. It was a shattering, mind-numbing blow which brutally tore apart hopes and dreams. Frank and the lads were devastated. Somehow, it would never be quite the same again.

'I was heartbroken,' says Frank openly. 'I worshipped the guy. He was totally adorable. Everybody you've ever heard of in motor racing turned out for his funeral. Nobody ducked it. And there were plenty of red eyes from the hard guys, I can tell you. It was a very moving event.'

Frank also pays tribute to his old friend by shooting down those critics who felt that Piers was in over his head, attempting to run too quickly when he didn't quite have the talent.

'I would say that's definitely not the case,' he insists with genuine passion. 'OK, perhaps he had been trying too hard earlier in his career, realising that he wasn't always taken seriously by the Chapmans and the Brabhams. But he had terrific car control and skill.

'You must also remember he wasn't driving for a premier team either. But he was extremely intelligent, always thinking about ways to enhance the performance of any car he was driving. A certain maturity was showing. Just remember that in 1970, working with Gianpaolo Dallara, they took a real junk shit box of a car in South Africa to be a midfield runner by Spain, then almost a front runner, tyres permitting, by the time he was killed at Zandvoort.'

Bubbles Horsley has no doubt that Frank developed a unique relationship with Piers. 'It was very much young men together, memories which went back to scurfing about with F3 cars on the continent, the camaraderie and boyish enthusiasm we all had for life. When we got to play in the big league, we never really recaptured that.'

Lady Sarah recalls: 'Piers and Frank got on together and understood each other so well. They were old friends and sustained a good relationship to the end. He was tempted by that Ferrari offer in 1970 and at one stage I really thought it might be a good idea. But Piers didn't want to leave Frank, and Jacky Ickx warned Piers about the political problems of being a Ferrari driver, so he eventually decided against it.

'There was interest from Lotus as well, but no, Piers stayed with Frank. The chemistry was there. They talked the same language. They were such happy times and everybody had such incredible optimism, even when things weren't going right.'

3

Enter Patrick Head

There were to be many turning points in the fortunes of Frank Williams and his team, not least the business ramifications which followed Piers's death. Frank remained as intensely committed to motor racing as ever, but now the ground was dramatically cut from beneath him. In the complex, unpredictable game of motor racing snakes and ladders, the partnership with Piers Courage had enabled him steadily to progress up the rungs of the ladder. But the death of the debonair Englishman sent Frank hurtling back down a snake to rock bottom. Effectively, he had to start the game again from scratch.

In an effort to sustain some of de Tomaso's enthusiasm, Frank attempted to sign up the brilliant young Brazilian star Emerson Fittipaldi. There was no chance. Lotus chief Colin Chapman had him under contract and he was specifically debarred from racing anything but a Lotus in any category. The de Tomaso project tottered along to the end of the season, Australian youngster Tim Schenken accepting the drive which at least gave him a leg-up into F1. But with Piers's death the spark had gone out and the moment was past for the Williams-de Tomaso alliance.

'It was a great shame,' muses Frank wistfully. 'De Tomaso had just done a major deal to sell his company to Ford, so there was talk about a little more technical help from Cosworth, perhaps an engine or two. We had also made a number of sponsorship contacts, admittedly on a very amateur level as compared with the way we do things today, but Piers was a coming man in a great sport and I think things were beginning to click for us on this front as well.'

Frank emerged from 1970 financially bruised and battered: 'The company was very heavily insolvent. All we owned were two engines, a transporter, some minor mechanical items, lots of debt . . . and no Piers.'

Nevertheless, Frank picked himself up and set about trying to re-establish the team as F1 contenders. With sponsorship from the

French Motul oil company he fielded an off-the-shelf March 711 for
Frenchman Henri Pescarolo, naively believing that things would continue their previous upward trend.

'You must remember that in those days I was starry-eyed, full of
enthusiasm for whatever I turned my hand to,' Frank explains. 'I
believed in Porridge, so I believed in the next one. Pesca had been good in
F2, extremely brave in the Matra at Le Mans, not lifting off at night in the
rain and so-on, so I was full of enthusiasm for him. But he wasn't quite
top F1 material and we never quite gelled. We were always struggling.'

As a businessman Frank developed into a remarkable rag-bag of
contradictions, as he was to prove over the next seven years. His capacity
for clinching a deal, of surviving until next week, of ducking and dodging
the creditors, of running his F1 team on thin air – all would pass into
Grand Prix folklore. But he could never quite pull off the big sponsorship
coup and, as a result, as the years went by and the debts accumulated,
paying last year's bills with next season's sponsorship monies became an
accepted part of his modus operandi.

On one occasion, Frank was beaten at his own game, albeit inadvertently, by the Ford Motor Company. Harry Calton, now in charge of
Ford's Public Affairs, recalls the episode:

'Back in the early 1970s I received a phone call from Walter Hayes
who said Frank wanted to buy a 15 cwt Ford Transit van, so this was duly
arranged and delivered. Shortly afterwards, I got a rather embarrassing
memo from the accounts department saying "Mr Williams's cheque has
been returned unpaid." I had the awkward task of ringing Frank to
explain. He was most apologetic and, within 12 hours, had a banker's
draft delivered to Ford's accounts department.

'By that time, the accounting mechanism had somehow managed to
re-present his original cheque and, this time, it was paid. So Frank
suddenly found that he'd paid for the Transit twice. Again, Ford's
accounting system had swallowed his cheque and he just couldn't believe
that it took six months before he could get reimbursed. I don't suppose
that happened to him very often.'

This was at a time when most F1 team principals were on Ford's free
list for the loan of a Ford Zodiac, a slice of largesse which Frank always
appreciated and never forgot. He was a great favourite among the hard-
working and conscientious staff at the Ford press depot at Brentford,
Middlesex, where these "freebie" cars were prepared and maintained.

Alf Belsen, who ran the depot for many years, remembers Williams as
always tremendously cheerful, always prepared to arrange passes if one
of the guys was going on holiday to a Continental Grand Prix. He
wouldn't say "yes", and then forget it, like some of his colleagues. It
would be done. The passes would be there. The lads at the press garage
found him delightful to deal with.

In 1971, Pescarolo's best placing was a fourth in the British Grand

Prix, and he also won the F2 Mallory Park International in Frank's March 712. But the whole programme was under-financed, sponsorship spread too thinly and the factory in Bath Road bursting at the seams. It was the beginning of a gentle downward spiral.

Frank hadn't been too impressed with March's standards of construction either, assuring *Motoring News* on one occasion that 'I'll never buy another March' which, of course, he didn't. Not until 1972, anyway.

He really wanted to build his own car again, get back to an exclusive arrangement similar to that which he enjoyed with de Tomaso. The opportunity arose when Politoys, the Italian model car makers who had been co-sponsors on Pescarolo's March, put up £40,000 for Frank to build and run a tailor-made F1 contender. There was insufficient room at Bath Road, but one of the team's mechanics, Bob Evans, got word of a new 5,000 sq ft factory becoming available on the outskirts of Reading. It was just the job and the team quickly transferred its operation to these new premises.

Lack of manufacturing facilities meant that the Politoys was manufactured with assistance from Gomm Metal Developments, a specialist sheet metal business in Old Woking which had previously carried out rebuilding work on Frank's F2 March chassis in late 1971. The car was finally finished in time for the 1972 British Grand Prix at Brands Hatch where Pescarolo celebrated its debut by writing it off. It was a trait the bearded Frenchman would repeat, smashing up Frank's March 721 on no fewer than four occasions. The team was on its knees.

In Part 2 (The Financing of an F1 team) the commercial intricacies of how Frank continued to operate through to the middle of 1975 on a progressively diminishing budget are recounted in detail. Suffice to say here that from the end of 1972 for the next three seasons, Frank Williams (Racing Cars) Ltd bumped along at the back of the field, punctuating a depressing series of retirements with the odd, unexpected finish in the top six here and there.

These fortuitous results earned valuable World Championship points, helping the team to get to the next race. But a succession of tired engines, tatty racing cars and second rate drivers purchasing rides with personal sponsorship that all too frequently failed to materialise, reduced Frank to the edge of bankruptcy. However he always managed to stay one step ahead of the bailiffs, even if unpaid bills occasionally meant that the telephone to the Bennett Road, Reading, factory was cut off. When it was, the boss kept in touch with the outside world by means of the public telephone box outside Reading Speedway track.

At the start of 1975, Frank was chatting on the telephone with Gianpaolo Dallara, who was now working at Lamborghini, and asked the Italian designer whether he had any ideas. Dallara told him that they had this very rich customer who kept telling them that he wanted to race a Lamborghini at Le Mans 'whatever it costs'. Frank pricked up his ears.

'Tell me about him,' he urged.

Contact was duly made with this character. He called Frank and they arranged that he should come up and watch the team contest the non-championship Daily Express International Trophy meeting at Silverstone. Frank says: 'I was in our garage, fussing about, when a dark shadow descended over the car. I looked up and there was this enormous figure in a short leather jacket, muscles bulging. The figure extended a hand. "Hello zer . . . I'm Valter. You must be Frank" – and that was it.'

Walter Wolf was an Austro-Canadian millionaire who had made his fortune in the oil equipment business. He was a shrewd man, a tough negotiator, but utterly captivated by what he saw, and he agreed to help Frank's team with sponsorship. Jacques Laffite was the team's number one driver, a promising rising star, and he helped the team stay afloat with a timely second place to Carlos Reutemann's Brabham in that summer's German Grand Prix at the Nürburgring.

'To start with Walter just paid for some engines, but increasingly he wanted to become a shareholder in the company,' says Frank. 'I was reluctant to relinquish any control. Yet he played a major part in enabling us to stay in business throughout 1975, of that there's no question at all. In the second half of the year he was very keen to buy the team, which was effectively insolvent, but we still retained membership of the Constructors' Association and that was worth a bob or two.

'In preparation for 1976 I was talking to Marlboro and they were prepared to pay £100,000 for us to take Jacky Ickx. That was a lot of money in those days as we could supplement that with additional backing, smaller amounts from other sources. I thought we had a reasonable chance of getting things sorted out until one day I thought "The hell with it, let's do a deal with Walter, 60-40. He can be King and I'll run the show." So that's how it worked out.'

At the end of the season Frank Williams (Racing Cars) Ltd was effectively metamorphosed into Walter Wolf Racing. The new organisation bought the under-developed, rubber-suspended Hesketh 308C programme, together with designer Harvey Postlethwaite, for £450,000 and embarked with optimism on the 1976 season. Things could hardly get worse. But they did.

Shortly before his decision to sell the controlling interest to Walter Wolf, Frank had signed up a promising young chief engineer called Patrick Head. Postlethwaite's arrival on the scene with the Hesketh package had the effect of demoting the newcomer to a secondary role almost before he had started.

Shrewdly, he stayed on, reasoning that he could learn from his more experienced colleague. It was a decision Frank Williams has had reason to be grateful for ever since. From March 1977, Patrick would become chief designer for Williams Grand Prix Engineering, the new company which was born at the start of that year, and an integral, indispensable part of the team's rise to World Championship winning capability.

Patrick Head was born into a world of motor racing and fast cars. His father, Col. Michael Head, had been a Military Attaché in Sweden between 1949 and 1951 where he bought an alloy-bodied XK120 straight off the Jaguar stand at the Stockholm Motor Show. Later he would be Director of Fighting Vehicles at the army's base in Chobham, Surrey, during which time Patrick recalls him running-in his competition cars on the facility's test track there.

Col. Head also enjoyed a stint as a military advisor to Sir Solly Zuckerman, the chief government scientist, in daily contact with all the service chiefs at the highest possible level. But it was as an enthusiastic club racer, preparing his machines in the garage alongside the family's Woking home. that Michael Head imbued his son with an eventual enthusiasm for cars and motor racing.

Something of a martinet, Col. Head decided that Patrick should pursue a career in the navy. 'It was a variation of Henry Ford's old adage,' smiles the Williams designer, 'in that you can do anything you like, my boy, as long as it's going into the navy.' In the absence of any ideas to the contrary, Patrick duly obliged, taking a naval scholarship at the age of 16 before going to Gosport 'to swing around on a few ropes, take an intelligence test and so-on.'

He spent only three months in the Royal Naval College at Dartmouth before buying himself out after a bit of a misunderstanding about career prospects with the engineering officer who had advised him if he went to Cambridge through the navy, he would be in the service for life. Patrick, who had anticipated staying in only until his early 30s, baulked at that prospect – inaccurate, as things transpired – and disentangled himself from the Senior Service. It cost him £195, all the money he had in the world.

This career detour unfortunately put him in bad odour with his father. He was unwelcome at home for a few years and only enjoyed a brief rapprochement with his father in late 1970, a few months before Col. Head succumbed to secondary cancer.

Patrick subsequently followed a convoluted path to an honours degree from London University. His need to come to terms with the economic realities of life was cushioned by a timely inheritance 'from a super old bloke known in the family as Cousin Alec, who was Irish, with huge jowls and a red nose!' This enabled him to pay his own way through university, in addition to building his own boat.

'This all gave me an independent arrogance,' he remembers with a touch of self-deprecation. 'I suppose it was partly responsible for me taking such a long time to pass my exams. I was a bit of a child of the sixties, living in a London flat, smoking pot, very Bohemian ... quite out of character, really.

'I have to say that the idea of working and achieving something was not a priority. I just wanted to have fun and enjoy myself. Even up to joining Frank in 1975 I wasn't committed to going motor racing. There didn't seem to be any pressure to buckle down and think of a career.'

He dallied with competition driving very briefly. At 17 he tried his hand at karting, then in 1969, during his last year at university, tried clubmans sports car racing. He came to an arrangement with Arthur Mallock, the man who pioneered the U2 sports cars, whereby he could use plans for the front half of the constructor's design and modify the rear end to accept a Lotus Elite differential, thereby endowing the machine with independent rear suspension.

'It was exceptionally heavy and rather complicated,' he recalls. 'I raced it briefly in 1969 and 1970. Clubmans cars are, in my view, pretty lethal machines; engine hard up against your leg, propshaft whirling round alongside your kidneys and the driveshaft a couple of inches from your back. It scared me witless!'

Notwithstanding his earlier pretence towards lack of ambition, as things transpired Patrick had more than five years' varied engineering experience in motor racing by the time he joined Frank Williams. Just after his father's death he joined Lola Cars at Huntingdon, one of Britain's most prolific manufacturers of proprietary racing cars across a wide range of formulae. He was subsequently occupied on an ambitious engine development project for Formula Super Vee, designed a neat little F2 car for Richard Scott and worked for Peter Agg's Trojan organisation on their T101 Formula 5000 car together with former Brabham designer Ron Tauranac.

Patrick was certainly not impressed by the Williams FW05, née Hesketh 308C, and privately vowed that, if this was regarded as a competitive Formula 1 car, he felt confident he could do better. He would get the big chance to prove his ability less than two years later.

With Jacky Ickx and French youngster Michel Leclere as the driving team, the Wolf-Williams cars were unmitigated disasters. After James Hunt had driven the car, under the Hesketh banner, for the first time in the non-championship 1975 Swiss Grand Prix at Dijon-Prenois, he was deeply concerned about the machine's idiosyncrasies. And things only got worse the following year, the team's problems being compounded by a number one driver whose motivation was sadly flagging.

Yet Frank, with his unshakeable determination and sometimes infuriating ability only to look on the bright side, seemed blind to the mounting problems. He should have seen the warning lights. Walter was OK, reasoned Frank. He understood.

In fact, it was quite the contrary. From where he was viewing the proceedings, Walter could see the good name he'd built up in the oil industry being squandered on a badly administered racing team fielding an embarrassingly uncompetitive product.

It was Frank's close friend Dave Brodie, one of Britain's leading saloon car drivers and an acquaintance from the Pinner Road days and who would later briefly become a director of Williams Grand Prix Engineering, who laid it on the line, as Frank now freely admits:

'Old Brode took me out to lunch and said "you'd better start getting some results, because that sort of man (Walter) will be very impatient . . . you'll be in big trouble". We said "No, no, Walter understands racing, he'll give us time". But Brodie was right and I was wrong. He was always more perceptive and streetwise than me.'

In the middle of the 1976 season Walter Wolf removed Frank Williams from the front line in an organisational shake-up that introduced former Lotus team manager Peter Warr into the equation. Walter was taking command, determined to mould the team into what he reckoned a competitive F1 team should be, not what Frank had let it drift into. Williams found himself reduced to the role of highly-paid sponsorship chaser, although in reality he soon found himself assuming the role of Walter's errand boy. High salary or not, it wasn't what he wanted. With absolutely no acrimony, he split with Wolf to go it alone.

When it was announced that Frank intended to re-establish himself as an independent team owner, it raised the spectre of another under-financed, hand-to-mouth operation scraping by at the back of the field. Surely, thought the critics, Frank has had enough of beating his head against the proverbial brick wall. But this time, it really would be different, not least because Patrick Head decided to go with him.

From the start of 1978, when Head designed the neat Williams FW06 which began to put the team on the map, Williams Grand Prix Engineering inevitably began to assume a distinctively different character. In the past, it had been Frank on his own, battling against the odds, but now Patrick would become an absolutely essential element in the equation. Over the following 12 seasons, as the team began to enjoy the good times, Patrick's influence and overall character became as deeply ingrained in the team's identity as the man whose name is carried by the cars.

No longer would Frank have to worry himself about the engineering side of the business. The team set up in new premises on an industrial estate in Station Road, Didcot, where the modest success achieved during 1978 acted as a catalyst to prompt dramatic expansion over the next couple of years. The key turning point would be 1979 when Head's magnificent FW07 design re-drew the parameters of Grand Prix car performance.

In the summer of 1978, the dramatic, World Championship winning success of Colin Chapman's ground effect Lotus 79 alerted every other F1 designer to the absolute necessity of exploring the intricacies of under-car aerodynamics. This was a major turning point in Grand Prix car design and anybody who failed to pursue it was effectively dead in the water to all competitive intents and purposes. Patrick applied an enormous amount of his own personal endeavour to developing an understanding of ground effect technology and came up trumps as a result.

'Undoubtedly when we did the FW07, a great deal of the basic thinking centred on what Lotus had done with the Lotus 79,' he explains openly. 'Although, to be honest, from the outset I really didn't fully understand the function of ground effect, and it became very clear to me at the end of 1978 that we needed to get some time working in a wind tunnel.'

Patrick had heard that Lotus did much of its aerodynamic development in the wind tunnel at London's Imperial College, so he contacted John Harvey, who ran the college's aeronautical division. He confirmed that there was a small amount of time available in the tunnel, although generally it was pretty heavily booked up. So Patrick went and used it, quickly appreciating that this would become an essential tool for F1 car design, but that it would be absolutely ideal if Williams GPE could obtain one for itself.

Casting back to his time with Lola in Huntingdon, the Williams designer recalled that Specialised Mouldings, who for many years serviced almost the entire British motor racing industry when it came to the manufacture of tailor-made glass fibre body components, possessed their own wind tunnel. So he rang the firm's boss, Peter Jackson, to inquire whether they might like to sell it. The reply was affirmative. A deal was struck and the tunnel, which the previous owners had discarded some time previously, was delivered to the Williams base in Didcot on a low-loader truck. Such were the limitations on space at the team's existing premises in Station Road that a lease had to be taken on additional, unadjoining premises, in order to accommodate this new technical luxury.

'By the time we acquired this tunnel, of course, it was too late to influence FW07,' Patrick recalls. 'And, in fact, the entire aerodynamic design of that car was based on a single week's work in the Imperial College wind tunnel – in what amounted to the first wind tunnel work I'd ever done in my life. Really, I hadn't got a clue what ground effect was all about and had to think very carefully about the whole project.

'One notable area we made a significant improvement on was the front wing set-up because the Lotus 79 had huge nose wings on it which damaged the airflow to the side pods. We twigged very early on that a ground effect design would really be better without front wings which is why we had tiny little neutral profile trim tabs on FW07 from the start and it even raced on a few occasions without any front wings at all.'

With Frank working hard on the sponsorship front, garnering funds from Saudi Arabia, Williams Grand Prix Engineering had assumed the outward image of a big budget team by the start of 1979, with the result that some observers simply could not understand why the first FW07 wasn't ready before the fifth round of the Championship, the start of the European season.

In reality, of course, the team could hardly expand quickly enough, particularly in the design department. In January 1979, the company was employing only 18 people in total, and Patrick's design department consisted purely of him and a junior engineer called Neil Oatley who had joined mid-way through the previous season, although their development capability was considerably strengthened by the recruitment of Frank Dernie as full-time aerodynamicist at the start of the season. The Williams FW06 had been totally Patrick's handiwork from the ground up and FW07 was also his own concept, although Neil was invaluable with engineering detail and Frank contributed considerably with important aspects of the latter stages of the design.

By the end of 1979, the Williams workforce had expanded dramatically to 45 employees and the team had narrowly been defeated in its quest for the World Championship. Not only had Regazzoni won the team's first F1 victory at Silverstone, but Alan Jones kept the ball rolling with impressive wins in the German, Austrian, Dutch and Canadian Grands Prix. They finished the year very much as the team to beat.

Over the years that followed, Patrick Head would forge a reputation as a designer which accurately reflected his whole demeanour. A succession of practical, sturdy, serviceable and consistently competitive machines sprang from his design department. If, within the F1 community, his designs were regarded as slightly conservative, the consistent level of success achieved by Williams GPE over the past decade has tended to underline that this is no bad thing.

'In the early part of my career I got cured of any idea of being egotistical from an engineering standpoint,' he admits. 'By that I mean in the sense that one might say "I'm going to prove to the world that my conceptual ideas are better than anybody else's". I think that attitude came about because I saw the damage that can be done to a company if one person over-indulges himself in conceptual ideas that don't work.'

In adopting this rationale, Head was thinking specifically about the way in which Colin Chapman had followed up the Lotus 79 concept by producing the aerodynamically complicated type 80 which proved a complete and utter flop.

'Chapman was such a big figure at Lotus, in complete charge and with an enormous reputation, that he could take a risk like that,' explains Patrick. 'But not only was the thing a disaster, but it went through the whole of 1980 with bits falling off and breaking, which is why Carlos Reutemann left them and came to drive for us. But while Lotus could arguably afford to take time off for such experiments, if we had endured a year like that, certainly in our early days, we would have been hard-pressed to survive. Granted, we had bad years like 1984, but we always managed to produce enough expectation for the following season. I learned early on that you've got to do a good solid job to survive and keep your credibility in this business.'

Patrick's measured approach to the development of the Williams F1 cars during the early 1980s laid a solid bedrock for future achievement. They were among the last front-line teams to embrace both carbon-fibre chassis technology and turbocharged engines. Yet when they made the switch, they did so with well-justified confidence.

Patrick became a significant shareholder and director of Williams Grand Prix Engineering in 1979. The relationship between Frank and his Chief Designer, now Technical Director, is based on a mutual recognition and respect of what they have both contributed to the overall equation of a successful business operation.

That's not to say that tensions don't build up between them. For Patrick, motor racing is overwhelmingly all about sensible engineering and the need for a lot of no-nonsense dedication and hard work. In their early years together there were some horrifyingly vociferous arguments between them in the Station Road factory. Legend has it that other occupants of the trading estate complained when Patrick's personal volume control was on the stops. They were asked if they could at least keep their factory windows closed when such frank exchanges of views were under way.

Yet there are other, more frequent, occasions when they take on the image of a couple of conspiratorial youngsters on a treat from school. Lunchtime meetings in Frank's office are often lighthearted, laced with delightfully indiscreet gossip. Basically they get on well for two people who have spent 13 years of their professional life squaring up to the same challenges in their chosen business.

Although Keke Rosberg would win the 1982 World Championship at the wheel of the Cosworth-engined Williams FW08, it was clear that the team was running against the overwhelming turbo tide and a switch to the latest breed of forced induction 1.5-litre engines was overdue. Yet Frank and Patrick sifted through all the options with meticulous care before making the correct decision. In 1981 they opened negotiations with Honda for the supply of turbocharged F1 engines.

At the start of the 1980s, there had been a sea change within the world of Formula 1 racing, indirectly triggered by the arrival of Renault, France's national racing team, on the scene three years earlier, armed with the first turbocharged 1.5-litre engine. This more or less coincided with Colin Chapman unlocking the secret of under-car aerodynamics and the subsequent division of Grand Prix racing into two separate factions.

Ranged on this side of the Channel there were the small specialist British teams as epitomised by Williams – high on technical ingenuity, but low on political clout within the halls of FISA, the sport's governing body, which from the start of 1979 had become the bailiwick of Jean-Marie Balestre. On the other side of the divide was a smaller group, essentially just Renault and Ferrari plus a few who chose to align themselves with these two influential teams.

The British-based teams formed the backbone of the Formula One Constructors' Association, the power base of Bernie Ecclestone. In a nutshell, he was the one individual most responsible for Grand Prix racing's rise to international popularity as one of the most popular televised international sports. Under his stewardship, FOCA had become a highly organised, well-drilled group of professionals, all of whom were totally committed to fielding cars in a full World Championship programme throughout every season. In terms of commitment to Ecclestone and the FOCA ethic, few disciples were more loyal than Frank Williams.

'Bernie was the leader and we followed,' he says respectfully. He is absolutely dedicated to Ecclestone's cause, although outsiders see Frank as much more of an establishment man than the feisty campaigner who was right at the sharp end of the battle against FISA in the early 1980s. His optimism that the sport's governing body has the capacity for even-handed and considerate handling of the sport's problems is freely expressed, even though it is not a view shared totally by even his two co-directors, Patrick Head and Sheridan Thynne.

Set in an historical context, the first few years of the new decade came to represent a complex transitional period during which the level and intensity of F1 became transformed by the arrival of major motor manufacturers in the role of engine suppliers to the major teams. At the time, however, it seemed as though the sport's governing body was discriminating against the FOCA-aligned entrants in favour of those turbo pioneers, Renault and Ferrari.

At the end of 1980, the sliding aerodynamic side skirts which were absolutely central to the success of the sophisticated ground effect cars, were banned by FISA on the grounds of safety. Moreover, the sport's governing body initiated this rule change without giving the two years' notice which was provided for in its own regulations. Formula 1 was thrown into a major panic.

Briefly, the FOCA-aligned teams toyed with the idea of introducing their own 'pirate' World Championship. At the start of 1981 a non-Championship South African Grand Prix took place at Kyalami to the old 'skirted' regulations, and Carlos Reutemann's Williams FW07B emerged the winner. But the race was never counted for the official World Championship. This came less than a year after Alan Jones had won the Spanish Grand Prix at Jarama, an event which was also disallowed Championship status following a major sanctioning dispute which represented another key move on the chess board of controversy between FOCA and FISA.

Despite peace apparently being restored to the Grand Prix scene by the introduction of the Concorde Agreement at the start of 1981, the first few months of 1982 saw controversy erupt yet again when the FOCA teams detected a subtle loophole in the regulations which would allow their relatively under-powered Cosworth V8-engined cars to compete on a more even footing with the more powerful, but heavier, turbos.

It had long been accepted practice that oil reservoirs be replenished immediately after a Grand Prix before the cars were weighed at post-race scrutineering. Now Brabham and Williams decided to fit their machines with water reservoirs, ostensibly for brake cooling purposes, which they sought to refill in the same manner. This enabled the cars to run under the minimum weight limit during the race and then be 'topped up' to an appropriate weight before being checked over afterwards.

FISA disallowed this practice with the result that Nelson Piquet's Brabham and Keke Rosberg's Williams, both Cosworth-engined cars, were disqualified from first and second places in the 1982 Brazilian Grand Prix. This handed victory to Alain Prost's Renault, which had finished third on the road, and triggered a boycott of the San Marino Grand Prix by all the FOCA-aligned teams.

'The only one to break ranks over this was Ken Tyrrell,' recalls Frank. Sponsorship considerations had obliged Tyrrell to swim against the tide, a decision which would put him permanently beyond the pale in the eyes of several members of the exclusive FOCA enclave.

Eventually peace was restored to the international Grand Prix scene and the turbo era steadily took shape with all the leading FOCA lights climbing aboard the bandwagon out of necessity. Brabham would forge a partnership with BMW, Lotus with Renault and McLaren with Porsche. Meanwhile, Frank Williams and Patrick Head steadily massaged their fledgeling relationship with Honda, the first tentative steps towards which had been taken as early as the week immediately following the 1981 Brazilian Grand Prix.

4

The big time: Honda and Renault

The long-term company policy developed and adopted by Williams Grand Prix Engineering over the past decade has been simple and straightforward, namely a continuing and overwhelming commitment to Formula 1 motor racing and seeking, on a year-by-year basis, to win the World Championship.

'We do not have a plan which says, for example, that by 1998 we will have a turnover of £300 million and will have swallowed up a couple of dozen companies within motor racing in the process,' explains Frank Williams.

'We keep our eyes open for opportunities, sure enough, but not in any way that could be seen to dilute our F1 efforts. Other projects would necessarily be subordinate to the main business of being competitive in Formula 1.'

On the face of it, this seems an understandable and straightforward philosophy. Yet achieving those aims, the very task of becoming a Grand Prix racing team which is consistently regarded as a front-running contender, has necessitated facing a succession of complex decisions, both technical and commercial, over an extended period. For example, with the boundless gift of hindsight, the manner in which turbocharged engine technology and carbon-fibre composite chassis development evolved throughout the 1980s seems extremely logical.

Yet, looking back to 1982, Grand Prix racing was in a constant state of flux, a condition of fluid uncertainty, racked by disputes between the constructors and the sport's governing body. In such a climate, making the correct technical decision was necessarily clouded by the ever present thought that whatever option was taken by a company like Williams, it could be rendered meaningless, useless and outlawed if FISA decided to spring another sudden rule change on the hapless competitors.

What had become absolutely clear, of course, was that there was no possibility of continuing into the turbocharged era with an off-the-peg customer engine like the Cosworth DFV. No engine manufacturer was providing such a service anyway and, even if such a source of supply had been available, few teams would have wished to share the technology any more than Patrick Head wanted to be second in a queue for the TAG/Porsche engine behind the McLaren team.

In fact, ever since 1979, Williams had been pursuing its own discreet engine development programme on the Cosworth DFV, using the services of John Judd's company, the Rugby-based Engine Developments organisation. This had been prompted by the obvious fragility of the DFV valvegear during 1979 and 1980 as the 3-litre V8 engine was squeezed to deliver ever increasing power outputs. In three years the Williams development boosted the V8's potential from around 480bhp to nearly 540bhp. But it wasn't enough to get a sniff of the new turbos.

So what were the options available? 'We could be a Renault customer, a Honda partner, a BMW customer or even a Matra customer,' explains Frank Williams. 'Matra had a tiny V6 on the stocks, but it was enormously expensive by the standards of the time. We were looking at paying around £3 million for a supply deal in 1982 for 1983.' Patrick Head recalls that its wide-angle vee made it unsuitable for potential use in conjunction with ground effect aerodynamics, even though flat-bottomed chassis regulations were introduced at the start of the 1983 season.

Patrick also examined the four-cylinder, single turbo BMW option to the point where the German firm supplied the team with a mock-up engine so that installational problems could be considered. But the TAG/Porsche reservations also applied to this project, for Williams would be sitting in a queue behind the Brabham team which had been in at the ground floor of the BMW F1 project. It was also prohibitively expensive.

Meanwhile, the Honda option was being discreetly and unobtrusively pursued. It was a long and rocky road which started when negotiations opened at the end of April 1981 and was not finally firmed up until a contract for testing and long-term race development of the Japanese company's twin-turbo V6 engine was signed on 22 February, 1983. The news was announced publicly by Frank Williams and Honda's F1 overlord Nobuhiko Kawamoto in August 1983 at the Austrian Grand Prix and the first Williams-Honda raced in the final race of that season, the South African Grand Prix at Kyalami.

Officially, it was a well kept secret in F1 circles. Unofficially, of course, rumours had been flying for months. Frank, always appallingly unconvincing when it comes to telling half-truths, attempted to throw the media off the scent. However, the author recalls one golden moment, about a month short of the official announcement, when Frank virtually conceded, ahead of time, that the deal was done.

Although he never had the inclination to become a pilot himself, the world of aviation has always held a considerable fascination for Frank and he meticulously kept a detailed record of all the commercial flights he took over many years, noting plane types and their registrations. Returning from Frankfurt after the 1983 German Grand Prix, I managed to persuade him to show me his most recent entries in the log. I knew precisely what I was looking for. After scanning the list for a moment, I remarked that there seemed to be an awfully large number of flights logged between Heathrow and Tokyo. 'You bastard, A.H.!' he grinned ruefully.

Frank remembers: 'The first formal meetings involving the possibility of a partnership between Williams and Honda for F1 racing took place in the Honda UK offices at Chiswick shortly after the 1981 Brazilian Grand Prix.

'We had originally set up the meeting between Honda's link man Alf Briggs and Mr Kawamoto for the Monday after that Brazilian race, but both Air France Concordes managed to break down and we couldn't make it back in time. The meeting was postponed but, when it finally took place, went smoothly enough.'

Honda went back to consider the outline deal. The next meeting with Frank Williams took place in Tokyo just after the 1981 Dutch Grand Prix at Zandvoort, but it was not until Christmas 1982 – 'after a lot of thrashing about' – that the deal was finally in place. Even then, there was a last-minute hiccup.

'Our chief accountant George Koopman drew attention to a potential anomaly in the agreement,' recalls Williams. 'He said to me "Frank, you've really got to insist on that particular point", so we sent a telex to them raising a query.

'Back came a telex from Kawamoto saying, in effect, "We've had enough, the deal is off." So we got in contact with Jack Brabham, whose relationship with Honda went back to the mid-1960s when he used their engines in his F2 cars, ate a bit of humble pie and the negotiations resumed. But they were tough, going into a lot of detail and always proved very specific about terms.'

That episode should also have served as a subtle warning. Although they were partners in the project, it soon became clear to many observers on the sidelines that Honda would seek to become the dominant force within any partnership it entered into. This quality would continue to manifest itself after the Williams-Honda alliance was broken up and the Japanese company forged a similar relationship with McLaren.

Massaging the personal relationship with Honda became something of a priority. Dealing with the Japanese culture was a major challenge and, in this connection, Sheridan Thynne recalls the enormous amount of assistance received by Williams from Mark Snowdon, at that time the right-hand man of Austin Rover Managing Director Harold Musgrove. At around the same time that Williams was starting to do business with Honda, Austin Rover was entering into its technical and production collaboration with the Japanese company. Snowdon quickly grasped how to deal with them.

Sheridan recalls: 'Mark had been entrusted with the task of handling AR's relationship with Honda and, as we gathered at the time, was rather more diplomatic with them than perhaps Harold Musgrove managed to be. Harold used to stir people up in Tokyo, and then Mark would follow up, smooth it all over and work out some sort of a compromise that was at least operable. He had more than a few suggestions as to how we ought to handle them and was very supportive, helpful and keen in easing it all along a bit.'

At the same time as these negotiations were continuing apace, Patrick Head was proving extremely conservative when it came to the adoption of carbon-fibre chassis construction, the Williams chief designer needing to convince himself totally that this was the correct route to follow. McLaren and Lotus had set the pace in this respect during 1981, but it would take another four years before Head abandoned aluminium alloy honeycomb in favour of this new material.

More speculation and controversy surrounded the application of carbon-fibre technology within the F1 world than just about any other single technical element throughout the 1980s. It had its roots in the 1960s when Government-sponsored, research programmes on both sides of the Atlantic, and in Japan, focused on the challenge of developing a new, lightweight and extremely stiff material for various demanding areas of aerospace technology.

During the early 1970s, carbon-fibre came to the notice of many people, including Patrick Head, with the publicity surrounding the problems encountered by the Rolls-Royce RB2-11 jet aircraft engine where the material had been used to manufacture the first-stage compressor fans.

In that application, while the fans worked perfectly well, it would only take the introduction of a small amount of sand or other abrasive material into the air flow through the engine for the epoxy resin to be stripped from the fans, thereby significantly weakening the blades. Head first encountered carbon-fibre in a motor racing application when the Hesketh 308Cs, inherited by Walter Wolf Racing in 1976, used the material in their wing support structures.

Becoming acquainted with the way in which the carbon-fibre filaments should be saturated with just the right amount of resin, 'laid up' in the best way to endow a chassis with the maximum possible impact-resistance qualities, and then oven-cured at the appropriate temperature, meant straying into a totally fresh technological area as far as Formula 1 racing was concerned. In such circumstances, Head's caution was absolutely understandable. While it would be nice to take a year off learning about fresh chassis construction methods, Williams still had to compete, and run competitively, in order to stay on the Grand Prix tightrope.

'You've got to remember, there was no accumulated fund of technical expertise concerning the use of carbon-fibre in motor racing on which one could draw at the time,' Patrick points out. 'Consequently, as far as Williams was concerned, one of the reasons for the slow introduction of such technology was that we had insufficient knowledge about its behaviour. One needed to know a great deal about structures, and be able to make very confident decisions when it came to laying up the fibres in specific directions, before starting on the manufacturing process.'

The realisation that this was fresh territory that needed to be explored in considerable detail led to Williams GPE employing Brian O'Rourke, a composites specialist with experience in the aviation industry, to oversee the company's development within this particular sphere.

Head also felt it was necessary to have adequate control over the manufacturing procedure within the Williams organisation before unreservedly committing the company to the manufacture of carbon-fibre chassis.

'There were also aspects of the behaviour of certain carbon-fibre/honeycomb materials which I wasn't terribly impressed about,' he recalls. 'In addition, we had experienced two massive shunts with FW06 and FW07 monocoques – at Watkins Glen in 1978 when Jones's car broke that hub shaft, and at Silverstone during testing in 1980 when Reutemann went straight into the vertical sleepers on the outside of Copse corner – and had been extremely impressed with the way in which our aluminium monocoques stood up to the impact.'

Ensuring that as much driver protection as possible was built into the cars he designed has always been a major priority in Patrick's mind since he began designing F1 cars for Williams 13 years ago. That, combined with a reasoned sense of what was economically prudent, and what wasn't, contributed to Williams being slow off the mark in setting up its own composites department.

'I've always attempted to take a practical approach towards the cost involved in producing an F1 car,' says Patrick. 'And I think in those days we were talking, I would reckon, of a cost increase of around 100 per cent between an aluminium and a carbon-fibre chassis.

'At that time I had something of a tendency to say "Well, this may be a little bit nicer, but will cost 10 times as much, so we won't do it". I had always tried to keep costs down to a reasonable level and recall being quite shocked when we had some carbon-fibre test panels made for experimental purposes and, when I got the quote, it seemed absolutely astronomic. I think that made me a little bit wary about dealing with sub-contractors from that point onwards, and I decided we would accumulate all the expertise in-house before embarking on a major carbon-fibre chassis development programme.'

As it turned out, the last aluminium alloy honeycomb Williams F1 chassis would be the Williams FW09, the first of the team's cars to use the

Honda V6 turbo engine. After years of installing Cosworth V8s into the engine bays of a succession of consistently effective racing cars, Patrick Head and his design team suddenly came back to basics when Honda finally delivered the first engine to Didcot in the spring of 1983.

When Head began to assess the situation, he must have envied his old friend John Barnard over at McLaren, starting with a clean sheet of paper and telling Porsche precisely how he wanted the detail design of the TAG turbo V6 laid out. What Patrick inherited for his first turbocar was a lumpy, untidy 80-degree $1\frac{1}{2}$-litre V6 which had metamorphosed from Honda's 2-litre Formula 2 engine.

Just like with carbon-fibre, there was no accumulated fund of experience which he could consult for guidance as to the manner in which the engine could be installed in the chassis. Although the tiny Spirit team had done some race development with the early Honda RA163 engine during the second half of 1983, prior to the debut of the first Williams-Honda, there was precious little that the senior team could learn from this preliminary dabble. The first engine arrived at Didcot in a box, together with two turbochargers. There was nothing else. Crucial ancillaries such as radiators and plumbing for the turbo and exhaust systems would have to be designed and developed by Williams.

After two years fighting the turbos with a Cosworth V8, Keke Rosberg was thrilled to be sampling the new Williams-Honda FW09 at Kyalami in 1983. In his view, having the new car ready for the final race of the season could only benefit the team's potential for the following year. He finished fifth on the car's debut, optimistic about unlocking further potential before the start of the 1984 Championship programme.

The development of the Williams-Honda FW09 provided a classic lesson of how consistent evolution significantly alters the way in which a racing car's performance is perceived by its driver. At Kyalami in 1983, the Honda V6 seemed quite a tame and manageable engine, in Keke's view. The FW09 seemed prone to slight understeer – in basic terms a handling imbalance whereby the front end of the car tries to run wide, away from the apex of a corner – the Finnish driver believed this could be sorted out through routine winter testing. However, things didn't turn out that way.

The Williams-Honda FW09 used in that first race was very much a development car. By the time Rosberg drove the car in the first race of the following season, Williams aerodynamicist Frank Dernie had helped to unlock more power from the Honda V6 engine by significantly improving its cooling system. Later in the season a more refined rear suspension system, with pull-rod activation of the spring/dampers replacing the original rocker arm arrangement, gave more grip to the rear tyres.

Suddenly, the Williams FW09 became a very different proposition. The Honda engine's abrupt power delivery, within an extremely narrow rev. band, became more obtrusive. At the same time, as a by-product of that very quality allied to the more efficient rear suspension, its understeering qualities became more pronounced going into the corners, snapping viciously to oversteer as the power came in with a bang.

Rosberg, shooting from the hip with a certain spontaneous lack of tact, blamed most of the trouble on the fact that the chassis was flexing. In fact, it was the cylinder block and engine mounts. Understandably, Keke's allegation annoyed Patrick Head who felt that the team's number one driver was a bit too inclined towards opening his mouth a split-second ahead of deciding exactly what was going to come out of it.

In fact, although Rosberg scored the maiden Williams-Honda victory in the 1984 Dallas Grand Prix, even Patrick Head would concede this was more a tribute to the Finn's remarkable physical resilience in the sweltering Texas heat than a reflection of any outstanding technical excellence on the part of the engine/chassis package. Moreover, as the 1984 season wore on, there was an increasing realisation on the part of Honda that they were not getting the job done. Changes would have to be made to their approach in 1985 if the Japanese motor manufacturer was ever going to make a worthwhile impact on the F1 scene.

Keke Rosberg credits Patrick Head with really shaking up Honda's ideas. 'Whatever the shortcomings of FW09, it was Patrick who really made Honda appreciate just what was required to get the job done in F1,' he asserts firmly. 'He was the man almost entirely responsible for making them raise the standard of their game. He educated them, if you like, into realising precisely what was wanted.'

Behind the scenes during the early part of 1984, the directors were privately beginning to feel desperate. 'To start with the mechanics were having to deal with up to six engine changes through every Grand Prix weekend,' Frank remembers. 'There was an increasing feeling within the company of "Oh, what have we gone and done", but Mr. Kawamoto, as the key man in the deal, got the message and quickly understood.'

Kawamoto was, and is, a committed Anglophile. A mechanic on the F2 Brabham-Honda project back in 1966, he had developed a deep-rooted appreciation of Anglo-Japanese relationships as well as understanding the ways of motor racing. Very approachable, and with a keen grasp of English, he was totally committed to racing, with a sincere belief in its value to Honda, both from a technical and promotional standpoint. Yet behind that affable front, Kawamoto was tough, ambitious and extremely clever.

Frank Williams recalls that, while Honda were 'thrilled to bits, when the partnership scored its first victory at Dallas, Kawamoto came to appreciate that a fundamental revision of the whole F1 engine programme was required after an ignominious showing in the 1984 Dutch Grand Prix at Zandvoort.

Frank says: 'The turning point really came at that race when Keke ran as high as third, only to roll silently into the Williams pit, right in front of Mr Kawamoto, out of fuel twp laps before the end. This came on top of three broken engines during practice. No question about it, he was highly embarrassed.

'Two weeks later, Mr Kawamoto brought his colleague Mr Sakurai to Monza where we also got through two engines a day thanks to a succession of piston failures – Friday, Saturday, Sunday morning warm-up, and in the race. The ignominy and mortification of seeing the debris at his feet was worth a hundred complaining telexes to Japan. Mr Kawamoto, in effect, said "right, we need a new approach" and immediately told Sakurai to get on with it.'

Up to that point, the Honda F1 racing effort had been something of a low-key operation, a pet project of Kawamoto, operated by Engineer Hagita who had been a mechanic on the motorcycle team during Mike Hailwood's great days riding for Honda almost two decades earlier.

'Hagi was a fantastic chap,' recalls Patrick Head. 'But they had a problem in the sense that they needed a more senior, fully developed engineering and management structure, rather than simply being entrusted to a mechanic/technician, to head up the whole project. So Hagi rather got swept aside to be replaced by Sakurai in charge with Engineer Ichida looking after the technical side'.

Yoshitoshi Sakurai would be Honda's F1 Racing Manager through to 1988 when he left the company's employ. He was calculating and ruthlessly dedicated to furthering Honda's success level, and his time with the company certainly coincided with the greatest period of achievement for the Williams-Honda partnership. Amusing company, yet perhaps rather direct, Sakurai did not seem as sympathetic or in tune with the European way of doing things and, after his departure from Honda, even the outwardly mild-mannered, diplomatic, Kawamoto ventured some subtly-aimed criticism of his methods during a conversation with the author in 1988.

Into the 1985 season, Williams had squared up to a battery of sophisticated, well-developed turbocharged opposition in the form of McLaren-TAG, the reigning World Champions, Lotus-Renault, Brabham-BMW and Ferrari. The team had moved into its spacious new factory at Basil Hill Road, Didcot, in June 1984 and Patrick Head's design team was now armed with the equipment necessary to tackle the manufacture of a carbon fibre monocoque. The result was the all-new Williams FW10, eight such chassis being manufactured during the course of the season.

The relationship of mutual trust between Honda and Williams Grand Prix Engineering developed steadily and was enhanced by the fact that an engine department was established within the factory at Didcot. This dealt with routine rebuilding of engines primarily for testing and practice purposes, thereby relieving pressure on the Honda Research and Development department at Wako, near Tokyo, which remained responsible for the race engine preparation and development. It was considered quicker to despatch development components to Didcot to build into the engines there rather than complete the entire task in Japan, as well as reducing the overall number of engines that would have been needed if some had, in effect, been permanently in transit.

'We welcomed their working here,' says Frank, 'because it led to close and worthwhile co-operation. For sure, they could be difficult to deal with, but they were nice people and could also be fun. Understanding precisely what they meant could sometimes be a problem and they were often very forthright. They were tough partners who didn't beat around the bush.

'The Honda mechanics seemed to like us and we liked them. We eventually established good communications at all levels throughout the group. Once you dealt with them successfully it became extremely rewarding; their bottom line was that they were going to win. There were no two ways about it.'

For 1985, Honda concentrated on producing engines with a 'softer' power curve to improve driveability, but the early part of the season saw them frustrated by a succession of turbocharger failures. The first race of the season in Brazil had seen Rosberg succumb to one such failure after leading the early stages of the race, while Nigel Mansell's debut for the team was a disappointment. The Englishman flew off at the first corner after a tangle with Michele Alboreto's Ferrari, later retiring with engine problems resulting from a damaged aerodynamic diffuser panel under the rear of the car.

Mansell atoned for this display of impetuosity by producing fifth place finishes in the Portuguese and San Marino Grands Prix and qualified alongside Ayrton Senna's pole position Lotus 97T at Monaco. Unfortunately, brake problems dropped both Nigel and Keke out of the top six by the end of this gruelling race, but Rosberg bagged the team's first win of the season with a typically effervescent performance through the confined streets of Detroit.

A week prior to this success, Honda made a tremendously significant step forward for the Canadian Grand Prix at Montreal. The introduction of the 'E' specification RA163 engine sharpened the overall competitiveness of the Williams FW10 technical package. Rosberg and Mansell finished fourth and sixth, the Finn managing this despite two pit stops during the course of the race to set the tone for the following weekend's success.

Back in Europe, the Williams-Hondas continued to prove fast, but hard on tyres, and the chassis eventually reached its peak of refinement at Brands Hatch where the Grand Prix of Europe took place at the start of October. A revised induction system on the engine allowed the rear bodywork to be reduced in height, improving the aerodynamic efficiency of the rear wing, and pull-rod rear suspension replaced the heavy rocker arm arrangement to complete the package.

In this specification, the Williams-Honda FW10s reeled off impressive triumphs in the last three races of the 1985 season. Nigel Mansell scored his maiden F1 victory in front of that adoring home crowd at Brands Hatch, following it up with an even more commanding success at Kyalami in the South African Grand Prix. Finally, Rosberg rounded off his association with the team by taking a well-judged victory in the inaugural Australian Grand Prix through the streets of Adelaide.

The Williams-Honda alliance finished the year taking joint third place in the Constructors' World Championship, equal with Lotus-Renault, beaten only by McLaren-TAG and Ferrari. It was heartening enough, but there was even more success to come – on track, at least – as the 1986 season beckoned.

Throughout the halcyon days of the turbocharged Grand Prix engine during the mid-1980s the Formula 1 technical regulations were gradually altered in an effort to cap the mushrooming power outputs, ostensibly in the interests of circuit safety. By the end of 1985, the Honda RA163 engine was producing well over 1,000bhp, using unfettered boost for the purposes of qualifying, although the requirements of relatively economical running necessarily demanded within the strictures of the 220-litre maximum permissible fuel load meant that this output was substantially lower for the race.

For 1986 the engine regulations would call for a restriction of turbo boost pressure to 4-bar, although the 220-litre fuel maximum would be retained, and Patrick Head's design team drew from their experience with the Williams FW10 to produce a totally new car, the elegantly functional FW11, widely regarded as one of the classic racing cars of its era.

Before Nelson Piquet and Nigel Mansell had the opportunity to give the new challenger its race debut, Frank Williams had his disastrous road accident. The physical consequences of this tragedy left him close to death for several weeks, and inevitably imposed severe limitations on Frank's mobility which many of his friends privately wondered if he was capable of coming to terms with. Up to that point, his whole being was so totally immersed in the business of motor racing that it was difficult to imagine how he could have found any time for a private life outside his immediate circle of confederates.

Yet as long ago as 1973, he had married Ginny Sawyer-Hoare, whose first husband Charles had briefly been a customer of Frank Williams Racing Cars when his Formula 3 Titan was maintained at the Bath Road premises in Slough.

Frank would be the first to agree that his family life had always been reduced to a subordinate role. Realising this, Ginny quickly donned a mantle of assured independence, shrewdly appreciating that social gatherings, family birthdays and even Christmas were not permitted to intrude on the business of Grand Prix racing.

Close friends joke good-naturedly that they sometimes find it amazing he was ever home long enough to father his three children, Claire, Jonathan and Jaime. Now suddenly everything changed. That active and independent man was transformed into a totally dependent being.

The 1986 season continued apace. Neither car finished at Imola, while unsuitable final drive ratios blighted their progress at Monaco with the result that Mansell could only trail home fourth, Piquet a disappointing seventh. Then Mansell got his score off the ground with victory in the Belgian Grand Prix at Spa, admittedly only after Nelson's retirement with engine trouble.

Once Nigel got into his stride, he reeled off the wins at Montreal, Paul Ricard and Brands Hatch. Then Piquet got second wind, taking the chequered flag at Hockenheim, Hungaroring and Monza. Then Mansell was on top again in Portugal before the two of them fumbled through the Mexican Grand Prix fourth and fifth, blighted by the need to make two stops for fresh tyres on this sun-baked, abrasive track surface.

Soichiro Honda, the company's founder, journeyed to Adelaide for the final shoot-out. The patriarch and his acolytes undoubtedly made the trip confident in the expectation of seeing either Nelson Piquet or Nigel Mansell take the Drivers' World Championship. As we will see in Part Four, through an interlocking and entirely unforeseen set of freak circumstances, the crown slipped from their grasp and was retained by Alain Prost. Honda was disappointed with the outcome. More seriously, though, Frank's accident had made them uneasy about the way in which Williams Grand Prix Engineering was operating.

'It's fairly clear that they were distressed about my accident,' Frank agrees, 'because of the effect it might have had on their World Championship attack. I also believe, with hindsight, that it was responsible for altering their view of Williams as a company. I don't believe they grasped that we had an efficient management structure, despite the evidence of their own eyes.'

Sheridan Thynne comments: 'At the first race he visited after Frank's accident, Kawamoto certainly asked Patrick and me who was going to run the company. They couldn't see that there wouldn't be a problem, that we didn't actually need an immediate replacement managing director.'

Unwittingly, through no fault of its own, Williams GPE had come up against one of the idiosyncrasies of Japanese business methodology. They didn't view life in the same way. In their view, there must be an established, identifiable framework – in this case management orientated. Things had to be done, objectives achieved. But they had to be done the right way, for what they saw as the right reasons. Honda couldn't grasp that the Williams company could function without Frank at the helm on a day-to-day basis.

'I think in Japanese companies, the managing director has what might be described as a well-defined, if symbolic, public relations and promotional role. In their view, you can't have a company without one. The fact that we were winning most of the races was ignored. They just wanted us to get in a replacement as quickly as possible.'

There was to be an added complication from the start of 1987, inasmuch as Honda had also decided to supply their engines to Team Lotus. Ayrton Senna would head up the driving squad with F1 novice Satoru Nakajima, who had done plenty of Williams-Honda testing back in his native Japan, included in the second car as part of the deal.

Williams got the clear message that Honda, whose admiration for the politically adept Senna was boundless, expected Lotus to trounce their new FW11Bs. However, despite its ambitious computer controlled active suspension system, the Lotus 99T wasn't in the same class and although Senna won two races, he was seldom more than a strong also-ran.

Meanwhile, in the wake of this mounting anxiety within Honda about the manner in which Williams Grand Prix Engineering was being managed, during the early months of 1987 the team began to suspect that their Japanese partners were contemplating a termination of the engine supply contract at the end of the year. This was obviously a matter of grave concern, for the deal ran through to the end of 1988 and, after the team's corporate antennae picked up disturbing signals at around the time of the Monaco Grand Prix, Frank grasped the bull by the horns and told Kawamoto what he believed they had in mind.

'He said nothing, but just smiled in a rather knowing manner,' Williams recalls. Just prior to the German Grand Prix at Hockenheim came the formal notification. Two weeks later, Piquet jumped ship and signed a contract to drive a Lotus-Honda for 1988. For Williams, the jigsaw was coming apart. Piquet would replace Ayrton Senna who now switched to McLaren, effectively taking the Williams engine supply with him.

Frank picks his words carefully when he reflects on the breach with Honda, unwilling to outline the details of the settlement which was eventually concluded with Honda to terminate the deal as amicably as possible under the admittedly strained circumstances.

'With hindsight, I suppose one could have taken a more aggressive legal stance with Honda,' he muses, 'but a settlement was duly reached, although, again with hindsight, it was grossly inadequate. Privately we thought we had a sound technical basis for our switch to a Judd naturally aspirated engine in 1988, but we were not wise enough to see that this was potentially a major disaster.

'It turned out to be the latter and, believe me, it brought the team to its knees. We were not quite on the floor, but the countdown had almost begun, if you like. The 1988 season was certainly pretty lurid thanks to Honda's clumsiness.'

For a short time there was the possibility that Honda might drop Lotus and supply engines to Williams and McLaren in 1988, but that would have meant Nakajima partnering Piquet or Mansell. Quite rightly, neither Frank nor Patrick were prepared to be put in a position where they were effectively consigned to second billing behind McLaren in Honda's list of priorities, so the suggestion was declined. Patrick Head, for his part, believed that Williams should have threatened Honda with legal action in pursuit of what they saw as their rightful claim.

Outsiders concluded that Honda were also irked that the Williams management had failed to impose team discipline on Mansell, a viewpoint fuelled by Piquet's outspoken comments on the matter. Much the same trend continued through 1987, the revised Williams-Honda FW11Bs, now running under the revised regulations with 4-bar permissible turbo boost pressure under a 195-litre fuel capacity limit, winning the lion's share of the races.

Piquet emerged as World Champion, but the season was something of an anti-climax when Mansell crashed and hurt his back during practice for the first Japanese Grand Prix to be held at Suzuka. By then the die had been cast. For 1988, Williams would be making the switch from turbo power to use a 3.5-litre Judd V8 engine under the new interim technical regulations which would see the turbos phased out by the start of the 1988 season.

Equipped with the Williams active suspension system which Piquet's FW11B had been fitted with for his winning drive in the 1987 Italian Grand Prix at Monza, the team was outwardly upbeat and optimistic. There was the feeling that such a light, agile machine with its transverse gearbox would be highly competitive against the turbos which, during their twilight year, would be further limited to 2.5-bar boost pressure and 150-litres of fuel.

As things turned out, the McLaren-Hondas of Ayrton Senna and Alain Prost won 15 of the 16 races in 1988 and Williams not a single one – the first time for 10 years that they had been away from the victory rostrum. The active suspension had proved both unreliable and temperamental, and although a switch to conventional springing on the eve of second practice for the British Grand Prix at Silverstone gave Mansell the equipment to storm home second in the race, by then he had signed a contract to join Ferrari for the following year.

'Basically we didn't do a very good job, it's as simple as that,' explains Patrick Head. 'We started the year quite optimistically with Nigel on the front row at Rio, running close to the leaders in the race before the engine started to overheat and all sorts of associated problems arose. To be honest, if we had started the season with a straightforward conventionally suspended car, we would have been in better shape. That FW12 was a bit of a pig's ear after we'd modified it for the British Grand Prix.'

Not to be caught short, Williams decided to finalise their driver line-up immediately after the Silverstone race. Barely a fortnight after Nigel signed for Ferrari, Thierry Boutsen was recruited to run alongside Riccardo Patrese in the 1989 Williams squad.

Although the turbo era came to end in 1988, the legacy of these forced induction engines lingered on. Their development had attracted a host of major engine manufacturers into Formula 1, thereby dramatically raising the technical stakes. Those who thought that the 3.5-litre naturally aspirated regulations would bring about a return to the previous status quo, whereby most teams purchased off-the-peg V8s from Cosworth Engineering, were not in touch with reality.

Barely a month after Honda and Williams made public their decision to split, Frank and Patrick started exploratory talks with Renault Sport at Estoril during the 1987 Portuguese Grand Prix weekend. Renault, the pioneers of turbo technology, had been out of the F1 arena since the end of the previous year when Lotus abandoned the French national car company's highly developed V6 in favour of the rival Honda unit.

However, Renault had not closed its eyes to the value of Grand Prix racing as a significant promotional and technical tool. Highly respected chief engineer Bernard Dudot and a small group of engineers were retained at Renault Sport's Viry-Chatillon headquarters, quietly working away on the development of a 3.5-litre V10 cylinder engine for the new naturally aspirated F1. They were not proposing to resume the operation of their own works team, which had dwindled sadly away at the end of 1985. However, they were interested in talking about the prospect of supplying engines to an existing organisation. Particularly a proven front line team such as Williams.

The deal was finalised in June 1988 and the first Williams-Renaults made their race debut in the 1989 Brazilian Grand Prix at Rio in the hands of Thierry Boutsen and Riccardo Patrese. Patrick had originally decided to build a new car to accommodate the RS01 V10 engine, but progressive development with the FW12 convinced him there was plenty of scope left in the car that had originally been fitted with the Judd V8 and this avenue was pursued throughout the season.

After a frustrating year, it was a relief to get back to a partnership with a major engine manufacturer and the team's achievements surged forward as a result. Boutsen and Patrese finished first and second in the rain-soaked Canadian Grand Prix and, in the final race of the season, Thierry took the new FW13, which had been introduced at Estoril, to an even more commanding win in conditions significantly worse than those he had experienced at Montreal.

One of the problems encountered with the first Renault engine was that it had not been specifically designed for a Williams chassis. Bernard Dudot and his engineering staff started developing the 67-degree V10 in April 1987, some 14 months before the partnership was officially sealed with WGPE.

This situation was rectified for 1990 with the introduction of a heavily revised RS2 version of the engine, not only offering more power, but the facility to be installed much lower in the chassis. An intensive development programme continued throughout the season, but while Patrese won at Imola and Boutsen in Hungary, the team inwardly knew they had slipped from the competitive high wire.

Williams had to raise the standards of its game. As you will discover in later pages, they settled down to do just that, from the viewpoint of driver strength, internal management restructuring and technical capability.

As far as they were concerned, 1991 was going to be different.

PART TWO

The financing of an F1 team

5

The way we were

There was a time when wealthy gentlemen of independent means bought themselves a Maserati or an ERA and sallied forth into Europe to do battle with Mercedes-Benz and Auto Union. During those balmy days of the 1930s, when money was a rather vulgar topic not spoken about in polite society, one either had the funds to take part on the international motor racing scene or one didn't. There were no halfway houses.

Independent wealth was the key. Sponsorship, as such, did not exist. Assistance might be obtained from fuel and tyre companies for the supply of their products, but this would hardly have made a dent on the prodigious expenditure required to keep an independent racing team on the road. There was no motor racing infrastructure as such, whereby a bright young talent could claw his way to the top of his chosen sport unless he or his family had considerable personal resources. There are very few 'rags to riches' success stories emanating from the 1930s in the way the likes of Colin Chapman and Frank Williams managed to put their reputations on the map in more recent times.

Dick Seaman, who rose to be Britain's leading international driver with a place in the Mercedes-Benz team, came from a wealthy background. His mother relentlessly bankrolled his racing efforts, even to the point of buying him an ERA with which to make his reputation in Continental races. Nor could ERA themselves, although small beer by the standards of the Nazi-backed German organisations, be compared with the sort of status enjoyed by the fledgeling Williams team during its dark years of the early 1970s.

Raymond Mays and Humphrey Cook, the architects of the ERA company, also came from very wealthy families. There was no scrimping, saving or living on borrowed sofas for the likes of them. When Mays was commissioned in the Grenadier Guards, just after the First World War, his mother rented him an apartment at the Savoy rather than have him go through the discomfort of staying in the barracks. Three decades later,

Charlie Crichton-Stuart may have laid claim to a more aristocratic background than Mays and Cook, but his flat in Pinner Road, Harrow, hardly ranked comparison. Different motor racing generations have suffered different levels of privation!

In the post-war era, the financing of Grand Prix racing changed dramatically. In the early 1950s we had the likes of Ferrari and Maserati financing their challenges through the manufacture of high-performance road cars in addition to the sale of single-seater and sports-racing cars to wealthy amateur competitors. In 1954, Mercedes-Benz made a return to the scene, totally financing a two-year F1 and sports car racing programme in order to reassert their reputation as a road car manufacturer of considerable stature and technical capability.

Grand Prix racing was not a financially self-sufficient business at this time. Britain's efforts during the mid-1950s were spearheaded by Vanwall and BRM, but these were subsidiaries of vast industrial empires and not expected to pay for themselves as going concerns. The Vanwalls, which would win the Constructors' World Championship in 1958, were not only the first British F1 cars seriously to challenge Ferrari and Maserati, but the whole *raison d'être* behind their existence was the burning ambition of millionaire bearings magnate Tony Vandervell to 'beat those damned red cars'.

Similarly, the BRM – which started out as a laudable, if ill-judged effort at producing a 'national British' Grand Prix car – was eventually rescued from bureaucratic bungling by the intervention of Sir Alfred Owen, whose family owned the Rubery Owen Group, a vast industrial empire which is now part of GKN. Although they owned their teams, both Vandervell and Owen were, in a sense, still sponsors. The keen business sense which had helped them build their commercial empires quickly alerted them to the possibility of Grand Prix racing as a form of marketing tool, an image-maker. Building F1 racing cars mirrored an image of technical capability, if not always excellence, and large sums of money were invested to that end.

The late 1950s and early 1960s saw another distinctive shift of emphasis. The availability of 'proprietary' Grand Prix engines from Coventry-Climax enabled a whole new generation of participants to try their hands on the Grand Prix stage without having to invest the daunting outlay necessary for an exclusive source of engine supply. Foremost among these newcomers were Cooper and Lotus – Cooper pioneering the way forward with a switch to rear-engined chassis design, and Lotus then picking up the torch to set fresh standards of technical ingenuity and imagination throughout the two following decades.

They were scathingly referred to at the time as 'special builders', and later as 'garagistes'. This somewhat disparaging label has unfortunately been perpetuated through to the present day by observers who should know better. It was this mould of specialist manufacturer from which sprang the Williams, McLaren and Brabham teams of the future, providing an opening through which motivated and highly enterprising people could thrust their foot into the Grand Prix door.

This shift in emphasis, of course, produced a very significant change in the funding of these teams. Without the luxury of financial under-pinning from a vast industrial empire, this new generation of F1 team had to live on its commercial wits. Generous contracts with tyre and fuel companies provided the lifeblood of Lotus, Cooper and Brabham for the first half of the 1960s, providing a crucial supplement to the money that was actually earned from the race prize funds.

From the end of the war right through to the early 1970s, race organisers effectively had to negotiate another key element in the F1 earnings equation with individual teams. Starting money was often a closely guarded secret between organiser and entrant. Moreover, the likes of Ferrari would frequently hold organisers to ransom with threats that the Italian team might withdraw its cars unless the financial arrangements were significantly improved at the last moment.

More damagingly for the image of Grand Prix racing as a whole, there was no obligation on the part of any team to contest every race. Thus when Ferrari withdrew from the 1959 British Grand Prix at Aintree, for example, thereby depriving the home crowd of seeing former Vanwall ace Tony Brooks in action as well as inflicting mortal damage to the Englishman's World Championship prospects, there was absolutely nothing the organisers could do about it.

The history books are littered with examples of races compromised by such bloody-mindedness. Only in the 1970s would the Formula One Constructors' Association, of which Williams would become a loyal and devoted disciple, impose an obligation on everybody to come along to every race. In retrospect, this was probably the single most crucial development to accelerate the image of F1 towards that of a top drawer international sport. Race organisers throughout the world came to learn precisely what they were getting for their money and consistent interest in the Championship battle was therefore sustained.

When Frank Williams stepped on to the Grand Prix stage with Piers Courage at the start of 1969, Dunlop was the single most crucial key to the viability of his project. At that time the tyre companies wielded tremendous power and influence.

'In 1969 we benefited from very substantial Dunlop support by the standards of the time,' recalls Frank Williams, 'and we also attracted the first Williams commercial sponsor from outside the orbit of the motor racing business. This was T.W. Ward, a manufacturer of machine tools.

'The contact was made initially by one of our mechanics, Bob Evans. He had met a man called John Halbert who was Managing Director of ABMTM – the Association of British Machine Tool Manufacturers – which acted as a marketing group formed by a consortium of diverse machine tool companies, of which T.W. Ward was one.

'John Halbert thought that Ted Williams, whose family owned Ward, could be the right person. He put it to them and they thought it was a good idea, believing that it would project a good image for their products. This was very avant garde thinking for the time. So Ted Williams came on board and off we went. We put a little Ward sticker in front of the windscreen of Piers's Brabham and banked their cheque. Ted remained a staunch financial supporter of the team until his death in 1979. He meant a great deal to us and made a really significant contribution – a very special bloke.'

Prior to this deal, Frank's enterprising sense of ambition had led him to make an approach to the US-based Reynolds aluminium company, the idea being that they were the sort of high technology concern that might be interested in becoming involved with Piers's graduation to F1. The way in which the pitch was made is instructive to recall, for it graphically illustrates the sheer optimism which Frank could bring to bear on such a project.

At the time – summer 1968 – Max Mosley was running his Formula 2 Brabham BT23C out of the Williams premises in Slough, fielding the machine as what amounted to an informal number two car alongside Courage's similar mount. A barrister with a reputation for considerable eloquence and mental dexterity, Max was the son of pre-War British Fascist leader Sir Oswald Mosley, and it was to Max that Williams turned for assistance.

'Since I had a degree in physics, he asked me whether I could give the impression that I was a highly qualified engineer,' explains Max with some amusement. 'He'd originally tried to persuade Robin Herd, with whom I'd been at university in Oxford, to go along with him. But Robin was working for Cosworth at the time and didn't feel he could do it, so I found myself roped in.

'Bruce McLaren also came along with us and the worst moment for me came at a party thrown by the Reynolds management at which I was introduced to their stress analyst, a Chinese fellow by the name of Mr Wang, or something similar. It was suggested that Mr Wang asked me some penetrating questions to check my credentials, but as things turned out he treated me to a monologue on the development of aluminium drilling bits for Alaskan oil fields so, thankfully, I didn't have to say a great deal. We really didn't know what we were doing, to be honest, and didn't get the sponsorship. Ironically, Bruce did pull off a deal with them for co-sponsorship of his Can-Am sports cars. It was quite a successful foray however, because Bruce paid Williams generous commission on the deal!'

The body blow of Piers Courage's death, and the subsequent termination of the partnership with Alessandro de Tomaso was a serious setback, but by no means terminal from a commercial standpoint. Yet even at the end of 1970, Frank was reduced to cheese-paring economies to balance the team's books.

In order to move some way towards reversing the financial deficit, he was forced to sell one of the team's Cosworth engines. It should be mentioned that two such V8s had been bought for the team prior to Piers's Tasman adventure at the start of 1969 by Derek Mackie, the owner of a textile factory in Belfast's Falls Road. He was another wealthy enthusiast, from the same mould as Ted Williams, for whose philanthropy Frank had every reason to be very grateful.

The realities of financial necessity began to pressure Williams heavily in 1971 as the whole emphasis of his team's operation altered. No longer could he afford the financial luxury of being a team chief in charge of his own destiny in the sense that he could pick and choose his drivers. Getting the budget together in order to stay in the Grand Prix game was the first and last priority. Whoever could come up with the budget got the drive.

The bearded Frenchman Henri Pescarolo came knocking on Frank's door with a proposal for a two-car March team in Formula 2. He had £23,000 sponsorship from the Motul oil company for such a programme and the deal was done. But with Ted Williams coming up with another £10,000 for an F1 project, Motul were persuaded to produce a further £15,000 to ensure that Pescarolo found his way into the cockpit of a Williams team March 711. This was further supplemented when Frank's good friend, Italian journalist Giancarlo Falletti, made contact with Politoys, manufacturers of die-cast models, who chipped in with a further £10,000.

At the end of the previous season Williams had also acquired a brace of second-hand March 701s which had been used by Pescarolo and Derek Bell in the non-Championship Argentine Grand Prix at Buenos Aires. Now these outdated racers became another minor profit centre for Frank Williams Racing Cars, being leased out to Motor Circuit Developments for British also-rans to handle in the British domestic non-championship races held at Brands Hatch and Oulton Park. This produced an additional income of £1,000 per race for Frank's struggling team.

Nevertheless, expenditure would run significantly ahead of income for the team in the years immediately following. Even with a modest workforce of 10 people, Williams was operating on the financial bone in 1971 and that trend would continue into 1972 when the team expanded to field a second car for Carlos Pace, the Brazilian's personal sponsorship adding only another £10,000 to the overall budget, despite expectations of much more.

Motul was happy to pay £40,000 to keep Pescarolo in play at the wheel of Frank's March for a second season, although the way in which he developed a penchant for crashing became a major headache. Meanwhile, Politoys put up around £40,000 for Frank to build a tailor-made machine bearing their own name, the design work of which was entrusted to Len Bailey. It was readied in time for the British Grand Prix at Brands Hatch where 'Pesca' managed to write it off on the opening lap. Things could hardly get worse.

At about this time, the Formula One Constructors' Association was becoming organised under Bernie Ecclestone's methodical control as a negotiating body to deal with the various race organisers across the world. The idea was to offer a package deal for a set number of cars and, in the case of races outside Europe, to provide its members with subsidised travel and air freight facilities. Membership of the Constructors' Association would only be open to bona fide manufacturers, rather than teams entering off-the-peg racing cars such as a privately operated March, but Frank conformed with these more stringent requirements from the start of 1973 when he built his own cars from the outset.

In 1973 he was fortunate enough to benefit from backing from the Philip Morris cigarette company, one of Grand Prix racing's most consistent benefactors over the last two decades, through their Marlboro brand which was then also being carried by the works BRMs. In addition, he was encouraged to become involved in a link with the Italian Iso-Rivolta car company, with the result that the Williams cars were entered in the World Championship as 'Iso-Marlboros'.

Marlboro were rather betwixt and between as far as their F1 sponsorship programme was concerned. In the second year of their sponsorship agreement with BRM, they were disappointed that the once-proud British team had only managed a single victory when the gallant Jean-Pierre Beltoise triumphed in monsoon conditions at Monaco in 1972.

For 1974, they had targeted McLaren as the team with whom they really wanted to forge an alliance. So what motivated them to go with Frank? 'Faith, hope and charity,' he replies with a grin. 'Faith in their future McLaren deal, hope that BRM would hit decent form – and sheer charity for Williams!'

With continued support from Politoys and the ever-loyal Ted Williams, plus sponsorship promised from Italian driver Nanni Galli to secure his place in the team alongside New Zealander Howden Ganley, Frank faced the new season with a budget in excess of £100,000. At a time when the front-running teams in Formula 1 were talking in terms of £250,000 sponsorship programmes, yet again it was not sufficient to get the job done.

Galli's sponsorship failed to materialise, so he lost the drive after a couple of races, and the Iso-Rivolta payments were frequently late arriving. 'It had seemed a good idea to align the team's image with an exotic Italian sports car,' Frank recalls, 'but it turned out to be a bad deal. They were supposed to be in for 1974 as well, but no money ever arrived.'

Marlboro's sporting director Pat Duffeler bailed Frank out mid-season with another £15,000 contribution, but it was still hand-to-mouth stuff for much of the year. And so the pattern went on through 1974 when that crucial introduction to Walter Wolf was made.

When Frank finally cut free of the Wolf organisation and became his own man again in time for the start of the 1977 season, he was starting from the bottom of the pile yet again. Even less so than before, he was hardly in a position to nominate the driver of his choice, so when Peter Macintosh, team manager of the rival Fittipaldi outfit, introduced Belgian driver Patrick Neve, who had around £100,000 available in sponsorship from the Belle Vue brewery concern, it didn't take long for the deal to be done.

Of course, Frank was by now out of the Formula One Constructors' Association ranks. His ticket to ride on that particular bandwagon now accrued to Walter Wolf Racing. Anyway, in 1977 his suckling team failed to qualify for membership on three counts: it was a totally new organisation, it did not take part in all the races, and it was not manufacturing its own car.

Buying a year-old, off-the-peg racer was the only realistic option available to Frank in the short term so, as Patrick Head installed himself in their new headquarters at Unit 10, Station Road Industrial Estate, Didcot, a deal was concluded to purchase a March 761 rolling chassis for £14,000. Frank had toyed with the possibility of purchasing one of the redundant Penske PC4s from the American-financed team which had closed its doors at the end of 1976, but this machine had a winning pedigree – John Watson had triumphed in the previous year's Austrian Grand Prix – and was expensive with a £20,000 price tag without engine or gearbox.

True enough, a March 761 had won the 1976 Italian Grand Prix in the hands of Ronnie Peterson, but somehow that cachet hadn't rubbed off on the price of the arguably less refined machine from the Bicester-based manufacturer. Despite all his unfortunate experiences with 'bought-in' March chassis during the Pescarolo era, Frank couldn't ignore a 33 per cent price saving and the deal was done. The jigsaw was coming together.

This was a time of high investment for Williams Grand Prix Engineering, as the new company was officially titled, but Frank had more than a passing degree of good fortune when it came to acquiring the equipment and materials he needed. To service Neve's F1 efforts, which kicked off at the Spanish Grand Prix – the fifth round of the title chase – he acquired three Cosworth DFV engines.

One was purchased from Italian Tyrrell privateer Alessandro Pesenti-Rossi, another from Bernie Ecclestone and a third, in a badly blown-up state, as something of a gamble from Penske. That last V8 had a hole in the side of its block and very badly deranged internal components, but it had a bargain basement price of £1,500. Frank duly sent it back to Cosworth engineering where it was rebuilt and sent back to Didcot together with an invoice of £3,500.

This caused some consternation at Williams GPE because Frank was absolutely convinced that the block needed replacement, a luxury which alone would surely have cost £2,000. As time went by, that situation increasingly bothered Frank, but it was only years later, when Williams had grown to the point where they were Cosworth Engineering's biggest single customer, that he remarked to one of their directors, Jack Field, that he thought there must have been some sort of accounting anomaly. 'That must be the first and only time anybody got something for nothing from Cosworth,' Frank chuckles.

Neve was obviously particularly excited by the prospect of competing in his home Grand Prix at Zolder, but his enthusiasm got the better of him during pre-race testing at the North Belgium track some nine days before the race. He crashed the March heavily on the Friday, and Patrick Head was left with the solemn task of telephoning Didcot to report that the monocoque had been very severely damaged.

Frank got in touch with March Engineering at Bicester who agreed that it would be possible to rebuild the chassis round its existing internal bulkheads and, in one of those breathtaking displays of commitment that is almost taken for granted within the F1 business, the car was reconstructed by the following Tuesday and was duly delivered back to Zolder at around midnight on the Thursday, in time for Neve to do his stuff at Zolder during the first qualifying session.

During this challenging and demanding time, Frank's friend Dave Brodie was an absolute tower of strength and assistance, aiding the new company in every way he could. 'Brode' had been one of Frank's confederates from the days in the Harrow flat and now ran a prosperous and successful metal plating business. With Frank's personal credit worthiness then running at a low level, Brodie assisted in a small way with introductions when it came to opening lines of finance. Brodie would be a director of Williams GPE from 1977 through to 1981.

Ted Williams was still there, as loyal a supporter as ever, and T.W. Ward not only continued to contribute in terms of hard cash, but also provided a capstan lathe for the factory and got their joinery department to help with the manufacture of workbenches at the team's new base.

At this stage in the new company's history, it was spend, spend, spend. Precious little was being earned by Neve's tail-end efforts in the Williams March, for there was no money to be picked up from the Grand Prix prize fund unless a competitor got in among the top 20 qualifiers. Neve managed this just once, earning less than £1,000 in start money, and the year's income from racing barely topped £15,000 in total.

By the mid-1970s, Grand Prix racing was operating within the structure of a complex system of prize fund payments which still applies to this day. Some 45 per cent of the total payout is based on the race positions at quarter, half and three-quarter distance, as well as the final finishing order.

Of the balance, 20 per cent reflects the order of the top 20 qualifiers on the grid at that particular event. The remaining 35 per cent is awarded on the strength of the position within the top 20 point-scoring competitors in the two immediately previous half seasons, allied to the number of championship points accrued up to that point in the year. Neve trundled round near the back of the Grand Prix fields until the end of the 1977 season, was thanked for his efforts and politely shown the door. On the face of it, there had been precious little to show from the efforts of Williams Grand Prix Engineering during that challenging first season, but behind the scenes the commercial reality was distinctly different. No longer had Frank ended the season with a huge deficit, living hand-to-mouth and looking optimistically for the next deal to materialize.

The summer of 1977 had seen the team make a major breakthrough on the sponsorship front. The first signs were modest and unassuming, but their long-term implications would be absolutely central to the success achieved by the team in the years to come.

Frank Williams had made his first contact with the Saudis.

6

Breakthrough with the Saudis

From the British Grand Prix onwards through the balance of the 1977 season, Patrick Neve's Williams team March 761 carried sponsorship identification from Saudia, the airline of the Kingdom of Saudi Arabia, on its rear wing. That an airline had chosen to become involved in Grand Prix sponsorship was regarded as highly unusual; the spectre of a car carrying such advertising being embroiled in an accident had, in the past, been sufficient to make companies wary of becoming involved in this fast-moving activity.

Frank Williams had been thinking in terms of exploring the oil rich kingdom of Saudi Arabia for future sponsorship, reasoning that there was a lot of potential finance available in that part of the world. Yet the links with Saudia had come about as the result of a lucky break rather than any shrewd and incisive forward planning.

'A guy I knew by the name of Tony Harris worked in the London advertising agency which handled the Saudia account,' recalls Frank, 'and he agreed to introduce me to Mohammed Al Fawzan, the airline's sales manager in Jeddah. At first glance he liked the idea and we invited him to come to the F2 Silverstone race in May, 1977. He liked what he saw and arranged for our new company to have a very small sponsorship deal on the rear wing of the March.'

It only amounted to a £30,000 deal, minimal beer even for a secondary co-sponsorship at the time and, although the Saudia involvement was expanded to around £100,000 backing for 1978, its most significant value was as a 'calling card' for Frank to use in his approaches to other Saudi Arabian companies.

'With that credential, I was in a position to talk to other influential individuals from a position of relative strength,' he admits. Moreover, the commercial respectability of Saudia was well worth accepting in exchange for a relatively small sponsorship contribution because it provided such a useful stepping off point in more wide-ranging sponsorship negotiations. What you had to remember was that these guys in the Kingdom to whom I was talking had never seen motor racing, apart from occasionally on the television.'

Saudia's sponsorship encompassed virtually the entire surface area of the Williams FW06 when Patrick Head's compact new design was unveiled to the press at Didcot in December, 1977. The event was given added status by the arrival, in a specially chartered helicopter, of Saudia's Director General, Sheikh Kemel Sindhi, later to become Saudi Arabia's Deputy Minister of Aviation. By such a visit, the Saudi establishment was, in effect, bestowing its seal of approval on Frank Williams and his enterprise.

It was at about this time that Charlie Crichton-Stuart entered the orbit of Frank Williams's motor racing activities for the second time in just over a decade. Their paths had rather diverged after 1967 when Charlie retired from driving to marry actress Shirley-Ann Field. He had flown Vampires in the RAF, and his business life now led him back into the world of aviation as a private pilot. In the years that followed, he would be employed behind the controls of an executive jet for Harrods boss Sir Hugh Fraser.

Early in 1974 it was planned that he should join Lord Hesketh in a similar capacity, but the pending fuel crisis led to Alexander Hesketh changing his mind and not in fact buying the aeroplane he had originally intended to. Charlie was now redundant.

'I messed about for a bit and then went to sell cars for H.R. Owen in Kensington,' he recalls lightheartedly. 'I was only there for eight months, but I met a lot of rich people, one of whom was a guy who was living here in the Dorchester Hotel called Prince Sultan bin Salman, who would go on to have the distinction of being the first Arab to fly in the Challenger spacecraft. I sold him a Ferrari.

'At this time, in late 1977, he was about 22 years old and went off to study at university in Denver where I took Frank to meet him. Frank said "I'll pay your fare, let's see if we can sell them some motor racing" and off we went!'

Armed with only a plastic scale model of Mike Hailwood's 1974 Yardley McLaren, Frank and Charlie duly arrived in the USA. Their sales pitch was a success and Prince Sultan agreed to forward the proposal to his family in Riyadh.

Frank Williams recalls: 'I got myself to Riyadh in January 1978, rang up Prince Sultan and he took me to see his cousin, Prince Muhammed bin Fahd, who was the second eldest son of the present King Fahd. He duly gave me an audience in his beautiful office and said "I will help you". There was no firm commitment, although we did discuss money. The whole thing was over in about 10 minutes and I went away with no more than the assurance that he would help. I was slightly over-awed by the very beautiful offices and the atmosphere of enormous power and wealth they exuded. I had about six or seven minutes in which to make my pitch, and I had been practising my speech for days . . .'

This introduction opened the door for sponsorship from Albilad, Prince Muhammed's own international trading company. Albilad's business interests in Britain were looked after by Jonathan Aitken, the Tory MP for Thanet, who, by curious coincidence, had been in the same year as Piers Courage at Eton.

Shortly afterwards, Williams received a telephone call from Jonathan Aitken and went to his London offices for a discussion. 'I gave him the full details of the company,' recalls Frank, 'and the next thing I heard was that the Prince was in London wanting to see us. So we loaded up FW06, hauled it up to London and unloaded it in the bus lane right outside his hotel. That's how the deal was done with Albilad.

'That represented a lot more of a step forward within the world of Saudi commerce. In 1978 we had a good healthy dollop of finance from Albilad – around £200,000 – and the following year, although the Prince didn't want to spend too much of his own cash, he did lean fairly heavily on his buddies and they contributed a very healthy budget, well into seven figures. A lot of other companies were happy to follow his lead. For example, Dallah Avco, a company involved in airport maintenance, put in a lot of money simply because Prince Mohammed asked them to do so.'

Others that fell into this category included Baroom, a steel and cement merchant; Bin Laden, the Kingdom's largest road builders; Siyanco, an engineering consultancy; and a relatively new trading company called Encotrade.

The expenses involved in fielding a worthwhile Grand Prix effort had increased dramatically since Frank and Piers set out on the F1 trail nine years earlier, as Williams explained at the time of FW06's unveiling:

'Running the Brabham cost between £40,000 and £50,000 for the entire season, relying on a couple of Cosworth V8 engines which could be rebuilt at £300 a time. Now we're thinking in terms of a budget 10 times that figure in 1978. A new Cosworth engine now costs £14,500 and we'll be using six altogether, with rebuilds now costing £2,500 a time, assuming that it's just a routine overhaul with nothing seriously wrong.'

Doing business in Saudi Arabia occupied a great deal of Frank Williams's time during 1979 and 1980. It could be a tedious and long-winded task. Frank quickly discovered it was necessary to balance just the right amount of pushing with suitable deference to those who controlled the purse strings.

'A lot of my approaches were speculative, admittedly,' Frank remembers. 'For example, one of the Prince's men would say "Siyanco is going to help you, ring them up". So I'd make a call to the company and perhaps had to do a fair bit of pushing and shoving before it was accepted that you would go round to their offices to see them. Even then you might go three times. That was simply par for the course. In Saudi Arabia, I soon discovered that the wristwatch is purely an ornament, not a piece of functioning equipment!

'The heat there was very uncomfortable. The flight from London used to get into Riyadh at about one o'clock in the morning, so it would usually be about three or three-thirty before I was through customs and settled into my hotel.

'I would then get up at about 11 in the morning, walk outside and – boof! – it was like walking into an autoclave. The heat drove me straight back into the air-conditioned comfort of the hotel. The air was dry and it was about 44-degrees centigrade, a really physical blow, I can tell you. Jeddah was a little bit cooler, but with much greater humidity. Believe me, it was extremely hard work.'

In the spring of 1978, Prince Sultan visited the Monaco Grand Prix in company with two of his friends, Prince Muhammed bin Nawaf and a young Franco-Saudi by the name of Mansour Ojjeh. Frank was absolutely determined that Alan Jones and FW06 put on as good a show as possible to keep them entertained and kept his fingers crossed as the Australian ran on the tail of the leading bunch, despite trailing an ominous and potentially expensive cloud of oil smoke for many laps.

The oil tank had sprung a leak and the Williams eventually crawled into the pits to retire, its lubricant exhausted. But Frank would rather have had his car performing well in this prestigious race than Jones taking the prudent course of action and retiring early in order to save the engine. Eight years earlier, Frank resolutely refused Alessandro de Tomaso's requests to run Piers Courage on half tanks in order to show well during the early stages of the same race. Now Frank could perhaps, retrospectively, have understood his point.

As it was, Alan switched off before the engine broke expensively, but the Saudis were definitely impressed and Mansour Ojjeh soon became involved as one of the company's most ardent and enthusiastic sponsors through his family's company, Techniques d'Avant Garde.

TAG is a Paris-based high technology company which forms a crucial conduit between the Saudi government and the rest of the world, carrying out all manner of wide-ranging business. It was founded by Akram Ojjeh, Mansour's father. One of TAG's most publicised business deals was the purchase of the *France*, the world's largest ocean liner, from the French Line and its sale to a Norwegian cruise company. They also represented the Saudi Ministry of Defence in arms deals, marketed the Canadair Challenger executive jet, and had tentacles which extended into many other areas of the Saudi economy, from farming to industrial enterprises.

The high technology image of Grand Prix racing appealed strongly to Mansour Ojjeh's ambitious sense of enterprise, and TAG would become the team's prime sponsor throughout 1980 and 1981. And again, it was

Charlie Crichton-Stuart who helped get the deal together. In 1979 he would join Williams as TAG's liaison man, quickly building up a strong and close relationship with Mansour and his family, spending a lot of time with him at the races when Frank and Patrick were otherwise occupied with the business of running the team.

From the touchlines, it's easy to conclude that the Williams team was somehow rather spoiled by the unique nature of the TAG sponsorship. The association with the image of Formula 1 in itself was almost entirely enough for TAG's purposes, although Mansour would use the races to entertain certain key friends and associates. There was little pressure on the team to take part in the sort of promotional activities which were to become such an integral, indispensable part of Grand Prix sponsorship arrangements during the years that followed with other companies.

As a result, Charlie Crichton-Stuart considers that TAG felt taken somewhat for granted and rather neglected, although the spectacular success of the Williams team throughout 1980 and 1981 certainly left them with no cause for complaint as far as on-track performance was concerned. However, just as they failed to romance Carlos Reutemann, so Frank's relative inexperience in these matters led him to spend less time than was perhaps prudent in massaging the Ojjeh's obvious enthusiasm for this spectacular sport.

Nevertheless, Williams recalls Mansour as 'a gem to deal with. Kind, approachable and very supportive. He was learning fast as a businessman, of course, although he was very much working for his father in those days.' By the end of the decade, with his elderly father now ailing, Mansour would be in effective control of TAG along with his brother Aziz.

Moving into the technically volatile 1980s, just as Williams were becoming embroiled in their negotiations with Honda for the supply of a turbocharged Grand Prix engine, so McLaren boss Ron Dennis arrived on the scene and virtually hijacked TAG from Frank's clutches. At the end of 1981, Dennis and his co-director Teddy Mayer had committed themselves to the extremely ambitious Porsche turbo engine programme for the McLaren team, but they had not got the necessary finance available to follow the project through on a long-term basis. Mansour Ojjeh was targeted as a likely investor and Ron's judgement proved spot-on.

'Ron was pretty quick on his feet,' concedes Frank, 'and he certainly did a very good sales job on Mansour. We were very unhappy about it, but that's Ron's modus operandi.

'Mansour came to me and said "I've told Ron that I want to do it, but I'll only do it if they agree to supply Williams as well". And Ron had agreed to those terms; he didn't have any choice, of course. But our noses were slightly out of joint, so we said we didn't really want to share anything of a technical nature with another team.

'We were looking for an exclusive deal with a manufacturer and, whatever the deal on paper, we quickly concluded that we would have been the second string Porsche team because McLaren's Chief Designer, John Barnard, was already well down the road to laying down his own detailed design requirements to Porsche for the engine.

'As a result, the TAG sponsorship began to reduce in 1983. To be honest, I told Mansour that the Porsche project would not work. I was quite wrong. In fairness to him, he believed in it and nothing would deter him. Whether this was sound judgement or just blind enthusiasm at the time, I'm not really certain.'

In addition, Patrick Head's objective opinion was that Porsche would not be able to do as good a job as Honda which, in strictly historical terms, was probably an accurate judgement, even though it did not look that way in the short term. Although the TAG-Porsche engine would power McLaren to 12 wins out of 16 races in 1984, at that point the Williams-Honda alliance had yet to reach its peak. By the time that Nigel Mansell and Nelson Piquet were dominating the scene in 1986 and 1987, the McLaren-TAGs were beyond the absolute peak of their competitiveness. Indeed, Ron Dennis was already targeting Honda as his potential engine supplier for 1988.

By 1981, Williams Grand Prix Engineering had shrewdly started to feel the way in which the commercial trend was moving, that the halcyon days of the Saudi involvement might well be coming to a close. This awareness was quickly grasped by Sheridan Thynne who had by this stage joined the team as the sponsorship co-ordinator specifically dealing with Leyland Vehicles, who had joined up as a major co-sponsor at the start of 1980 and whose contribution is examined in more detail within the next chapter.

Sheridan's career path into stock broking had left him less than fulfilled. In the early 1960s he had raced a Mini with sufficient lack of success to convince himself that the World Championship was not beckoning. But while he had abandoned all thoughts of a career behind the wheel, his enormous passion for motor racing remained undimmed. Almost single-handedly, or so it sometimes seemed, he would keep the letters page of *Autosport* magazine filled with pithy correspondence throughout the 1970s.

He joined Williams in 1980, fed up with the way in which the stock-broking profession was administered by its governing body. Perhaps rashly, he believed that Grand Prix racing might be a better prospect from that particular standpoint. It wouldn't take him long to discover that it wasn't necessarily the case.

'By 1981 the team had seen which way the wind was blowing and made a conscious decision to go west, so to speak,' he explains. 'The Saudi sponsorship finally died in 1984 when the sun was setting on their vast oil wealth and there was suddenly the need for quite a lot of cost-cutting in the Kingdom. Mansour had stopped at the end of 1983, pursuing his interests with McLaren, so we decided to make a switch. This involved switching our involvement with Mobil, for example, from the Saudi Arabian arm of the company on to a more international basis, as well as making approaches to such companies as Canon, Denim and ICI.'

To judge precisely what the Saudi Arabians had achieved from their sponsorship of Williams Grand Prix Engineering is best summed up by a little cameo during the state visit to Britain by King Khaled in 1981. The Williams team's partnership with the Saudis was then virtually at its peak, Frank was among the guests invited to Buckingham Palace when the Queen held a state banquet in honour of the visiting sovereign.

Despite his team's achievements, Frank confesses that he wasn't quite certain as to why somebody like him had been invited to such a lavish function. He struck up a conversation with another guest, a Member of Parliament, and actually advanced this tentative query as they chatted together.

'Mr Williams,' said the MP, 'I suspect that the reason you're here is that your team is one of the handful of companies to have enjoyed a really successful business relationship with Saudi Arabia.'

That was it in a nutshell.

7

The challenge of the commercial era

As far as Williams Grand Prix Engineering was concerned, the beginning of the 1980s saw the company taking what is now seen as something of a pioneering role in the development of non-tobacco sponsorship within Formula 1. The Saudi Arabian connection had been absolutely crucial in getting the team on its feet, but it became increasingly clear that such patronage could not necessarily be relied upon in the long run. None of the Saudi sponsors was using the association with WGPE for any conventional commercial marketing viewpoint. It was image-making by association: successful in its way, but not a business route to a pre-planned objective.

Throughout the 1970s, Grand Prix racing had been awash with sponsorship, notably from the cigarette companies who realised that investment in sport offered a viable and effective means of recouping coverage they were increasingly debarred from achieving through conventional television advertising. Colin Chapman had pioneered the association between Grand Prix racing and cigarettes back in 1968 with the Gold Leaf Team Lotus partnership which later developed into the highly effective John Player Special promotion which is still associated in many people's minds with the sport some years after it came to an end.

However, the Williams team's first foray into non-Saudi sponsorship came not with a tobacco company, but with the commercial vehicle off-shoot of Britain's nationalised motor company. Through a fortunate set of interlocking circumstances, combined with a shrewd display of judgement on the part of the key decision-makers involved, Williams would benefit from major co-sponsorship from Leyland Vehicles, the bus and truck manufacturers, throughout the highly successful 1980 and 1981 seasons.

Not only did this partnership produce considerable benefits to both sides – which is, after all, the whole purpose of a sponsorship deal – but it effectively delineated the ground rules by which Formula 1 sponsorship programmes in general, not just with Williams, would develop throughout the ensuing decade. In that respect, the Leyland-Williams deal was a trendsetter.

The story started when Steve Herrick, Overseas Sales Director for Leyland Vehicles, paid a chance visit to the first practice session for the 1979 Long Beach Grand Prix in Southern California.

'I was trying to do a deal to sell Leyland bus chassis to an operator in Los Angeles and I took a day off to go and watch the cars practising through the streets of Long Beach,' he recalls. 'I remember being quite impressed at the performance of the Williams driven by Alan Jones; this was at a time when the Renault turbos seemed to be blowing up left, right and centre. But, of course, this was before Frank's team had won a race. I left on Friday evening to fly back to the UK, but began mulling over a few ideas in my mind.'

In 1979, Leyland Vehicles was entering an ambitious and optimistic phase of its development. There had been a major management change and the division's fortunes were now being guided by the capable influences of Chairman David Abel and the Sales and Marketing Director, Frank Andrew.

They faced a considerable challenge in re-establishing Leyland as a credible name in the commercial vehicle export market. They had to make headway in the European market if the company was to have a worthwhile and viable future. At that time their biggest export market was Nigeria, where they had sold in the region of 10,000 trucks. But Europe seemed to remain impregnable. Depressingly, surveys initiated by the company revealed that many people thought that Leyland was a sub-division of General Motors. They knew Rover and Jaguar, the car-making divisions of the company, but the Leyland name was not widely identified with commercial vehicles.

'Even more importantly,' says Herrick, 'we had just come off the Arab black list for the first time since the late 1940s' – when the state of Israel was established – 'and it was a time when Saudi Arabia was almost eating commercial vehicles. Almost literally, when the ashtrays were full or they got dirty, they were driving them out into the desert and abandoning them. The petro-dollars were flowing round the Middle East like never before and we just had to find some means of getting our foot in the door of that market, competing with the big German firms, Mercedes-Benz and M.A.N., who were by then well entrenched.'

Herrick's attention was drawn to the identification on the 1979 Williams; TAG, Albilad – the Saudi Royal Family's international trading company – and the link with the Ojjehs. He went back and persuaded Leyland that a co-sponsorship deal with the team would reap truly worthwhile benefits. He admits that many people in his company thought he was mad. After all, Williams had yet to win a race. But after Regazzoni won at Silverstone, unlocking the floodgates of success in the second half of 1979, it became a lot easier to get the deal arranged.

In 1980 and 1981, the Williams cars would run as 'Saudia Leylands' in recognition of this sponsorship tie-up. For the truck makers, it worked a treat. This wasn't a case of flashing the Leyland name across television screens of the world to increase brand awareness. It was a carefully thought-out strategy to reach a very specific end result.

'The deal with Williams gave Leyland an almost overnight entrée to the companies we needed to be in touch with in Saudi Arabia,' continues Herrick. 'But there was something more intangible as well. We wanted to be associated with British success. Later benefits included the obvious one of providing our salesmen with a firm and interesting talking point during their negotiations, not to mention the effect it had on morale in the truck plants. But those benefits really came later. It was getting the initial contact with those people who made the buying decisions that made the Leyland-Williams association so very worthwhile.'

In retrospect, he acknowledges that meshing the interests of the Saudis with those of Leyland was quite a tricky business, doubting whether it could be repeated in the 1990s. 'It was a close-run thing whether they could co-exist at the time,' he reflects. 'I don't think that the partnership could have gone on too long. It was a case of an old-style autocracy versus a hard-nosed commercial concern. But we didn't want to frighten them away because it was that very association with them that we were after!'

With the arrival of the Williams team's first serious Western commercial sponsor, Sheridan Thynne finally joined the company on a full-time basis. Over the previous two or three years the stockbroker had given a lot of consideration as to how major Formula 1 sponsorship arrangements could be made to work on a consistent, regular basis, and how best they could be capitalised upon by both parties involved. In 1980, he was able to start putting his thoughts into practice.

'When I joined the team it quickly became quite clear that the considerable surplus funds available to our Saudi-Arabian patrons was not something we could necessarily expect on an open-ended basis,' he remembers. 'Consequently, the collaboration with Leyland Vehicles, and later with Mobil, represented a change to a situation where we had to provide tangible commercial benefits to investing companies. That was something I understood, was able to explain to potential sponsors that I understood, and could work with them on achieving these aims.

'Roughly at the same rate as the Saudi's surplus funds were diminishing during the early 1980s, we were able to introduce fresh interest – in the form of Denim, ICI, Canon and so on – to fill the potential vacuum.

'The Leyland Vehicles' association was a classic case of things happening at the right moment for both parties. Trying to raise their profile in Europe, where they were not well regarded at the time, was helped by the fact that it is very easy to identify potential customers who might purchase commercial vehicles in significant numbers. It was also easier to pinpoint the decision-makers in Europe, partly because motor racing there is an ABC-1 activity which is not touched by the slightly downmarket image which the sport suffers from in the UK.

'I believe that the Leyland deal was one of the best managed sponsorship programmes Williams ever became involved in. They benefited from tight, centralised control in the UK, knew precisely how they would run their campaigns at individual races, and did not have any European offshoots intervening to alter, or interfere with, those plans in any way.'

There is, of course, another major factor to include in the commercial equation. Through the 1980s, the budgetary requirements of a front-line Grand Prix team were expanding at quite considerable speed, far in excess of inflation, and the whole business of targeting a suitable company which could benefit from the quite considerable investment that was increasingly required, became a specialised business in itself.

In 1980 the Williams budget had been around £2.25 million at a time when the team was paying for its own Cosworth engine supply. Ten years later the budget had expanded to around £15 million, in addition to which Williams GPE benefited from the supply of Renault V10 engines in just the same way as it had enjoyed the use of Honda turbos between 1984 and 1987.

In his new role as Commercial Manager, and in close collaboration with Steve Herrick, who joined the London-based CSS Promotions during 1982, Sheridan Thynne assumed the responsibility for targeting potential investors who might be interested in becoming involved as Williams sponsors.

Together, they have evolved a scrupulously detailed and painstaking technique when it comes to the task of pinpointing a company for whom co-sponsorship of the Williams team would offer a significant advantage. Herrick basically finds the target company and devises most of the tactics for reaching it, while Sheridan works to fashion the package whereby Williams GPE seeks to meet the marketing objectives of that company. Having achieved that, it is up to their respective teams to keep the sponsors happy, a task which is considerably aided by CSS's Williams PR lady Ann Bradshaw. It is a full-time job.

For example, between them, Herrick and Thynne launched a three-year campaign to work towards securing Labatts as a team co-sponsor. They did not actually speak to the company until they were 18 months into that programme, by which time they had acquainted themselves in minute detail with the intricacies of the drinks company's position in the market place. This in itself illustrates the way in which tackling potential investors had moved on to a professional level since the amateurish days of the late 1960s and early 1970s. When the first tobacco companies arrived on the scene, many people in the sport reached the mistaken conclusion that, if motor racing worked for cigarette makers, it would automatically work for any other company. If readers care to flick through the pages of motor racing magazines of the time, they will find instances of drivers and teams complaining that they got no response from sending proposals to 'over 100 companies.' Very few gave any thought to what those individual companies might specifically gain from a motor racing involvement. In such a team's over-optimistic view, just having their names on the side of a racing car would somehow confer some magical benefit. And if it didn't, no matter; by then the money would be in the bank. The simply enormous sums of money involved as Formula 1 racing moves into the 1990s are of an order to render such a casual approach worse than useless. Badly planned sponsorship proposals can lead to unsatisfactory relationships that not only are not renewed, they also prejudice that sponsor against ever getting involved in the sport again.

The track record for Williams GPE's sponsor relationships through the 1980s reveals a number of productive, long-term associations which have endured despite the various pseudo-political ructions to which Formula 1 has been subjected from time to time. Clearly, they are satisfied customers. That they are so, is down to good planning and foresight.

Herrick and Thynne both make the point that it is not as difficult as one might think to identify those companies who might be interested in what they are selling. There are probably between 35 and 40 concerns, world-wide, who could raise the necessary budget and for whom a Formula 1 sponsorship programme would be worthwhile. In this connection, we are talking about front-line, blue chip corporations, not in any way what Herrick describes as 'peripheral' organisations. The two men make detailed proposals to no more than three or four such companies during the course of the year, having done considerable homework beforehand.

'Three or four times a year I find people saying to me "you should really approach such-and-such a company. Their Managing Director, or whoever, really loves motor racing". And I never make the approach', says Sheridan with some amusement.

'I firmly believe this to be the wrong approach. In targeting that very small number of companies, we are making a big effort to try to identify organisations which have marketing aspirations which Grand Prix racing can realistically deliver.

'Canon and Labatts, the Canadian brewery which joined us as co-sponsors in 1990, are two examples of those. To a large extent all our sponsors fall into this category. So while there may be a certain appeal in having one company that might just have surplus funds available at a particular moment, such an arrangement is unlikely to continue for a long period. One of the great benefits of having sponsors who have been with us for seven or eight years is that we can point to them as examples of companies whose original decision to become involved was not taken by a single director who simply loved racing, but the Board of Directors who believed the whole project was definitely viable.'

Steve Herrick feels that the only time they misjudge a pitch to a potential sponsor in when there are factors involved that they cannot be aware of, even within the scope of their detailed prior investigation into that company's business.

'It may be that there are some personal directives within the company that we are not in a position to know of,' he says, 'such as a decree from the Chairman that they are going to support a golf match or a tennis tournament, or whatever. Sometimes we encounter companies that have adopted very firm anti-motor sport directives, but they are few and far between and our own homework has tended to identify if this is likely to be the case long before we make a presentation.'

What Herrick and Thynne are offering is international branding. Potential sponsors have to decide whether to spend their money on a straightforward 'above the line' advertising campaign, or become the focal point for an advertising campaign. This tends to be the basic question facing the companies rather than which one of several sports they are likely to choose.

If the targeted company is keen to become involved in sports sponsorship, Herrick is in no doubt that Formula 1 is in a class of its own in terms of credibility as a global proposition.

'If you want an international sport which is annual, world-wide and attracting on-going interest throughout the year, Grand Prix racing is in a class of its own,' he states unequivocally. 'The only things in the same league are the World Cup and the Olympic Games. But they have their limitations.

'As far as the World Cup is concerned, it only takes place once every four years. You can't guarantee which countries will end up in the final. You are not being offered a sponsorship deal as such. It's just a perimeter board position and, while a company gets saturation coverage for a short time, the cost involved for being one of eight co-sponsors is not far off the entire team budget for a year's Formula 1 racing.

'In the case of the Olympic Games, it is the most expensive of all the sports. You pay $30 million to be a sponsor and you can't do anything with it, apart from knowing you have exclusivity in terms of marketing and promotion. No Olympic stadium is allowed a sponsorship banner, so you have to project your company's name by spending at least that outlay again to derive any advertising benefit. That is a phenomenally expensive proposition. Again, it happens only once every four years and its effectiveness as a tool depends to a large extent on who is going to be taking part.'

There, in a nutshell, is one strong factor supporting F1. International athletics meetings of any stature can never positively guarantee the quality of their field. Those competitors in the Grand Prix World Championship have to compete in all 16 races. Promoters and sponsors know that they will have a 26-car field, come what may, with all the established stars taking part.

By contrast, golf is seen in some quarters as elitist and not popular in all countries. Tennis also has its limitations. If you sponsor motor racing, it is the only major international sport that allows you to sponsor the competitor. In every other sporting area, you have to sponsor the event.

'As an example, try thinking who the sponsors are of each individual Grand Prix,' grins Steve Herrick. 'I guarantee that anybody outside the business will have difficulty mentioning them. But then think about which team Marlboro sponsors, which team Canon sponsors, and so on. I think you will find that more people will be able to answer that question correctly.

'There may be some things wrong with Grand Prix racing, but one of the things that is right is that it makes no pretence at being non-commercial. It does not have mealy-mouthed rules where people take the money with one hand and prefer to say that they didn't with the other. That's what is wrong with the Olympics. It's the closest thing to the Arts, for example, where they don't really want to accept sponsorship, but financial needs oblige them to do so.'

Sheridan Thynne takes up the point: 'The appeal to many people is the extent to which the F1 World Championship season is enduring. The season lasts for eight or nine months, with previews and follow-ups throughout the media, and this continuity proves particularly suitable if you are building a marketing and promotional programme. It goes on for 52 weeks of the year and none of its rivals can offer that.'

This continuity of interest proves of particular benefit for sponsors who do not want a large impact for a short time, but are seeking a sustained programme. Labatts, who are involved in a fast-growing world-wide acquisition and marketing programme, have found this prospect of being in the public eye for long periods a particularly compelling reason to have become involved as one of the Williams GPE co-sponsors. Thynne has a very clear picture in his own mind as to what Williams GPE is selling to potential sponsors. 'We are a businesslike, front-running Grand Prix operation,' he states, 'a specialist engineering company whose end product is F1 motor racing more than simply a racing team. We have a good record of working with sponsors to identify peripheral things that they can do outside the sport, based on their involvement with us, that can help them sell their product.'

In trying to project the company's serious, technologically sophisticated image, Sheridan invites potential sponsors to visit the Didcot factory as early as possible in the negotiating process. He believes that half an hour spent walking round the premises can tell them more about the company, and what F1 racing with Williams really means, than all the audio visual presentations could ever convey.

The team's sponsors basically fall into two key groups; those who like the association with the image and are keen on increasing their market awareness, such as Canon, Labatts and Camel cigarettes, and those who can point to a direct engineering spin-off such as ICI and Mobil.

In the case of Mobil, who were involved with the team for 10 years up until 1989 when the switch to Renault power meant a change to Elf fuel and lubricants as part of the deal, the Williams link offered a platform from which to market Mobil 1, their synthetic lubricant. This proved particularly successful in connection with the European market where it has been established that customers are more prepared to pay premium prices for premium lubricants than they are in the UK.

The association with ICI began on a purely promotional basis before later extending into collaboration on technical matters, one example of which was the development of a carbon-fibre composite gear selection fork for use in the Williams transverse gearbox.

'In addition, they have become associated with us on a number of other very advanced high technology projects,' explains Thynne, 'and we believe Williams GPE has brought them two specific benefits which may not be immediately obvious.'

He continues to explain that ICI like to enthuse their technical personnel with high technology projects and have been impressed by the speed and reaction time which is a necessary element of the Formula 1 business. During discussions about the composite gear selector fork, some drawings of a conventional fork were produced and the ICI men said they would come back in about six weeks' time to deliver the first prototype.

They then asked the Williams personnel how long they would need to test it, assess the results and respond. The answer was 'about three weeks.'

Sheridan says: 'That reaction almost stopped the ICI people in their tracks. We were offering a response time which they found almost unbelievable. They were used to dealing with, say, the aircraft industry where, in similar situations, they would have been told to come back in two years. It was exciting for ICI to push their boffins in a situation where they had to react quickly themselves. They found that particularly appealing.'

The other valuable function fulfilled by a Formula 1 sponsorship programme is the facility for introducing senior people in one company to their opposite numbers in other companies, forging a link which quite often leads to business being done between them. Sheridan recalls a very specific example of how this can come about:

'ICI had a relationship with a company in America called Collins & Aikman who were trying to supply some seat materials to the US automobile industry. The team had an invitation to a cocktail party thrown by Chrysler's Advanced Engineering Division and we managed to arrange it so that two guys from Collins & Aikman attended. I introduced them to senior representatives from Chrysler, business cards were exchanged and that subsequently led to new business. In this respect, we are very attentive to the need to introduce one sponsor to new business areas – either sponsor to engine supplier, for example, or sponsor to sponsor. We try to do that on quite a regular basis.'

Selling sponsorship in Japan, however, was to post quite a significant challenge for Thynne and Herrick, even though by the time they started negotiations with Canon, the major international photographic and office equipment company, in 1983, Honda was represented on the international Formula 2 racing scene and soon to make the move up into F1.

'The Japanese market had to be educated as to what Formula 1 was all about,' recalls Herrick. 'They had seen it briefly on the television and had it in the back of their minds that James Hunt had done something at Fuji back in 1976, but they didn't really seem to know what.' Eight years had passed since that Japanese Grand Prix where the English driver clinched the World Championship, but Formula 1 had since not paid any further visits to Japan and few major companies had seemed to notice its absence. Convincing Canon that Formula 1 would be a worthwhile project in which to invest, took Thynne and Herrick somewhere in the region of 13 months between making the first approach and signing the contract.

Once aboard, Canon would become a totally committed and highly enthusiastic major sponsor of the Williams team's efforts. Herrick felt that those negotiations with Canon highlighted a distinct trend which he was to encounter again in the future, namely that the fundamental challenge wasn't to sell involvement with Williams, it was to sell the whole concept of Formula 1.

'Once we had persuaded them that F1 was a good idea, the business of selling Williams GPE as the specific vehicle, if you like, by means of which they got involved, was less of a problem,' he explains. 'A lot of our time in Japan was going through the basics, introducing F1, what it means in Europe, its attractions and its potential benefits to the company.

'While the Canon negotiations are an extreme example, most of the new clients we have brought in need to be educated as to how they can use F1, after which it follows on relatively easily that Williams are perceived as possibly the most outstandingly competent team available to them in this respect.'

Canon's dignified Managing Director Masahiro Tanaka explains the attraction succinctly: 'There were three main reasons behind choosing motor racing for our sponsorship. Firstly, Canon aims to be a global enterprise, catering for many different cultures throughout the world. Formula 1 provides a common culture, a focal point for the enthusiasm and attention of different people in many countries of the world. We can project to them an image of high quality, that of a reliable, high technology product.

'Canon also manufactures cameras and there are few sports more spectacular to photographers than motor racing. This is a uniquely attractive sport on a world-wide basis and we have stayed with Williams for six years, with a contract through to 1991, because we admire their enterprise and enthusiasm. We never considered owning a team of our own, so our relationship with Frank Williams and his colleagues is ideal for our purposes.'

Mr Tanaka was speaking from within the Canon hospitality area at Suzuka, during the 1990 Japanese Grand Prix. A quick glance around bore witness to the spectacular success and expansion of the sort of corporate entertainment facilities which Leyland Vehicles and Williams had effectively pioneered a decade earlier.

Unquestionably, Canon squeezed every drop of benefit from its association with Williams. At Suzuka, they were not only entertaining key guests from the camera and office equipment business, but also providing facilities around the circuit where amateur photographers could have their films processed, their cameras serviced, borrow long lenses and even use fixed-mountings on which to attach their own cameras in order to get better views of the circuit.

Intriguingly, when Honda abandoned its association with the Williams team at the end of 1987, Canon did not seem in the slightest bit concerned about this breach. To Western eyes, one would have expected an expression of concern and disappointment at the severing of relations between two great Japanese dynasties. But to reach that conclusion is to misunderstand the complicated ethos of the Japanese business community.

The Canon company is a conservative, long-established and traditional Japanese company of the old school, one of a handful of major international concerns with deeply entrenched roots. There are hidden elements which seem to influence the relationship between these establishment firms and newcomers such as Honda who, somewhat contemptuously, are regarded as the arrivistes of the country's business community. Honda is perceived as what Herrick describes as a 'GI bride' type of company which made its name in the US export market before returning to make a significant impact on the Japanese domestic scene. As a result, in some quarters of the country's business community, they are perceived as being not quite the ticket.

A glance at the 1991 Canon Williams FW14 tends to confirm that

Williams do a good job in meshing together the various requirements of a wide variety of co-sponsors. Aesthetically, the car's colour scheme may not be particularly pleasing, but great attention is paid to giving investors value for money commensurate with their percentage contribution to the overall budget.

Sheridan Thynne goes to some lengths to defuse theories about there being a prime position on a Grand Prix car as a general rule, pointing out that such cross-referencing is impossible to value objectively. That said, the side pods are a particularly popular position, but WGPE strives to have a quantifiable range of values. If one company is paying, for example, about two-thirds of another, they go to some lengths to ensure that the ratio of exposure on the car is about the same.

Occasionally, as Patrick Head recounts, a situation arises where a technical change to the car's specification upsets a carefully organised sponsorship livery: 'At the start of 1990, Labatts was sold space on either side of the monocoque ahead of the side pods, but our development programme resulted in our extending the side pods to the point that their original position was just not there any longer.

'So we were asked whether we could lengthen the side pods by another eight inches to accommodate their identification there. We tried the set-up in the wind tunnel, but it was considerably less effective, so we compromised with a four-inch extension. Rarely do things occur like that!'

In order to ensure long-term financial stability for the team, it has been a conscious strategy to have at least two major sponsors on the car at all times. Renewal of sponsorships is also arranged so that they overlap, thereby avoiding the potential cashflow problems that could be posed if a couple of backers declined to renew with the team at the same moment. A great deal of forward planning and careful consideration is expended on dealing with such matters. 'We think we have particularly good relationships between all the co-sponsors,' concludes Steve Herrick.

As far as corporate hospitality at the circuits is concerned, this is an expanding area which seems set to grow even further into the 1990s. The number of people entertained from race to race varies enormously. For example, at the first two races of the 1990 season, in Phoenix and Brazil, ICI were the only sponsors to avail themselves of the facility. At the other end of the scale, Silverstone and Monza probably see close to 1,000 guests being entertained by different co-sponsors, in different ways, at different places within the circuit. Over a period of a race weekend, they will all receive a visit from Frank Williams, Sheridan Thynne or one of the drivers.

Within the WGPE Marketing Department, Sheridan has a couple of able assistants helping on this front, but his own status as a director of the company is of particular significance when it comes to entertaining very senior company management (VVIPs in corporate jargon). It may be that these people wish to entertain a handful of extremely important customers, in which case the team provides an exclusive table outside the Williams motorhome in the paddock where up to six such highly valued guests can be entertained in an exclusive team environment.

The collaboration between Williams and Renault has been characterized by the development of a pleasant and easy-going relationship. WGPE treat them as a sponsor in terms of the level of service they are accorded, and they have access to whatever advice they may require from Sheridan Thynne's department. Perhaps significantly, they have proved far more receptive to suggestions from the team than Honda ever did during their tenure as the Williams engine suppliers.

Mindful of the need for its sponsors to benefit as much as possible from their involvement even when they are away from Grand Prix meetings, the team have two show cars which are made available on a free loan basis, the sponsor only paying for transport costs and the relevant insurance. Sheridan tries to encourage a situation where they are only used selectively, on important occasions, such as international trade fairs, rather than, for example, straightforward Renault dealer promotions where the novelty value could easily be diluted.

Possibly the most enterprising and unusual venture on the promotional front has been the establishment of a state-of-the-art Conference Centre and Grand Prix collection within a new building in the Didcot factory complex. This was the brainchild of the company's former Commercial Executive Colin Cordy who left Williams at the end of 1990 to set up a Formula 3000 racing team in partnership with the team's ex-manager Michael Cane.

These facilities offer an unparalleled opportunity for the team's collections of Grand Prix cars, ranging from the original FW06 through to the full range of Honda-engined challengers, to be displayed in a stunning environment. At the same time, it enabled the company to build an impressive conference facility with a unique atmosphere.

With up-to-the minute electronic presentation equipment, video systems and projectors, this is not only of benefit in terms of major sponsorship presentations to large numbers of people, but also has a secondary commercial application. 'Open evenings' are being offered to accredited car clubs and other official associations whereby guests can come along, have a drink and a buffet supper, while learning a great deal about Williams GPE and the way it does things.

'The original requirement was simply for a long-term home for our collection of F1 cars,' explains Frank Williams, 'but we needed a good, sound business reason to spend a lot of money on a building. Colin Cordy came up with the proposal because he anticipated a useful amount of business from the outside world. Equally, he saw it as a means of pleasing our sponsors by demonstrating to them that the company is very professional in its business attitudes to them and their requirements.'

The ultimate test for Williams Grand Prix Engineering, of course, is whether their sponsors find it quantifiably worthwhile, in a highly commercial business environment, to invest the sort of money required by a Formula 1 programme. Overwhelmingly, the answer must be in the affirmative.

As an example, ICI, whose fibres division had originally become involved in Grand Prix racing to have a reason to invite the manufacturers of sports clothing to meet them, worked out the cost effectiveness of Formula 1 television exposure and were extremely gratified by the result.

They found that in 1988 a total of 76,229 minutes of television coverage was broadcast, across more than 90 countries. In a good season, they concluded that the Williams cars, carrying their identification, would gain 20,000 minutes of coverage. In an average season, this would be reduced to 5,000 minutes.

However, for the outlay of their £2.5 million sponsorship budget, they could have had only a minute and a half of advertising time through conventional television advertisements. On that same basis, a good season for ICI in Formula 1 would have cost a staggering £32,400 million to translate into regular television advertising.

PART THREE

The factory as a business

8

Design and technology

In 20 years, the whole design and manufacturing process in Grand Prix racing has changed beyond recognition. Time was when a designer would virtually lock himself away for the winter at his drawing board and come up with a new car concept almost singlehandedly. As we have already seen, this was effectively the case when Patrick Head conceived and produced the first 'proper' Williams – FW06. That was a familiar situation throughout the 1970s. Even a prestige team like Lotus only had a handful of design draughtsmen attempting to translate into reality Colin Chapman's meteoric concepts.

Going into the last decade of the 20th century, Grand Prix car design techniques among top-line teams like Williams have evolved to levels of esoteric excellence on a par with those to be found in the aerospace business. The image of a Formula 1 factory as a dark, dank backwater, crowded with mechanics in oil-stained overalls, jostling each other as they seek to improvise with worn out components, is as far from today's reality as a Tiger Moth is from a Learjet. Walk into the Williams headquarters today and you will find a spotlessly clean, unobtrusively efficient, state-of-the-art facility crammed with up-to-the-minute machinery and specialist equipment.

The Formula 1 design process is a non-stop treadmill. The day never comes when Patrick Head and his colleagues rule off, sit back and think 'Right, that's this year's new car finished; let's now get on with the racing. We'll come back to think about next year's package next August.' With a research and development department running parallel medium- and long-term technical developments in conjunction with a self-contained test team, one of the gambles is how late to leave it before finalising the design of a new car and initiating the manufacturing process in time to get the machine on to the grid for its target race debut.

If most Grand Prix cars look very much the same to the uninitiated eye, that is because they have been spawned by a package of highly detailed and specific technical regulations which, more or less, dictate the overall configuration of the machine. So when Patrick and his colleagues set out to refine what has gone before, they are working within tight limits, bearing in mind the need for strict conformity with the rule book, the need to package driver, engine and fuel load within a set of claustrophobic dimensions and, from their standpoint, the burning desire to make the end result that bit better than the opposition.

Over the past decade, the position of the rule makers and the car designers has tended to polarize, with each facing the other across an understandable divide. The enormous increases in car performance, through both the development of turbocharged engines and a wider understanding and application of aerodynamics, produced such a leap forward in lap speeds that FISA, the sport's governing body, is always trying to think one jump ahead of the designers in order to restrict their freedom.

Meanwhile, the instinctive competitiveness without which a Grand Prix team would be dead in the water, leads its designers to probe ever more ingenious methods of speeding up the cars. Head concedes that it is an uneasy situation and that the relationship between FISA and the teams is not always a comfortable one:

'I must admit that I am concerned that FISA tends to regard the chassis constructors as rather wicked, self-serving people who are doing this awful thing of trying to make the cars go faster so that they become more dangerous,' he states. 'In reality, a great deal of our time is involved in meeting, and often exceeding, the constructional requirements which are, generally, evolved by the teams at FISA's request.

'As an example of this, early in 1990 we were all asked to get together and propose new rules regarding limitations on cockpit restrictions, and various other design aspects, which we duly did. These were submitted to FISA who seemed quite satisfied with them. We then went away and started working on finalising the designs of our cars for 1991.'

Suddenly, at the Italian Grand Prix, FISA President Jean-Marie Balestre popped up and strongly hinted that a fresh set of technical regulations might have to be implemented for 1991, accusing the constructors of having failed to advance proposals for reducing the speeds of the cars. In the same breath, he said that 'in the opinion of all the doctors, almost all the drivers and the other technicians, it is imperative to modify the cars.'

Such knee-jerk outbursts make Patrick Head, and indeed most of his colleagues in other teams, start to shudder. Ever since the start of the 1980s, they believe, there has been a gulf of understanding between FISA and the constructors on what is precisely involved in the wholesale re-design of a Grand Prix car at short notice.

One of the problems which tends to complicate the situation is that although fundamental changes to the F1 chassis regulations cannot be made without two years' notice according to the terms of the Concorde Agreement, the book of rules which governs the way F1 is conducted, FISA has a means of circumventing this requirement. There is a clause which allows immediate rule changes to be initiated on the grounds of safety and, in Patrick's view, this has been called up far more frequently than has been justified over the past decade.

It was used by FISA in 1980 to prohibit sliding skirts, prompting such a row and briefly jeopardising the whole future of F1 to the point that Williams GPE accepted a commission from Rover to design the Metro 6R4 rally car simply because both Frank and Patrick were worried that there might not be any future for Grand Prix racing as they knew it. This project is described in more detail later in the narrative, but the very fact Williams, took it on at all is indicative of the highly strung relationship between FISA and the teams. It can certainly make for a nerve-wracking design environment.

Head would like to see the relationship between FISA and the F1 constructors develop into a more genuine, workable and willing collabo-ration. 'I would certainly like to see more engineering input from the teams,' he says, 'and I see absolutely no reason why it could not happen if managed properly. But it's like everything else that's badly managed . . . there's a consistent lack of attention to the details involved, followed by a massive over-reaction. That seems very disappointing. It also makes me angry to even talk about.'

As the design department expands, and the process of manufacturing intricate and specialist components increases, so the potential for unex-pected problems crops up once more. In 1989 and 1990 for example, Thierry Boutsen suffered a couple of suspension breakages of the sort which might have been understandable – if not acceptable – in the old days when Patrick and the team were on a steep learning curve.

'I like to think that some of those things would not have happened if I had been right on top of the day-to-day design process in a hands-on sense,' Patrick Head reflects. 'But when you get to a company of this size it's very difficult to be right on top of every single thing that is happening.

'A lot of my responsibility nowadays is to develop systems and methods to ensure that less experienced designers, who may not have understood the implications and consequences of the design changes they make, have their work filtered. To do that without giving the whole place massive constipation – that's to say without an unacceptably long delay between designing a modification and it finding its way on to the car – is extremely difficult.

'In that respect, there are not many types of engineering activity in which the initiation of design action, and the need for somebody – in this case the driver – to go out and depend on it for his safety, are so close together.'

One can sense that Patrick would like still to be in total control, working away at the drawing board himself, but the sheer volume and intensity of specialist design work in today's F1 environment makes that an entirely unrealistic prospect. At any one time, the Williams GPE design office may be working on two or three parallel developments, yet their lead time for getting them into competitive action may vary enormously.

At one end of the scale these can include fairly routine items such as a revised upright for the suspension, while long-term developments – such as reactive suspension and the electro-hydraulic gearchange system used on FW14 from the start of the 1990 season – may take shape over two or three years.

'I do try to do some hands-on design work on particular aspects of the car,' he explains, 'but generally each engineer gets a specific package to deal with. I will usually write a brief for them which outlines the direction which I want them to pursue, and why a particular thing is being done. It amounts to a brief as to what we are trying to achieve, but I try to leave them some scope for putting a little bit of their personal stamp on a component.

'They will then start away and we will have periodic meetings as and when necessary. Perhaps one of them will say "I'm a bit stuck on this, can we have a meeting?" So we try to sort it out. There is occasionally the situation where they say "Look, we've examined it and we can't get such-and-such a component through there, or can't do it in the way you suggested". If I reckon it is possible, I'll take a copy of how far he's gone and have a crack at it myself. In those circumstances, I might find a way of doing it or say "You're right, we can't do it, so let's have a look at a different solution".

'I suppose I'm the only co-ordinator between the wind tunnel, manufacturing processes and what eventually happens out on the circuit. I have to link everything together and, hopefully with some accuracy, predict what long-term technical requirements we will need in the future as well as what's needed on the cars for the next few races.'

Patrick admits that he doesn't check every drawing that goes out, with the result that, very occasionally, he may change direction on something that is quite late down the road in a situation where parts may even have been manufactured. In that case he might take the view that, while it hasn't been made quite the way he would have done it, the component will be perfectly serviceable. Therefore he will let it go.

One key reason behind the expansion of the technical side in F1 is the growth in specialist fields such as carbon-fibre composites, aerodynamics, transmission and suspension development. They all have specialists working on particular aspects of the car's performance, all knowledgeable to a level which probably exceeds the central designer's knowledge in each of those fields. Patrick's job has, increasingly, required him to have sufficient knowledge of all such aspects of the development to keep them properly co-ordinated and working in harmony.

Of course, with a design department now employing 16 people, budgetary control is a matter of paramount importance. It's no secret that Williams turns over more than £1 million a month. It wouldn't have to go far off course in this respect to end up in big trouble.

'I get a set of accounts every month,' Head explains, 'and that enables me to monitor expenditure against budget. If one area is over-spent, then we will have a look at it and decide whether the reason for it is acceptable or not. It often happens that the underspend areas match the overspend.'

'Obviously, we predict our expenditure on the basis of the previous year's budget and sometimes the person making that prediction is not fully conversant with the technical programme. If, say, we've done a completely new gearbox during one year, the following year, although we may be running exactly the same gearbox, the accountant will just extrapolate the figures. Conversely, there may be more expenditure in a particular area than there has been during the previous season.'

Aerodynamic considerations have always been an important element in the design of any Grand Prix car, but with the advent of ground effect technology they became of absolute paramount importance. We have already seen how Patrick Head was alerted to the pressing need for William GPE to install its own wind tunnel in 1979 and reliance on such facilities has continued to snowball throughout the 1980s.

During his spell as the Williams team aerodynamicist, Frank Dernie expressed the view that it was difficult to reach an accurate conclusion as to whether a full-scale wind tunnel would be a more accurate proposition than one using scale models.

'Nobody has the data to reach an accurate conclusion either way, in my view,' he commented. 'I have some indications, though, that a full-sized wind tunnel does not always produce the same sort of results we get with the car when it is out on the circuit. For example, attempting to duplicate a situation where a car is accelerating from 100 to 150mph in about three seconds is a tremendously difficult thing to do.'

When FISA banned sliding skirts from the underside of F1 cars at the end of the 1980 season, having a wind tunnel facility aided Williams enormously in the task of developing efficient profiles for the side pods which would work relatively well under the new regulations, where there would now be a less predictable air flow beneath the car.

Extensive wind tunnel testing of the FW07 revealed an area for potential improvement which was incorporated into the design of FW08 at the start of 1982. The trend away from rocker arm front suspension to a pull-rod arrangement did not reflect a theoretical belief that this was a better system in itself. But it was established that those rocker arms, together with their fairings, were generating an unwanted degree of uplift, so the more compact and tidy pull-rod arrangement allowed airflow towards the side pods to be significantly less disturbed.

Many designers saw the 1987 season as a considerable turning point in the development of flat-bottomed aerodynamics – the ingenuity of Patrick Head, Frank Dernie and other rival designers having just about regained the sort of aerodynamics downforce which was lost when the flat-bottom regulations were introduced at the start of 1983. Dernie estimated that the Williams FW11B-Honda, in its highest downforce specification, was developing downloads comparable with those generated by the Cosworth-engined FW08C in its fast circuit, low downforce guide. Redressing the balance had virtually meant doubling the drag during that five-year period, but the prodigious power output of the Honda turbo engine overcame that problem.

By 1990, Williams GPE were carrying out their aerodynamics development in two wind tunnels, using a quarter-scale model in their own at the Didcot factory and a 40 per cent scale model in the University of Southampton facility. By the middle of 1991, when their new 25,000 square feet building to house the Research and Development Department is completed, it will contain an even larger tunnel in which they can test half-scale models. This facility should be the fastest 'low speed' wind tunnel in the world and, as such, should endow Williams GPE with an outstandingly accurate and effective design and development tool.

'In order to achieve dynamic similarity – that's to say an accurate representation in the wind tunnel of how the car's aerodynamics will behave out on the circuit – the closer you can get to full-scale conditions, the less the margin of disparity will be,' Patrick explains.

'Also, each tunnel obviously has a cross-sectional working area and, depending on the amount of blockage caused by the model within that section, you get errors in the result you end up with. This results from the air speeding up as it approaches the blockage, in this case the model. Obviously, when a car is out on the circuit, there is no such restriction to the airflow.'

Williams employs five specialist model makers to produce the scale models for wind tunnel purposes and Patrick explains that they may make two models for each tunnel during the course of the year. This enables testing to continue even while one of the models is back being altered. The budget for this crucial item in the overall scheme of things is in the order of at least £800,000 per year.

Having digested and assimilated the information gleaned from the wind tunnel work, since 1986 the design department at Williams Grand Prix Engineering has benefited from the installation of a comprehensive computer-aided design/manufacturing (CAD/CAM) facility. All chassis design work since the advent of the FW11 has been carried out using this system which enables fresh standards of detailed finish and fine tolerances to be achieved for the installation of all the various components which need to be packaged within an F1 chassis.

The system allowed the designers to view a three-dimensional picture of the proposed chassis layout on a computer screen, and then experiment with various details without ever having to cut metal or carbon-fibre to make a prototype component. For checking such crucial subtleties as radiator ducts, or deciding whether it was worth trying a new rear wing, the system's installation contributed to a much more economical use of the engineers' time.

Once the designer had satisfied himself with the basic configuration he had achieved on the screen, quarter-scale drawings could be created from which the team's model maker could manufacture the quarter-scale wind tunnel models. If problems were then encountered, and minor modifications were required to the model, it was easy for the designer to go back to the computer scale, produce a revised drawing and have the changes duplicated by the model maker. Even so, a large part of model development is still done using lumps of filler and sticky tape, and probably will be for many years to come.

Once the basic shape had been finalised, the aerodynamic department would hand their findings over to Patrick Head who, in conjunction with his design staff, would make final judgements as to the overall dimension of the chassis and precisely how the chassis would be manufactured from the viewpoint of just how the carbon-fibre composite materials would be laid up.

On FW11 it was quite a challenge to make the cross-sectional area of the monocoque as small as possible, trying to make up for the fact that the 80-degree Honda V6 was significantly larger than its main rivals such as the TAG-Porsche and Renault V6s.

Frank Dernie says: 'It was fascinating to be able to take, say, the engine management control box, and then take sections and check clearances, and even be able to show that we would have to remove some of the honeycomb within the engine cover to make it fit properly. It was that precise and detailed. Prior to that, of course, something like that might have to be improvised by the mechanics during the course of the car's assembly. Now it can be done before the manufacturing process has started, so a lot of time in the prototype shop can be saved.

'We could take sections and decide "that's a good space, we can put the water pipes through there" or "the gear linkage is going to foul that component there". Being able to look at all these things in quite substantial detail before you cut metal or start laying up carbon-fibre obviously saves time and money.

'The CAD/CAM process also gives you all your dimensions automatically and doesn't generate drawing errors. For example, in the old days a draughtsman might have wanted a $\frac{1}{4}$in hole, but drew a $\frac{1}{8}$in hole by accident. With this system it can't happen. It's almost self-checking in the sense that errors are easier to pinpoint.'

This machinery also provides for a direct link between the design stations and the machine shop. The precise geometric dimensions of complex components can be transferred directly into the computer programme governing the operation of those machining centres, leaving the operator to decide only which additional tools he will need to fit in order to complete the job.

The use of such CAD/CAM design systems has led to the area of finite element stressing, a detailed structural analysis of complex composite parts. The facility to carry out this intricate work has been steadily developed, initially on the various metal components employed in the chassis.

The unremitting pace of development throughout the 1980s, both in terms of aerodynamics and engine power output, produced a new breed of car capable of developing up to 3-G acceleration on a given radius of curvature at a particular speed. Since the way in which the aerodynamic, chassis and suspension components interact forms a crucial element in the handling of a racing car, it became a prime requirement that the basic monocoque structure should be endowed with tremendous stiffness.

When the first carbon-fibre composite Williams FW10 was built prior to the start of the 1985 season, it was considerably stiffer than the FW09, its immediate predecessor which was built round an aluminium alloy honeycomb chassis. As an illustration of this fact, in the cockpit area a 65 per cent increase in torsional stiffness was achieved for the same weight of component. It also followed the latest trend of the monocoque walls effectively doubling as the outer bodywork, making for a complicated moulding which was manufactured in two stages.

Using newly installed high temperature pressure vessels, called 'autoclaves', the outer skin was cured at the maximum autoclave pressures of 7-bar (100lb/sq.in). These two sections were then hot-wired together. The first stage sees an average of six plies (more in some areas) being high pressure cured in the mould, then the honeycomb and hard point inserts – on which various suspension and other component mountings are fixed – are hot cured into position at medium pressure. Finally, an equal laminate, usually of six plies, is hot cured at medium pressure to the inside of the honeycomb. Bulkheads and floor panels are then assembled and cold bonded into position.

Despite those early misgivings over the performance of carbon-fibre composite materials in a racing application, Patrick and his colleagues have long since satisfied themselves as to its suitability and its use has been quickly expanded to other key chassis components. The frontal impact tests, to which all F1 chassis are now subjected under the FISA regulations, have gone a long way towards allaying any worries on this particular score.

Undertrays are also manufactured from carbon composite, the requirement being that they should be light, rigid, easily removable and capable of sustaining any amount of 'kerbing' on the part of undisciplined drivers. During the height of the turbo era they were also required to endure close proximity to red-hot turbochargers as well as being subjected to the exhaust gases from the engine. By the same token, rear wings must be light, easily adjustable and capable of sustaining aerodynamic loadings in the order of 100 times their own weight. Again, carbon-fibre has come to provide the ideal medium for manufacturing such components.

The opportunity to seize every available technical opportunity is of paramount importance for a team to retain its competitive edge in this business. So when Williams was facing that mounting battle against the turbo brigade, towards the end of 1981 Patrick Head came up with an imaginative solution to improve the performance of initially the FW07 and latterly the FW08.

After carrying out some detailed calculations, Patrick reached the conclusion that the very large contemporary rear tyres used by F1 cars were responsible for something in the order of 40 per cent of the machine's overall aerodynamic drag. His wind tunnel investigations had suggested that a six-wheeler, using four small rear wheels to do the driving, would offer a significant performance improvement.

The rival March team had made a prototype of a similar system back in 1977, but lacked the necessary funds to develop the concept. Head, however, pressed on with his interpretation of the theme.

Hewland, the Maidenhead-based specialist gear manufacturers who have been at the heart of most British F1 transmission systems for more than 20 years, offered some assistance with the package, drawing on the experience with the March six-wheeler which was by now being used by amateur driver Roy Lane on the British hillclimb scene.

The new rear end set-up was centred on the conventional two-wheel-drive car's rear axle centre line, so the leading rearward axle of the six-wheeler was placed four inches ahead of the regular position and the driveshafts angled forward to cope. The rearward axle was driven by an additional final drive unit added on to the back of the transmission package.

The prototype Williams FW07D six-wheeler was sampled by Alan Jones at Donington Park just after his victory in the 1981 Caesars Palace Grand Prix at Las Vegas, his final triumph for the team. He was impressed, but its rocket-like acceleration and outstanding grip were not in themselves enough to persuade the tough Aussie to revoke his retirement decision.

The system surfaced again during 1982 when Keke Rosberg tried an FW08, similarly equipped, during testing at Paul Ricard. Patrick had to re-think the concept to overcome the difficulty of packaging the aerodynamic underwings, but the whole project came to nothing when six-wheelers were specifically banned at the start of 1983. It was an ingenious solution and its prohibition was one of those pre-emptive moves by the sport's governing body which makes the role of an F1 designer such a potentially frustrating task.

Williams GPE has continued to make significant progress in transmission development, a six-speed transverse gearbox being introduced in
1988 for the Judd-engined FW12, and further developed through to 1990
on the Renault-engined FW13B. For 1991, Nigel Mansell and Riccardo
Patrese are racing the new FW14 equipped with an ambitious new
electro-hydraulic gearchange system.

Unquestionably, working with Patrick Head in the Williams design
office has been beneficial to the future careers of several senior engineers
who are now with other teams. The track record of the 'old boys' from
this particular academy is impressive to say the least.

Neil Oatley is now number one man with McLaren; Frank Dernie
went off to assume total responsibility for Team Lotus fortunes as their
technical director, and is now with Ligier. Other graduates include
Enrique Scalabroni at Lotus, James Robinson at McLaren, Ross Brawn
at TWR Jaguar and Sergio Rinland at Brabham.

'I suppose you could say we have had quite an effect on the pit lane,
really,' says Patrick. 'There are pleasures to be gained by working with
other people. I don't know whether those who have moved on have good
or bad memories of their time with Williams, but Frank Dernie was here
for nine years, Neil for seven, so you're not talking about short-stayers.
They all went away because they were offered significantly more money
and wider responsibilities.'

9

Administration and management

'This is just like any other business, really – if you stop growing you die. One of the great things about being at the sharp end of the F1 business is that Williams Grand Prix Engineering is investing considerable amounts of money in the future of the company. The whole culture of the place is geared to motor racing with high calibre craftsmen, great engineers and excellent management, all of whom have a tremendous interest in motor racing and, especially, in the company.'

That's how the Williams GPE ethic is summed up by David Williams, the firm's General Manager. He is in charge of the operations as a whole, presiding over the factory in which Production Manager Tony Pilcher is responsible for the shop floor manufacturing processes by which the cars are produced.

While Frank, Patrick and Sheridan are the key decision makers when it comes to overall company strategy, Formula 1 racing on the scale pursued by Williams GPE has long since outstripped the capability of one individual to oversee every aspect of the engineering operation. Just as, well prior to his accident, Frank fully realised that the technical complexities of operating the team in the Grand Prix pit lane had far exceeded his own sole capability, the situation within the factory itself has become even more involved and specialised. Professional business management fulfils a role every bit as crucial as does innovative engineering.

David Williams joined the company in the second half of 1988 and has a firm grounding in engineering management. His responsibilities at Didcot involve the operations of the manufacturing facility as well as the research and development programmes.

'My job is to administer the whole operation,' he explains. 'This theoretically leaves Patrick and Adrian Newey, the chief designer, to concentrate as much as possible on their specific projects, on innovative concepts and future developments rather than being bothered with all the hassles of getting things made and getting the various programmes up and running.'

Unquestionably, this is a wide and extremely challenging brief. The General Manager's responsibilities range from co-ordinating the various departments involved in physically building the racing cars, plus having all the spares and equipment required for their efficient operation in the right place at the right time, budgeting for the factory's overall operations and for investment in new equipment, and the investigations into the application of new materials which may be of practical use at some time in the future.

A glance round the Williams GPE factory reveals several specialist departments, all working independently, yet all contributing to the overall end result. One of the most complex, and recently established, is the composites shop where all aspects of the manufacture of carbon-fibre components, from complete monocoques to minor ancillaries have been dealt with since the first CFC Williams FW10 chassis was manufactured at the start of 1985.

This area now includes two large autoclaves, the key pressure vessels in which the complex carbon-fibre chassis are 'cured' at the appropriate temperature, and various smaller ovens accommodating other items which, while requiring curing at high temperatures, do not necessarily need the process to be carried out under pressure. This department produces the monocoques, undertrays, bodywork sections and aerofoil sections and is subject to the most stringent quality control and technical examinations imaginable.

Central to this operation is the 'clean room' where the environment is air conditioned with the atmosphere constantly filtered and controlled to provide conditions where the temperature-sensitive aerospace materials that are used – carbon-fibre, kevlar and various types of resins and adhesives – can be worked upon with minimal chance of becoming contaminated.

'Composite materials are very difficult to inspect when the actual component is finished,' explains David Williams. 'You can only really monitor the manufacturing processes. They are not like components made of metal which you can check by stress-testing or X-ray examination. Proper quality control during the manufacturing process is the only guarantee you can have that the carbon-fibre component is going to perform properly in the field – short of actually destroying the component completely!' Williams GPE does not monitor the quality of the actual carbon-fibre materials, simply purchasing it to a particular specification. It arrives with a 'certificate of conformity' which declares that it meets with that specification.

A total of 15 skilled craftsmen are employed in the composites shop, many of them versed in the traditional manufacturing techniques of sheet metal fabrication. Williams GPE recruited many of its previous generation of fabricators from the aircraft industry, notably from the Royal Aircraft Establishment at Farnborough, and many of those men are still with the team, having transferred to embrace the intricacies of carbon-fibre work. In addition, there are plenty of younger people, some of whom have joined from rival teams, others from the aerospace industry and some whom the company has trained itself.

Nothing is spared in terms of the latest equipment. One item of machinery introduced in 1991 is a six axis 'robot' which can trim the carbon-fibre components to very fine tolerances, a time-consuming task if it is to be carried out by the workforce.

As an example of this machine's potential, David Williams cites its application in finishing the carbon-fibre undertrays and aerodynamic diffuser panels which form an integral feature of any contemporary F1 chassis design.

'We make something in the order of 100 of these components a year,' he says, 'and while this may not amount to manufacturing industry proportions, it represents a quite considerable output to a company of this nature. They take about four and a half hours each to trim by hand, to get them to the exact prescribed shape once they have been taken out of the mould. The robot can carry out this task in about eight minutes.'

After preliminary trials, the robot has now come into regular use, just one example of how specialist machinery can take the drudgery out of a repetitive job and release craftsmen to carry out more skilled and innovative work elsewhere in the factory.

Such machinery does not come cheap, of course. The sort of figures involved in purchasing machine tools on this scale may send a shudder down the spine when one considers the rather arbitrary fashion in which FISA seem capable of changing the technical regulations at a stroke, rendering obsolete thousands of pounds' worth of carefully manufac-tured components. For those die-hards who believe that racing teams are merely competitors, and should therefore be willing subordinates to a sometimes unpredictable governing body, the figures involved in equip-ping the Williams factory should stop them in their tracks.

The basic cost of such a 'robot' is around £95,000 plus another £20,000 'for a bit of kit that goes on the end for the high speed routeing.' And that doesn't include the £10,000 for the special enclosure into which the machine has to be installed to satisfy the factory's safety regulations. Going one step further, even the smaller of the two autoclaves, installed by Williams during 1990, cost £85,000. This is extremely serious engi-neering involving considerable budgets.

Before the carbon-fibre composite monocoque can be manufactured, the factory's pattern shop will be called upon to manufacture the 'bucks' from which the chassis mouldings are produced. In years gone by, hardwood was used for this purpose, but now Williams used a 'composite wood' material called Eurol which is more suited to the purpose since it will better withstand the temperatures to which it is subjected during curing in the autoclave. It is also environment-friendly in the sense that it is a synthetic product and eliminates the need to purchase hardwood, which is not only extremely expensive but also involves a small step in the destruction of the rain forests.

The Williams GPE factory shop floor destroys any pre-conceived image of the small, understaffed racing team as a tiny business with versatile personnel optimistically turning their hands to any task. This is big business. There are safety considerations, the need to conform to the Factories Act. Happily, the factory inspectors usually emerge from the premises on Basil Hill Road with smiles of approval on their faces.

'They always manage to find something wrong,' grins David Williams. 'But generally they look around our place and say that it's a pity that much of the rest of British industry doesn't take a leaf out of our company's book. We put great store by cleanliness, high standards of equipment and investment, but at the end of the day we have to conform.

'The attitude Frank and Patrick take towards the place is very positive, just the sort of attitude that Japanese companies, for example had tried to adopt in general industry. It's efficient, and it doesn't really take a great deal of effort to be clean and tidy as well. This approach sets the whole tone for the working environment and the employees.'

The Williams machine shop continues the high technology message. Within this hive of activity, some 16 specialists work away on a mixture of computer numerical and conventional machine tools, a mixture of milling machines and turning centres. Again, talking in terms of financial commitment, the most recent addition to the line-up is a large, Japanese-made machining centre. This had a basic price of about £200,000 to which can be added another £50,000 or so to equip it with a range of specialist tools and to train up an operator.

'This sort of outlay will not surprise many people in general engineering,' concedes David Williams, 'although it may surprise a lot of people who turn up to spectate at motor races. But we're working in an environment where the cost of an average lathe is in the order of £35,000 and even a bog standard turning lathe, the sort budding engineers might have used at school and which we might entrust to an apprentice, will set you back about £15,000.

Although many of these machine tools are computer programmed by the machinist to carry out a pre-set task, there are still a lot of jobs in the manufacture of a Formula 1 car where there is a need to produce one-off components. In such a case it is frequently easier to get a skilled man to do it straight off rather than waste time programming a machine for the purpose of making a single item, or a small run. However, the computer programmed machines are becoming more user-friendly all the time and David Williams can foresee the day when virtually every tool in the machine shop will be equipped with this facility.

The machine shop does everything except produce the original forgings and castings. These are bought in from outside suppliers, but from that point onwards every component is manufactured within Williams GPE.

The fabrication shop is responsible for producing the exhaust systems, all metallic structural items such as bracketry, suspension uprights, wishbones, anti-roll bars, radiators, oil tanks and general pipework. But even that is becoming ever more automated with, for example, pipe bending machines that can be programmed directly from the CAD/CAM stations in the design department.

'This is of enormous benefit when it comes to guaranteeing absolute consistency of dimensions,' says David Williams. 'Once we have produced the first exhaust system for a prototype car build we can repeat the same standards with much greater dependability and accuracy than in the past. If we're sending spare parts, perhaps, to the other end of the world, this at least enables us to know that when they arrive they should fit onto the car without any tweaking or surgery away from the factory.'

The model shop, meanwhile, involves the application of similar skills. Again, very skilled model and pattern makers are needed to produce the highly detailed models for aerodynamic testing. These are not toys by any stretch of the imagination, but intricately detailed representations of the full-sized car which must be absolutely accurate if the aerodynamic test programme is not to be a fatally flawed process.

In producing components for the cars, the overall philosophy is to try and keep stock in hand to a reasonable minimum. This is not a manufacturing concern where, if current components are not used when the product is contemporary, there will always be a demand for stock to equip older machinery. Once a Williams Formula 1 car is outmoded, there is no real purpose in holding a large stock of its component parts.

The factory tries to operate a system whereby, at the end of a racing season, the team is down to the minimum stocks necessary to see it through the winter testing. 'We don't want to have redundant components on our hands,' says David Williams, 'so we try to keep it as close to the bone as possible.'

The General Manager also plays a key role in financial planning within the company, meeting with Frank Williams and accountant Duncan Mayall sometimes as often as once a week, more usually once a fortnight. There are also monthly budget meetings which Patrick always attends. They operate an informal, but efficient, system of monitoring expenditure.

'It's not really a case of having an agenda in the formal sense,' explains David Williams. 'Frank may just say "David, how are you doing at the moment?" and I'll say that I've got some free time. So Frank will reply "Right, get hold of Duncan and we'll get talking".

'I'm employed to run the company from this point of view and, if there's a problem, I'll try to deal with it. If we have an overspend area, then I'll have to sort it out with Patrick and find a way in which we can manipulate the budget to accommodate it. In all these areas I will be keeping Frank fully in touch with developments.

'You've got to keep on top of this all the time. For example, in 1990 we spent something like £153,000 just on gear ratios, and for 1991 we are switching to new gears specially manufactured to our own design for a number of beneficial technical reasons. This means that the expenditure in this area is going to leap to around £200,000. That's just for the gears, mind you. The figure doesn't include the transmission casing, the final drive or even the input bevels.

'This sort of expenditure level is probably only matched by three other teams in F1 at the present time – Ferrari, McLaren and Benetton – and it serves as a measure of what is required if you are going to compete at absolutely the top level.'

The factory's operation as a tight, lean business enterprise also takes into account careful financial planning in line with the company's long-term strategy. Basically, Williams GPE works on a three-year programme in terms of its planned investment in equipment and facilities. This is updated annually, so at any one time the team has a very detailed schedule for the year immediately ahead, a slightly less detailed schedule for the second year, but fairly specific from the point of view of which way the company wants to go, and a basic outline of the third year priorities.

'These requirements are, in turn, interlinked to our sponsorship requirements over that period,' adds David Williams. 'Once we have decided what we need to be doing from the technical point of view, Sheridan and Frank then have an idea of how they will tackle the long-term budgeting.'

Research and development is the lifeblood of any Grand Prix team operating into the 1990s, and Williams GPE plans to have its new facility in working order by the middle of 1991. The new premises will be home to the model-making shop, prototype work on the reactive suspension, electro-hydraulic development work, the electronics department and expanding work into structural testing of composite materials.

Even with all these facilities accommodated, the new building should have about 12,000 sq ft of immediate surplus capacity to provide for expansion plans several years into the future. In turn, this will enable the main factory to be re-organised with more room available for all the other departments. All this stands as testimony to the fact that Frank, Patrick and Sheridan love and live motor racing to the point where a substantial portion of the company's income is invested in long-term projects.

'You've only got to glance round the factory to see the level at which investment is taking place at Williams GPE,' says David Williams. 'In

1990 our capital investment programme ran at just under £3 million and it is scheduled to be of the same order in 1991. We're talking about new machine tools, new equipment for the test team and so on. That's got nothing to do with the financial outlay involved in building or operating the cars. It is totally separate.'

Of course, it is not simply the ability to design, manufacture and assemble Grand Prix racing cars to superbly fine standards of precision and finish that distinguishes the workforce at Williams GPE. They also display a tremendous resilience and commitment when it comes to working under pressure, at short notice.

David Williams comments: 'The whole culture of the place is geared to motor racing and, consequently, they understand the need for quick response and first-class standards of work all the time. There is little need for a manager to go round looking over their shoulders saying "that's wrong, it's not up to standard" because the people who work here know when something is wrong, so they will scrap it and start again off their own bat if they make a mistake.'

Occasionally, of course, the factory will be called upon to work miracles overnight. Possibly the most celebrated example of this came in the summer of 1988 when, after a frustrating first qualifying session for the British Grand Prix at Silverstone, an overnight re-design of the suspension system for the Judd-engined FW12 was initiated at short notice by Patrick Head.

Up to that point in the season, the team's performance had been badly compromised by the strains of trying to make the computer-controlled reactive suspension system sufficiently reliable. Not only had the system's erratic behaviour confused and unsettled the drivers, Nigel Mansell and Riccardo Patrese, but the system showed a worrying tendency to break suspension components by hammering against its end stops, spread pools of hydraulic fluid across the pit lanes and become stricken by deep-rooted electrical malfunctions.

At Silverstone, the problems seemed bad enough for Patrick to press the 'go' button for an instant fix to get the team through its home Grand Prix. What followed was a classic example of how a top Grand Prix team can salvage something worthwhile from the apparent depths of technical disarray, a quality which calls for nerve, calmness under pressure, and a sure-sighted vision of what is called for in a tight corner.

It was a relatively straightforward task to equip the FW12C rear end with conventional steel springs in place of the reactive system, but the front end, where the tiny hydraulic jacks were mounted inboard atop the monocoque, represented a substantial challenge.

Thirty minutes or so after the end of the first qualifying session, Patrick drove out of Silverstone after calling the factory on his car phone. The purchasing department was instructed to look in their catalogues to find a source that could supply tiny disc springs of the appropriate rate, and a company in Worcester was contacted only a few minutes before closing time.

The factory owner was persuaded to take them home that evening and a messenger was immediately despatched from Didcot to pick them up. Working throughout the night, the Williams GPE factory adapted the FW12 front suspension struts to accept a piston fitted with a small damper valve and the reactive system bump stop was replaced with the new disc spring.

In the small hours of Saturday morning the first units were completed, tried on the factory's damper test rig and were whisked back up to Silverstone for installation on the team's spare car which by then had been stripped out in anticipation of the new components. Mansell tried them on Saturday, pronounced them fine, and a second car was converted thus for Patrese on Saturday night. In the rain-drenched race, Mansell rewarded everybody's effort with a storming drive to second place behind Ayrton Senna's McLaren-Honda.

This is recalled as one of the most celebrated examples of the Williams GPE staff rising to the occasion, but in reality it only received such wide-ranging publicity because it involved Mansell at Silverstone and the team was operating in front of the home crowd. As David Williams points out, examples of the workforce's commitment to getting the job done at all costs are happening all the time, even though outsiders get to hear little about them.

'If there is a problem at a race in Europe, for example, we might get one of the race engineers – or Patrick, if he's there – ringing back to Tony Pilcher, our production manager, telling him that something needs to be modified urgently,' says the factory manager.

'In these cases the telephone call may well be followed by a fax, possibly with a sketch of the changes that need to be carried out. There are always staff at Didcot over a race weekend to deal with just such a possibility.'

'When we have received the details of a proposed change, we may have to get an engineer down from the drawing office if we can't quite understand what is required. Then we might need to do some testing of our own. For example, a radiator might need to be checked on our flow rig. Then the component needs to be manufactured. If any outside components are deemed to be necessary, the purchasing department would obtain the specification from the engineers in the drawing department first. The production manager would not act on his own without making such a reference.

'Then it would be a question of sending out a van to pick up the necessary parts. You know, it's amazing how many factories you can get opened up on a Saturday if you've got a few decent team tee shirts in the back of the car.'

Once a new or modified component is completed, Williams GPE will get on to Rapid Movements, the specialist freight forwarding company which has served the F1 community for many years. They will pick it up, transport it out to the European circuit and deliver it by hand to the chief mechanic.

When it comes to such close knit operation, there is considerable inter-dependence between those personnel away at the circuits working with the racing team and those who toil loyally back at base. Under such circumstances it might be understandable if tensions built up. Those who are factory-based might conclude that the racing team members are really having a wonderful time, swanning round the world – while the men in the pit lane might risk drawing the conclusion that the factory staff don't really understand what real pressure is all about.

To head off such potential 'them and us' polarisation, the Williams GPE management takes an enormous amount of trouble to involve and inform its employees about all facets of the business, particularly in areas outside their immediate orbit. The company also offers a degree of flexibility over working hours, the premises being open for the workforce from 6:30 to around 22:00. Some come in at the crack of dawn and leave between 18:00 and 19:00. Others, perhaps those with families, start slightly later. Most home-based staff work between 55 and 60 hours a week which obviously includes an element of overtime which is not available to the racing team staff but they benefit from the higher basic salary instead.

There is a very small management pyramid which, in itself, enables the workforce to keep in touch with the decision-making processes. Beneath the company directors, as far as the factory is concerned, there is David Williams and the heads of department. The company pursues an 'open door' policy inasmuch as everybody is accessible to everybody else if there is a problem to be sorted out.

David Williams hosts staff meetings at regular intervals with representatives from the various departments within the factory, sitting them round a table to talk through any minor problems that may have developed and, hopefully, head off some that might be festering.

There is a well-established information system whereby David keeps the staff informed of what is going on in the company generally, what plans are in the pipeline, what may be happening in Research and Development, for example, in addition to furnishing news about any projected building plans that affect the premises or the imminent arrival of new plant and machinery. When the purchase of a major new machine tool is envisaged, the department foreman and staff who will work it may have a chance to visit a trade exhibition in order to have an advance look at the equipment.

'As far as the "us and them" syndrome is concerned, I'm happy to say it doesn't really exist here except within the context of good-humoured ribbing and leg-pulling,' says David Williams. 'But everybody in the firm, from the apprentices to the cleaners to the factory-based design engineers, will all get the chance to go on a working visit to a Grand Prix. It enables them to see the results of their own endeavours in action and rams home the message very firmly that the race team is not on holiday!'

It may be surprising, but many of the factory staff return in a slightly overwhelmed frame of mind, wondering how on earth the members of the race team can subject themselves to the pressure of Grand Prix weekend after Grand Prix weekend. Remarks such as 'I don't know how they stick it' or 'It's not really fun, is it?' can be heard quite frequently in connection with these visits.

These observations mirror a realisation of just how intensive and competitive the whole business of Formula 1 at the sharp end of the grid has become. Even David Williams, who has been to several races, but does not hail from a motorsporting background, understands their feelings.

'The thing that struck me was just how little you can see from the pit lane,' he reflected. 'Being involved at that level of intensity is not really fun in the accepted sense, is it? The whole business put me in mind of that famous remark of Bill Shankly's in connection with football – "This isn't about life and death: it's far more important than that!" – and I think that could be very aptly applied to the Formula 1 business.'

As a telling counterpoint to the levels of engineering excellence which Williams GPE applies to its activities, the story of the company's one significant foray into the world of specialised sub-contracting for other organisations is worth scrutinising in some detail. As previously mentioned, Williams were approached in 1980 with a brief to produce a competitive rally car for Rover and, as the future of the F1 business seemed clouded with political uncertainty at the time, an arrangement of this nature seemed a shrewd way of hedging their bets.

Patrick Head recalls: 'It is clearly very difficult to do F1 on a full-time basis and get involved in any detail with another project in a different area, but I suppose we took on the Metro project through force of circumstances. Rover's competitions boss John Davenport asked us whether we could shoe-horn a Rover V6 engine – which was literally the 3.5-litre V8 with two cylinders chopped off – into the front of a Metro.'

Williams GPE agreed to look at the project and it soon became quite clear that, to get the engine in, the driver would virtually have to sit in the back seat. Their team driver Tony Pond came down, tried it for size and immediately said "There's no way I could drive this thing quickly through a forest stage – I can't see the front end from where I'd be sitting." Clearly, we had to think again.'

At about this time the four-wheel-drive Audi Quattro was about to burst on to the international rallying scene and Patrick, who had briefly worked with British 4WD pioneers Harry Ferguson Research many years before, reckoned this was the way to go.

'So we turned the whole thing round with the engine at the back, the gearbox ahead of it with drive to both the front and rear wheels,' Patrick continues. 'We presented the concept to Rover and they said "This is great", pushed the "go" button and off we went with the project. We finished it in about a year, delivered three prototypes to Rover in about November 1981 – six months' development with Williams's assistance.'

The Rover competitions department eventually managed to persuade their board that they should launch a serious rallying programme, by which time they realised that this little V6 developed a wholly inadequate 220bhp or thereabouts. They then faced the challenge of sitting down and developing a new engine, a more powerful 3-litre V6, before concentrating on how to produce 200 of these machines to conform to the international Group B rallying regulations. In the meantime, changes in tyre dimensions meant that bigger wheel sizes than originally envisaged had to be incorporated into the design, giving the eventual Metro 6R4, as the car was designated, an 'up on stilts' outward appearance.

Today, visitors to the Williams Conference Centre and Grand Prix collection are able to see a Metro 6R4 on the mezzanine display level. All lumps and slats, humps and spoilers, it represents a curious strand of production car engineering far removed from the sleek, wind-cheating profiles of the Grand Prix cars below which demonstrate the true height of the Williams team's technical heritage.

The whole Metro 6R4 project was a novel diversion, an interesting technical challenge at a time when the company's capacity for innovative engineering briefly looked as though it would need to focus in new directions on a long-term basis. Happily, since those troubled times in the F1 business during the early 1980s, Williams Grand Prix Engineering has been able to rid itself of such side issues and concentrate on what it does best.

10

The racing team away from home

In the distant days of the austere mid-1950s, the struggling Connaught team was attempting to establish itself as a force within Formula 1, its cars travelling round Europe in a pair of converted ex-London Transport Green Line single decker buses. These elderly AECs were slow, ponderous and unreliable. Frequently they would break down as they breathlessly tackled steep mountain passes, compounding the problems of moving round the Continent during this pre-autoroute era.

Alan Challis, Williams GPE's seasoned and friendly chief mechanic up until the end of 1990 when he took over a key factory-based position, began his motor racing career as an apprentice with the now-defunct BRM team, working from their headquarters at Bourne in Lincolnshire. He well remembers when they took delivery of their Leyland Royal Tiger transporter in time for the 1960 Belgian Grand Prix. With its underfloor-engined configuration and spacious cabin for the mechanics, it was regarded as the last word in luxury.

In 1964, Frank Williams himself delivered Jochen Rindt's new Formula 2 Brabham from London to Vienna, driving a van towing a trailer. Any employee in 1990 who should complain, however lightheartedly, about any trans-European schedule with the team's state-of-the-art Renault turbo articulated transporters will get short shrift from the boss and a quick résumé of the Vienna delivery story!

'The yardstick is that in 1963 Jochen persuaded me to do that delivery trip,' grins Frank with some relish. 'We left the Brabham factory in Weybridge at eight o'clock in the evening, got the midnight boat from Dover to Ostend, left the Belgian coast at five o'clock in the morning and arrived in Vienna just before nine o'clock that same evening. Remember, although Germany had its autobahns, there was precious little in the way of trunk roads in either Belgium or Austria.'

By 1990, Williams GPE had its operational life running to a more ordered and predictable pattern. Prior to a European Grand Prix the two elegantly stickered Williams team transporters are loaded up with their precious contents, one carrying a brace of lovingly prepared Williams-Renault FW13Bs, the other transporter only accommodating a single car as part of its interior length is taken up by the team's de-briefing and conference room.

All three cars will have been fitted with freshly rebuilt zero-mile Renault RS2 engines delivered from the Renault Sport headquarters in Viry-Chatillon late the previous week. On the face of it one might have imagined it to be more logistically expedient to deliver the engines direct to whatever circuit is hosting the next race, but from the viewpoint of efficient use of the manpower available, the team prefers to leave base with the cars all ready to practise, save for the addition of fuel, oil and coolant. Spare engines, tools and associated ancillary components are stowed within lockable compartments, with side access, beneath the transporter floors.

The transporters, crewed by two drivers apiece, will probably travel from Portsmouth to Le Havre from whence they will get on to the European trunk road system, arriving at the circuit either late on Tuesday night or first thing on Wednesday morning. The actual organisation of an F1 paddock itself is an operation which takes precise timing, meticulous planning and the unstinting co-operation of all the team personnel involved.

The Formula One Constructors' Association has drawn up comprehensive rules for parking the transporters and associated team motorhomes, the transporters backing up behind their pits in a regimented order which reflects their position in the previous year's Constructors' World Championship. A team's status and level of achievement within the F1 community is measured in territorial terms once inside the circuit.

Paddock capacity at European Grands Prix is increasingly becoming a problem as the Formula 1 business continues to expand. It is now a question of somehow squeezing several quarts into a pint pot. Each team is theoretically allowed one motorhome, but with major engine suppliers now such a crucially important cornerstone of the Grand Prix game, room has to be found to accommodate their motor homes as well.

Thus Williams has its own motorhome and so does Renault. It's the same for McLaren and Honda, Benetton and Ford. The Williams team unit is painted a muted dark blue, stirring memories of Piers Courage's Brabham, and is equipped with an electric lift on its staircase to enable Frank's wheelchair to be winched inside. This is the innermost of inner sanctums, and any outsider invited to enter – be they senior Renault personnel or press men about to receive a slice of Frank or Patrick's mind – can count themselves a member of a privileged elite.

On the Thursday morning before the race, team personnel fly out. The mechanics leave on an early flight from England, the intention being that they should arrive, fairly fresh, in the paddock by noon. A number of travel companies tend to the team's requirements on this front, Williams GPE tending to use Bob Warren Travel in Arundel, Sussex, a firm which has a long track record of catering for the F1 community's sometimes idiosyncratic movement schedules.

Frank Williams, Patrick Head and the senior staff – probably co-director Sheridan Thynne and chief designer Adrian Newey – will fly separately in the team's private jet, one luxury which Williams has allowed himself in the wake of his 1986 road accident. The limitations on his mobility made the prospect of travelling, even in the first class section of international airliners, a frustrating, awkward and distinctly uncomfortable task. The interior of the Learjet has been specifically adapted for his requirements and he now uses it even for journeys as far afield as Japan and Australia. 'I must be one of the few Grand Prix team members to have visited the Aleutian Islands,' muses Sheridan Thynne in connection with one of these trips, 'although at the time I wasn't entirely certain where they were!'

By Thursday lunchtime the transporter is in place with its awning rigged up alongside, the cars are in the garage and either just returned, or just being prepared, for official scrutineering. This can take place at any time between 10.00 and 18.00 on the Thursday, the cars being checked for dimensional conformity with the regulations, their safety equipment and other routine details.

The rest of the day is spent, in Frank's words 'pottering' round the cars. The chassis set-up needs to be checked over and perhaps there are some extra components, which have come out 'hand baggage' with the mechanics, that need to be fitted before Friday morning's first free practice session. There will be a meeting with Goodyear technical personnel to discuss the tyre compounds available and their likely performance characteristics on this particular circuit track surface. And the team's tyre man will have delivered the wheel rims to the Goodyear compound where the tyre company's fitters will mount the necessary rubber in preparation for the following day.

Operating under the overall direction of Alan Challis up to the end of 1990, the team allocates three mechanics per car for each of the three cars. There are a couple of electricians and a couple of sub-assembly guys, plus a number of Renault engine technicians. There is seldom much tension between them, but a lot of car-to-car rivalry.

Challis, being rather older than the average man in this sort of job, was consequently imbued with an aura of senior status. He was respected among his colleagues and acted as a calming influence if any tension looked like puncturing the surface of the work in those pit lane garages.

Race mechanics are a highly motivated and committed breed who work long and, by most people's standards, pretty unsocial hours. But they have a zeal and passion for the job which many find difficult to fulfil in a conventional working environment, and they are remunerated on a higher salary level to the 'at base' factory workers to take into account the fact that they are away from their families for long periods. In addition, they will get their bed and breakfast paid, plus a daily subsistence allowance. This is increased specially for the Monaco and Japanese Grands Prix where costs are substantially higher.

Generally, the mechanics will be ready to climb aboard a handful of hired minibuses and head for their hotels between 18:00 and 21:00, leaving the cars standing in the pit lane garages and the transporters locked up. The Formula 1 teams tend to rely on circuit security, although there have been occasions when Williams have been on the receiving end of technical espionage, believe it or not, and Williams occasionally have been known to hire their own personal security man when they need to be absolutely certain that nobody will come snooping. Grand Prix racing is technical warfare of a highly sophisticated order.

Three laps into the 1979 Austrian Grand Prix at Osterreichring, the enthusiasm of Lotus boss Colin Chapman to find out some details of the Williams FW07 chassis dimensions spilled over into one of the most embarrassing episodes in recent years. He despatched his team manager Peter Collins to 'measure up' the spare FW07 which lay alongside the Williams transporter in the paddock while the entire team personnel were occupied in the pit lane.

Collins was caught in the act and sent off with a flea in his ear. For the next couple of races a formidable security advisor, 'Mac' McGowan, was recruited to keep prying eyes from getting too close. Chapman might not have been forgiven, but Collins certainly was. In 1982 he would join Williams GPE as team manager, a task he tackled with admirable professionalism and commitment for three years before moving to a similar position with the Benetton team.

Subsequently there were to be a couple more occasions when subterfuge turned to downright pilfering, a far more serious business. In 1981 at Rio, a rival team stole a set of dual rate springs which were being prepared for Carlos Reutemann's FW07B, while at Spa in 1986 some FW11 front wing end plates went missing. The following season, one particular red car sported front wing end plates which looked suspiciously familiar to the Williams crew. But although the pit lane gossip continued, there was nothing much more than circumstantial evidence to suggest the components were removed with malice aforethought.

Mindful of these lapses of integrity on the part of their rivals, when the team fielded the active ride suspension system at Monza in 1987, a couple of factory personnel were taken with the race team and slept at the track. Circuit security is generally pretty good, but on this occasion Patrick Head didn't want to take any chances.

The team generally brings just a single spare car, prepared to identical specification as the two designated race machines, because that is as much as the team's operational logistics can generally cope with. At certain crucial events, such as when both Mansell and Piquet were in contention for the Championship towards the end of both 1986 and 1987, the team brought along four cars in order that both men should have a spare available, but this is generally the exception rather than the rule.

'Adding a fourth car to the equation adds a disproportionate amount of extra personnel and effort to the point that the whole thing becomes rather top heavy,' explains Frank Williams, 'not to mention the extra pressure it puts on room in the paddock and pit garages. We inevitably take four to our home race at Silverstone, though, where it's just a case of hauling the car "up the road" and we generally have a fourth available at Monaco, usually a test car which is scheduled to be wheeled out for development work at Paul Ricard, which is just along the coast, on the Monday after that race.'

These facts notwithstanding, in order to provide for the possibility of a serious accident, and the consequent need to rebuild a car, the team always takes along 'the tub in the box'. This is a spare monocoque, completely prepared with instruments, plumbing and steering, round which the other components of a badly crashed car can be assembled to bring the team's machinery up to numerical strength during the course of a Grand Prix weekend.

One classic example of how this emergency technique could be initiated was seen at Suzuka during the Friday prior to the 1987 Japanese Grand Prix. After running wide on a corner during the first qualifying session, Nigel Mansell spun back across the track and crashed his FW11B very heavily and spectacularly into a tyre barrier on the right-hand side of the circuit.

The car was pitched into the air, landing with a spine-jarring impact which left the English driver in excruciating pain. He was taken off to hospital while the Williams crew, uncertain whether or not he would be fit enough to continue competing, built up the FW11B round the spare monocoque and had the whole thing ready to fire up by 20:00 that same evening. As it turned out, Mansell could not return to the fray, thereby guaranteeing the Championship to team-mate Piquet, but as an example of the well-ordered, disciplined and pre-planned manner in which the Williams team operates when faced with a sudden technical emergency, it was copybook stuff.

On Friday morning, the tension and pressure begins to build up. Stretching ahead is a punishing and intensive schedule which will culminate in the green light flickering on early on Sunday afternoon to signal the start of the race. From that point onwards, the fortunes of Williams GPE will be in the hands of the drivers, be they Riccardo Patrese, Thierry Boutsen, Nelson Piquet, Nigel Mansell or whoever. But up to that crucial turning point a monumentally complex, interdependent team effort is called for.

The mechanics will receive an alarm call in their hotel at around 06:00. By 07:30 they should be at the track where they are fed and watered. The management – Patrick, Sheridan and the engineers – generally arrive about half an hour later. Frank naturally takes longer to get ready and usually appears mid-way through the first 90-minute free practice session. The cars are checked over, warmed up at about 09:40, 20 minutes before the start of that session, and the drivers run through a preliminary briefing with the engineers.

The objective, of course, is the best possible position on the 26 car starting grid, but the fastest times are usually set on Saturday during the second qualifying session, fine weather permitting, and there are other equally crucial considerations to be taken into account. The need for an optimum, flat-out qualifying lap which sees the car performing at its absolute peak must be balanced against the challenge of working out the correct race set-up.

The first untimed session is something of an exploratory affair. The drivers will be seeking the best chassis adjustments for the circuit, and the prevailing conditions. This is based on a sequence of ideas to make the cars quicker, drawing on input from test sessions at the circuit. Towards the end of that session, both drivers will also usually do a few laps on the soft compound qualifying rubber just to get a feel of how the tyre compounds are performing in preparation for the hour-long qualifying period between 13.00 and 14.00.

That brief taste of qualifying rubber is crucial from the viewpoint of choosing the right tyres for the first official timed session. While an unlimited number of tyre sets can be used in the morning, regulations permit only two sets per car to be selected for the afternoon. Once chosen, they are stencilled with the car's race number, so there is no going back on a driver's choice in this area once the session begins.

By now the drivers are getting tense and focusing singlemindedly on the serious business of the day. In the interval between the two sessions the team does its best to insulate them from the outside world, giving them perhaps a light lunch in the privacy of the Williams team motorhome. This is not the best time for journalists to engage them in heavy conversation. Nor for the engineers, come to that!

Patrick Head says: 'Once you give the drivers a sniff of qualifying rubber during the morning session, their brains tend to go out of gear. Trying to talk to them about race set-ups between the untimed and timed sessions, particularly on a Saturday, is really to waste your time. Your man is thinking only about that blinding qualifying lap he's hoping to string together in the afternoon and, to be honest, you are probably de-tuning him by trying to talk to him about other things at that time. I don't think people outside the team, particularly journalists, can understand that because they don't have the privilege of getting sufficiently close to the situation.'

Driver psychology continues to pose something of a challenge throughout that first, hour-long qualifying session. Assuming Williams's men have opted for two sets of qualifying tyres, they face the prospect of two really quick laps during which the tyres are at their absolute optimum level of performance, producing the maximum potential grip. Strategy now comes into the equation and the team likes its men to get out early on the first set, before the track is too crowded, and get a decently competitive lap under their belts.

This is asking a lot from any driver. He has to wind his concentration up tight, produce a really quick lap, then retire to the seclusion of the pit lane garage. There are two sides to this particular coin. By doing his first run early on, he guards against the possibility of the track getting covered in oil should a rival's engine fail. It that happens, then he will be thankful he made that early run.

However, it is also the case that the racing line develops more grip as more cars lay more rubber debris on the track surface. In addition, the longer he waits for the second run, the more he may benefit from a slight drop in ambient temperature which will allow the engine to produce fractionally more power and the second set of tyres to have a marginally enhanced endurance span. In order to capitalise on this, the team is effectively asking the driver to go off the psychological boil for about 45 to 50 minutes before hyping himself up again for one last effort.

'The ideal situation, assuming the conditions are consistent, is for one run to take place between five and ten past one,' says Frank Williams, 'with the drivers going out again with about 10 minutes left to go. But if somebody does drop oil with 20 minutes of the session left, you're in trouble. It's a question of judgement, of making a shrewd gamble, and keeping your eyes on what the opposition is up to.'

Perhaps even more so than in the race itself, the tension can be felt shimmering off the pit lane like a heat haze during an official Grand Prix qualifying session. The concentration is intense, the air thick with Formula 1 technical patois.

'One notch off the rear wing for Riccardo . . . it looks like Senna's Es are graining on the outside edge . . . Mansell's found a clear one . . . Alboreto's screwed him . . . Berger got an Osella just before the chicane . . . what about a third run on a mixed set . . .' To the lay ear this is a cacophony of disjointed, breathless chatter. To the insider, it is a flowing narrative of informed comment and thinking-aloud speculation. If things go well during the first qualifying session, the team has cleared the first hurdle. If there is a mechanical hiccup, and time is lost, then the knock-on effect can dog a driver right through to Sunday's race.

Suddenly the chequered flag is out and the drivers eventually retire to the peace of the team's motorhome for the second detailed de-brief of the day. The first will have taken place about 30 minutes after the morning's free practice session has ended, the second about an hour after the qualifying session. These are crucially important technical meetings between the men behind the wheels and the engineers who need to interpret, with prescient accuracy, the drivers' observations about how the cars have been performing.

Many years ago, Frank Williams evolved a check list system which is still employed to good effect by Williams GPE in the field. A driver is invited to make comments about the car's performance by means of a succession of prompts. Clutch? Gearchange? Brakes? His memory is jogged about every aspect of the car's behaviour.

'It's all simple stuff,' says Frank, 'but it's amazing how well the system works. The guys' heads are spinning after they've come off the circuit, and they may have a lot they want to say. But if you simply say "How did it go?" you may just get a reaction like "oh . . err, it was OK" when, if they'd thought about it for a little longer, they might have a major point to make.

'By prompting them, you might get "Oh, yes . . . the clutch is slipping slightly at high revs" which they might, or might not, have forgotten if you'd invited them to make just a generalized comment. I remember Jacques Laffite losing the rear bodywork of his FW09B during the closing stages of the 1984 Portuguese Grand Prix, after making two time-consuming pit stops to try and fix the problem, depriving him of a very possible finish in the points. Afterwards, he said "Oh God, I meant to tell you that the bodywork was flapping slightly in the warm-up". He'd forgotten to mention it and the securing clips had eventually broken. That's precisely the sort of thing we are trying to guard against.'

As far as the drivers' attention spans for such de-briefs are concerned, Frank insists that 'Thierry and Riccardo both brought a lot of brain power to bear and were not prone to distractions. By contrast, Keke and Nigel could be a bit superficial but, having said that, Nigel once skipped a de-brief altogether at Silverstone in 1987 – and the following day he went out and won the race. So that rather took the wind out of our sails!'

As a result of the de-brief, a job list is produced which the chief mechanic will take away and begin initiating. The same Renault V10 engines remain in the cars overnight, assuming that there has been no significant failure, and the mechanics will reckon to get away to their hotels at about 20.00 if all goes to plan on a Friday evening.

On Saturday, the routine is repeated throughout the day, but with one significant difference. The 90-minute free practice session in the morning is spent working out a race set-up, which means both cars will spend time running with substantial fuel loads on race tyres. This is where the schedule can get rather tense, because if some problem on Friday has prevented the team from reaching its optimum qualifying set-up, some-how all the work will have to be squeezed into the Saturday morning programme as well.

Second qualifying takes place in conditions of even more psychological intensity than Friday's session. During that first hour the drivers' efforts are bolstered by the underlying knowledge that there is one more chance tomorrow. On Saturday, it is the final throw of the dice, the last opportunity to make certain of a place up with the front runners in the starting line-up.

Over the past three seasons, Ayrton Senna's immensely powerful McLaren-Honda has tended to make a habit of buttoning up pole position. Indeed, incursions on to the front row by the McLaren team's opposition became the exception rather than the rule throughout 1989 and 1990. It was a re-run of the situation experienced in 1986 and 1987 when the Williams-Hondas gained a reputation as Grand Prix racing's most consistent pacemakers.

Bearing these facts in mind, when Thierry Boutsen and Riccardo Patrese qualified first and second on the grid for the 1990 Hungarian Grand Prix, it was a time for guarded celebration within the team's ranks. Celebration, in the sense that a front row start is an ever more important factor in deciding the outcome of a race result in the currently super-competitive F1 environment. Guarded, inasmuch as any technical failure that causes a retirement is doubly disappointing if your car is running in the lead rather than further down the field.

On race morning, with freshly rebuilt engines now installed in all three cars, the pressure increases even more. There is a half-hour warm-up session in which the race set-up is checked again and final decisions are taken over the race tyre choice, again in conjunction with Goodyear. Another de-brief follows, and then it is a question of keeping the drivers away from as many outside demands as possible, apart from the obligatory briefing from the Clerk of the Course. In the past, several drivers have taken a somewhat laid- back attitude to this particular engagement, but in 1991 instant exclusion from the meeting will be the penalty applied for anybody who fails to turn up for the entire duration of the briefing. Previously such a breach of the rules attracted a 'nominal' $2,000 (US) fine.

For the Williams drivers, of course, there will inevitably be demands on their time during the course of the weekend from the sponsors. Balancing these obligations with the need to let them relax in the immediate run-up to the race requires careful judgement and the need to strike a suitable balance. On Saturday night it is the aim of Sheridan Thynne to have the drivers back in their hotels by 21:00 from any sponsorship function and, similarly, they are not encouraged to stray too far from the motorhome on race morning. Throughout 1990, Thierry and Riccardo usually attempted to sleep for around half an hour before going to the warm-up.

With about 40 minutes to run to the start of the race, the drivers are strapped in their cars in the pit lane garages. The pit lane exit opens with half an hour to go, at which point the drivers can cover a minimum of one reconnaissance lap to bring them round to the starting grid. If they wish to have more than one lap, they must trickle through the pit lane at what the regulations stipulate as 'greatly reduced speed'.

They must keep their wits about them at this point, because excessive speeding in the pit lane between these laps attracts a further penalty of $10,000 for a first offence – and $20,000 for any subsequent transgression during the same World Championship year!

During the last few minutes of track time before the start, the radio link between the drivers and their engineers can prove almost therapeutic for the competitors. Patrese regularly chats during the reconnaissance laps, almost literally talking himself into a position of calm in what is a private, one- to-one relationship with his engineer.

Once the race starts, driver behaviour varies considerably in this respect. Mansell has a reputation for talking virtually non-stop over the radio. Piquet, by contrast, hardly ever spoke. The systems are usually very difficult to keep operating reliably, subject as they are not only to enormous G-force loading, but tremendous vibration.

Generally the engineers will not initiate a conversation with the drivers unless it is absolutely necessary, but merely reply when they are called upon to do so. However, at Adelaide in 1986, Patrick Head was literally screaming for Mansell to come in for fresh tyres when the Englishman suffered that celebrated 200mph failure. On a more frivolous note, during qualifying at Montreal when the radio systems were in their infancy, the light-hearted Jacques Laffite sang 'Happy birthday to you' over the line to Neil Oatley, much to his engineer's red-faced embarrassment!

By the time the cars have finally taken their place on the starting grid, the race strategy will have been worked out as far as possible. If tyre changes are anticipated, the two drivers will be scheduled to come in separated by a two- or three-lap interval. The Williams men will also check with the other teams occupying pits in their vicinity to try to prevent a situation where rival cars inadvertently snarl up the whole procedure with an impromptu traffic jam.

Once the starting light flicks to green, the engineers and team management can only watch and monitor the proceedings. Their job is done. It's now almost totally down to the drivers, although the mechanics are under a great deal of pressure when it comes to tyre stops. A sticking wheel nut, or a malfunctioning compressed air hammer drill, can affect the outcome of a Grand Prix as surely as a major error of judgement on the part of the driver.

Occasionally, a situation will arise which is not specifically covered by the rule book. At the 1989 San Marino Grand Prix, the race was flagged to a halt after five laps following a major accident when Gerhard Berger's Ferrari crashed heavily on the fast Tamburello left-hander beyond the pits, erupting into flames.

Early days: an unfamiliarly hirsute Frank Williams wrestling with the Cosworth engine of Jonathan Williams's Lotus 22, Solitude, West Germany, 1963.

Frank at Oulton Park in 1964. The Austin transporter immediately behind him belongs to Ken Tyrrell, later to become one of the Williams F1 team's great rivals.

WHO IS FRANK WILLIAMS?

HE SELLS RACING CARS...

AND GUARANTEES THEM

Telephone: HARROW 0460/7854 (Middlesex)

This advertisement for Frank's racing car business appeared in Autosport *magazine during March 1967.*

Frank (right) and Piers Courage take a dip during the 1968 Argentine F2 Temporada series.

Jonathan Williams prepares to climb aboard the Frank Williams Racing Cars Brabham BT23C prior to scoring FW's first Formula 2 win in the 1968 Monza Lottery. In the background, goggles round neck, stands a youthful Max Mosley. Below, Jonathan hangs on in the lead ahead of Henri Pescarolo's Matra during his battle for victory.

Above left: *Learning about F1. Frank updates his records in the back of his team's transporter during the 1969 German Grand Prix at Nürburgring.*

Above right: *That golden partnership: Frank (left) and Piers together.*

Right: *Piers Courage, 1942–1970.*

Putting his name on the map: Piers steering Frank's F1 Brabham BT26 towards a magnificent second place in the 1969 Monaco Grand Prix.

Frank (left) and Piers (right) confer with de Tomaso designer Gianpaolo Dallara during practice for the 1970 South African Grand Prix at Kyalami.

Tragic afternoon: Piers and the de Tomaso at speed in the 1970 Dutch Grand Prix at Zandvoort, the race which claimed his life.

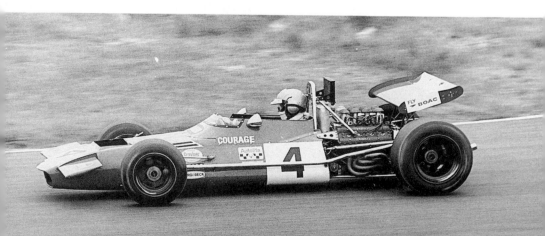

In 1971 Frank picked himself up off the floor and fielded this March 711 for Henri Pescarolo. Here the Frenchman heads for a promising fourth place in the British Grand Prix at Silverstone.

Williams greets motorcycle racing star Giacomo Agostini (left) at Silverstone during 1971. He considered giving the two-wheeled champion a chance in cars and even arranged a test for him in one of his Formula 2 March machines.

Signing up promising youngsters was no problem for Frank, but keeping them was quite another matter. Brazil's Carlos Pace, seen here in Frank's March 711 in the 1972 Belgian Grand Prix, was one who signed for two years, but left after only one.

New Zealander Howden Ganley was a steady and unspectacular performer in Frank's Iso-Marlboro during 1973, but he came close to scoring the team's first Formula 1 win in a confused Canadian Grand Prix. Below, Ganley files along ahead of Jackie Stewart's Tyrrell behind the pace car at Mosport Park; despite initial post-race elation, the official lap chart eventually placed him sixth.

Saving the bacon! Frank's team was probably at its lowest financial ebb in the summer of 1975, but Jacques Laffite helped pay some outstanding bills with a timely second place in the German Grand Prix with this plodding Williams FW04.

Austro-Canadian oil man Walter Wolf (left) bought the team for 1976, but probably wished he hadn't. It was a disastrous year for driver Jacky Ickx, here strapped in the cockpit of one of the former Hesketh 308Cs which were purchased in an effort to get the job done.

Williams re-born. In 1977 Frank split with Wolf to set up Williams Grand Prix Engineering, fielding this March 761 for Belgian journeyman Patrick Neve. Note the 'Fly Saudia' identification on the rear wing — the start of something big.

Start of a great partnership. Frank (right) with Patrick Head and the first Williams FW06, outside the new factory on Station Road Industrial Estate, Didcot.

Getting the job done. Alan Jones proving what could be done with the FW06 as he moves through the field to challenge for the lead at Long Beach in 1978.

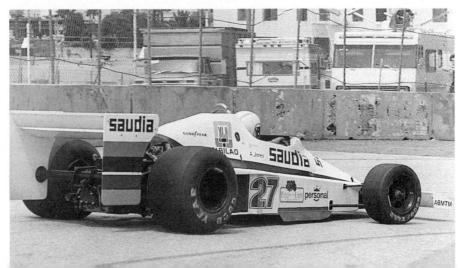

Victory at last. Clay Regazzoni waves from the top of the Silverstone winner's rostrum, in company with second and third place men Rene Arnoux (left) and Jean-Pierre Jarier. His Williams FW07 (below) took over at the head of the pack after team leader Alan Jones retired with a water leak.

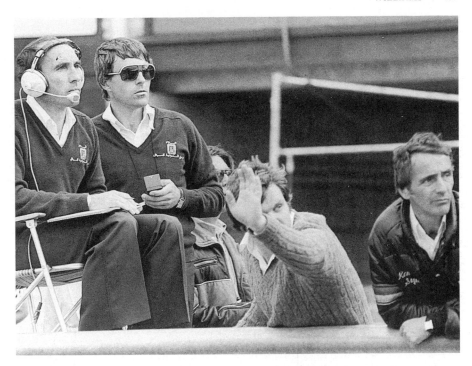

From left to right, Frank, Dave Brodie, Patrick Head and Charlie Crichton-Stuart watch impassively as Alan Jones takes the flag to win the 1979 Dutch Grand Prix at Zandvoort. Right, the man who helped put Williams GPE on the map celebrates that victory.

Alan Jones and the Williams FW07 proved formidable contenders across three seasons. Above, the rugged Australian battles with Gilles Villeneuve's Ferrari T4 en route to victory in the 1979 Canadian Grand Prix. Below, on his way to a storming win at Brands Hatch in the following year's British Grand Prix.

Partnering Jones in 1980 and 1981 was the introspective, cerebral Carlos Reutemann. Here the gifted Argentinian is seen in the process of winning the 1981 Belgian Grand Prix at Zolder.

After Jones and Reutemann unexpectedly retired from the sport, it was left to Keke Rosberg to assume team leadership early in 1982. He's seen here again at Zolder where a slight mistake on the penultimate lap prevented him from repeating Reutemann's 1981 victory.

Dynamic partnership: Nigel Mansell and Nelson Piquet were paired together in the Williams-Honda line-up for 1986, dominating the season to win the team another Constructors' World Championship.

Piquet steers his Williams-Honda FW11 towards victory in the inaugural World Championship Hungarian Grand Prix at Budapest in the summer of 1986. The Brazilian was a stealthy, intelligent performer during his time with Frank's team, but became paranoid in his belief that the management favoured Mansell.

During practice for the 1987 Japanese Grand Prix at Suzuka, Mansell crashed heavily in the Williams FW11B. Although, as it transpired, he was unable to race, the Williams mechanics had the damaged machine completely repaired and ready to go again later that same evening.

Tense moment: at a mid-race tyre stop, everybody has to pull together in a finely timed team effort. Here the Williams crew service Nigel Mansell's FW11B-Honda during his winning drive in the 1987 Spanish Grand Prix at Jerez.

Riccardo Patrese and Nigel Mansell file through the waterfront chicane at Monaco in their Judd-engined Williams FW12s during the 1987 Monaco Grand Prix. Having lost the Honda deal at the end of the previous season, this was a highly frustrating year in which the team failed to win a Grand Prix for the first time in a decade.

Frank with Williams GPE Commercial Director Sheridan Thynne, an old friend from the early days.

Patrese climbs aboard the Williams FW12-Judd during practice for the 1988 San Marino Grand Prix. Note the immaculate state of car, driver and pit lane garage. F1 had come a long way in terms of image during Frank Williams's time in the business.

Factory backing again: Frank and Patrick Head (centre, standing) pose beside a mock-up of the Renault RS1 V10 cylinder engine which the team adopted from the start of the 1989 season. With them are Bernard Dudot (left) and Bernard Casin from Renault Sport.

Thierry Boutsen gives the new Williams-Renault FW13 its maiden outing in the 1989 Portuguese Grand Prix at Estoril. The Belgian would go on to win that year's rain-soaked Australian Grand Prix.

Haven of tranquility: the drawing office at Williams Grand Prix Engineering, with David Brown, Nigel Mansell's race engineer, in the centre.

Thierry Boutsen leads team-mate Riccardo Patrese in the 1989 Belgian Grand Prix at Spa ahead of Alessandro Nannini's Benetton. Boutsen finished fourth, but Riccardo spun off the road after a collision while lapping Michele Alboreto's Lola.

The team's current purpose-built factory in Basil Hill Road, Didcot, was opened by Michael Heseltine in June 1984.

Clinical environment: the race preparation shop is immaculately clean and well-ordered. This shot, taken in January 1991, shows one of the team's FW13B-Renault cars just back from a winter test at Paul Ricard.

One of the giant, specially designed Renault articulated transporters which carries its precious load of Williams F1 cars round Europe during the height of the Grand Prix season.

Williams Technical Director Patrick Head at his drawing board, January 1991.

Aerodynamic develop-
ment is one of the most
crucial keys to the suc-
cess of any Grand Prix
car design. The
Williams team was
among the very first to
have its own wind tun-
nel for this purpose, in-
stalled in 1979. It will
be superseded by an
even more modern tun-
nel during 1991. This is
to be installed in a
brand-new research and
development centre.

Expensive equipment in
the Williams machine
shop includes this
computer-programmed,
multi-purpose machin-
ing centre which
represents the very
latest available
technology.

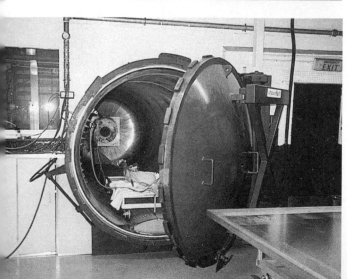

A key element in the
manufacture of carbon
fibre composite com-
ponents are two
'autoclave' high
pressure ovens, the
larger of which can con-
tain a complete F1
monocoque.

The Williams Conference Centre and Grand Prix collection includes this priceless display of the team's Formula 1 machinery from years gone by including (upper picture) the experimental FW08D six-wheeler prototype which was tested during 1982.

The Metro 6R-4 rally car is the only non-F1 interloper in the Williams collection. To date, it represents the company's sole foray into sub-contracting work for a major car maker.

Into 1991: The Eurol pattern (top) from which moulds are manufactured for the new Williams FW14 challenger which Nigel Mansell will drive this season.

The first completed carbon fibre monocoque for the new car.

In such a situation, the rules call for the competing cars to return to the starting grid – not the pit lane – where they must not be worked upon prior to the restart. Unfortunately, Boutsen's Williams-Renault FW12C, which had been right behind Berger at the moment the Austrian left the road, had sustained a puncture from flying debris and now reappeared on the grid with a deflated rear tyre. Moving the machine into the pit lane would, on the face of it, entail immediate disqualification, so the only way out of it seemed to be for Thierry to start the race with that punctured tyre still in place, limp round to the pits and have it changed at the end of the opening lap.

This quite clearly would have been an absurdly dangerous proposition. In very much the same boat were Alex Caffi and Olivier Grouillard, in a Dallara and a Ligier respectively. They had tangled on the third lap and arrived back on the grid similarly crippled, the former with a punctured tyre and the latter a damaged undertray. Apparently oblivious to the rules, the Ligier mechanics immediately set about replacing the damaged undertray on Grouillard's car.

Williams team manager Michael Cane asked FISA race director Roland Brunseyrade for advice on the matter and he directed them to push Boutsen's car into the pit lane, change the wheels and start from there. The Dallara team did the same with Caffi's car, so he and Boutsen joined in after the main body of the field had left the grid for the restart.

Five laps into the race, Grouillard's Ligier was duly black flagged and disqualified, following which the French team put in a protest against Boutsen and Caffi. It seemed hard that these two competitors should be excluded from the results – they finished fifth and seventh respectively – after racing hard all afternoon but, in retrospect, it was just as well they were permitted to complete the event.

Quite rightly, on subsequent appeal the Williams and Dallara were reinstated to their rightful finishing position, but it had been a highly complicated and unsettling affair. 'I think in circumstances like that FISA needs to have a contingency plan whereby a designated official is responsible solely for dealing with the mechanics of a restart, and any anomalies that might arise of the sort that Boutsen encountered at Imola are specifically separated from those responsible for dealing with the original incident and its repercussions,' observes Sheridan Thynne. 'It's quite clear that the FISA officials were all totally absorbed by the aftermath of the Berger accident on this occasion and there was the very real risk of a major misunderstanding, which could have resulted in an undeserved exclusion, when the need arose for a snap decision over what to do in a situation not specifically provided for by the regulations.'

Once the race is over, the intensity of effort and concentration drains away almost immediately the chequered flag is produced, giving way to a sense of anti-climax unless the team's car has emerged triumphant. Otherwise, there is no gentle let-down.

The cars which have survived to the finish, streaked with oil and grime, are directed into the *parc fermé* where nobody from the teams is allowed access to them for up to an hour after the race. The winning machine is scrutinised in detail, along with a random selection of other machines. A fuel sample is taken for scientific analysis to ensure conformity with the laid-down specification and FISA officials may choose to seal the winning car's engine. It will then subsequently be examined by representatives from the sport's governing body on its return to the team's base.

Within an hour or so, the Williams management will be making tracks for the local airport, Frank and Sheridan trying to drag Patrick away from the business of the day – the Technical Director is notoriously difficult to prise away from the circuit – and the business of packing up the cars starts in earnest.

The remaining fuel is pumped from the tanks, tyres stripped from their rims and returned to the Goodyear compound. Within about four hours, the Williams rigs are almost ready to roll. In many EEC countries there are limitations governing the use of heavy commercial vehicles during the weekend, but trucks carrying sporting goods gain exemption and the Williams transporters fall into this specialist category. By 21:00 on Sunday evening the two articulated transporters are in the queue heading for the paddock gates. Generally, they will be back at Didcot by Tuesday morning from most European races, although the long haul back from Spain and Portugal adds another day to that estimated arrival time.

Of course, transporting the cars round Europe could be regarded as the easy bit. When it comes to packaging them up for the long haul races outside Europe – to Phoenix, Brazil, Mexico, Canada, Japan and Australia – the travel arrangements involve packing and preparing the cars for shipment on the Formula One Constructors' Association charter flights.

The man who controls this business is FOCA's Alan Woollard, one of Bernie Ecclestone's key right-hand men, and he has been involved on this specialist project since the pre-jet era when propeller-driven CL-44 freighters, carrying a modest 10 F1 cars apiece, were chartered for the marathon two-day grind down to Buenos Aires when the Argentine Grand Prix opened the F1 season in January.

Nowadays, the Williams team's equipment and tackle contributes to the cargo load on one-and-a-half Boeing 747 freighters, or two-and-a-half DC-10 freighters, depending on what is available on the charter market. Throughout the Wednesday prior to the first flight's departure – some 10 days before the relevant race – virtually each hour will see at least one team transporter arrive outside the freight terminal at Gatwick, Heathrow or Stansted, bearing the cars. In addition, there will be a handful of high- sided trucks carrying the steel containers of engines and spares.

Whereas in Europe the Williams transporters double as giant toolboxes and mobile workshops on wheels, every single item required for the long-distance races has to be itemised, logged and packed away with meticulous care.

'It takes three or four people the best part of a week simply to box up all the containers before we take them to the airport,' explains Alan Challis. 'We are regularly transporting around 120 boxes to all the races outside Europe.'

Once the transporters have been moved out of the way at the airport, it is time for the cars to be loaded on to wooden pallets, then secured within the aircraft. It takes two and a half days to pack a fully loaded Jumbo jet with all the equipment and paraphernalia required for a Grand Prix and, at the arrival destination airport, the whole procedure has to be carried out in reverse.

Such high value machines as Grand Prix racing cars, and their engines, cannot move round the world without each having an international carnet – effectively a passport – on which they are described in detail, and their chassis and/or engine numbers recorded for cross-reference purposes. But the FOCA system works well. By the time the Williams mechanics step off their planes in Brazil and make their way to the Interlagos circuit in Sao Paulo, their cars and equipment will be all laid out in the appropriate pit awaiting their arrival. The whole thing is incredibly well organised. Without Alan Woollard and his colleagues, Grand Prix racing just wouldn't exist outside Europe.

Getting the cars there is only part of the equation. The specialist fuel required by today's breed of F1 car – manufactured by Elf in the case of the Williams team – is transported to the non-European races in a separately chartered Boeing 707. The tailor-made brews have to be packed in 50 gallon drums, this being the maximum permissible individual consignment according to the understandably stringent regulations which govern the air transport of such volatile liquids.

While Williams invariably relies on the FOCA charter arrangements, there have been moments when the team has struck out on its own. One such memorable excursion ended in unexpected frustration.

In an effort to gain advantage over its rivals immediately following the 1982 Long Beach Grand Prix, Williams decided to send one of the FW07Cs back to Europe as cargo on the scheduled Monday night British Airways flight, rather than wait for the FOCA charter the following day.

The intention was to get the car to a European test as quickly as possible, but an hour or so out of Los Angeles the flight received a bomb scare warning – and the 747 made an unscheduled landing at Winnipeg. That in itself produced an unfortunate dilemma.

The Boeing could only leave Winnipeg with a full fuel load for the non-stop run to Heathrow, or a full cargo load which would have meant it stopping in Montreal to take on additional fuel. Not wishing to subject the passengers to another delay, British Airways decided that the Williams team would have to be the losers.

The FW07C was off-loaded. It ended up travelling by road to Toronto where it was then loaded on to another flight, before eventually being repatriated about eight days behind schedule!

PART FOUR

The drivers

11

'Do you give me your word ... as a foreigner?'

Many cinema-goers will have curled up with delight when, in a scene from *Murder on the Orient Express*, Sean Connery, playing the buttoned-up Scottish army officer, inquires of a swarthy guest to whom suspicion has attached those memorable words: 'Do you give me your word ... as a foreigner?'

Frank Williams recounts that line with a genuine relish. Spend a few hours chatting in his company, and you're left in no doubt that he retains an underlying belief that the British are different, a cut above those 'foreign johnnies'.

He is quick to correct anybody who speaks about Union Jacks – 'Union flags!' – and at the height of the FOCA/FISA dispute which almost tore apart the very fabric of Grand Prix racing in the early 1980s, he insisted that a notice be placed prominently on the door of the team's motorhome which read 'British Press welcome here'. Bear this in mind, and one can reasonably conclude that Piers Courage provided a definitive role model for what Frank believed a Grand Prix driver should be: Debonair, dashing, blue-blooded ... English.

The relationship between a Grand Prix driver and his employer is the most fundamentally crucial single element within the entire make-up of a Grand Prix team. All the technical factors can be in place, the necessary finance, the logistical back-up – but if a driver is in any way unsettled in his relationship with the team, the potential is there for far-reaching and wearying aggravation.

On the face of it, you might be forgiven for thinking that employing a racing driver is quite a straightforward business arrangement. The team selects the man it wants, makes him an offer and the driver then accepts or rejects the proposal. This is not quite the case. Such predictable parameters may apply when Williams Technical Director Patrick Head is interviewing a young draughtsman for the design department, but racing drivers are more difficult to stereotype. They don't conform to any standard specification. They can have emotional qualities one is not aware of until they have been employed, and may display strengths and weaknesses which do not become apparent until it is too late. They may have egos which need to be sat on, or surprising shortfalls of confidence. The only thing that is certain is that they are all different one from the next.

When Mercedes-Benz and Auto Union were dominating the European international racing scene in the 1930s, it was quite a routine procedure to hold test sessions during the off-season in which a large number of aspiring drivers were tried, assessed and rejected. In the 1990s, if team owners are considering a change of driver, they have sufficient facts and figures about a potential candidate's previous form to be able to reach the decision without even needing to give the driver a test in their own car.

When Frank Williams signed up Alan Jones at the start of the 1978 season, he turned over the rugged Australian's racing CV in his own mind and made a firm decision even before the first Williams FW06 was even completed. Jones had won the previous year's Austrian Grand Prix at the wheel of an uncompetitive Shadow, thanks to tenacity and a sliver of luck. It was obvious that the guy had potential.

Similarly, when twice World Champion Nelson Piquet signalled he was on the market in the summer of 1985, Frank didn't think twice about recruiting him as a successor to Keke Rosberg when the Finn indicated that he would be transferring to McLaren the following year. Yet in the seven years that had elapsed between signing Jones and signing Piquet, Williams had changed beyond recognition from a fledgeling constructor to a consistent World Championship challenger. There would have been no more likelihood of Frank taking a chance on a Jones in 1985 than there would have been of a driver of Piquet's proven calibre agreeing to join Williams in 1978.

The backdrop against which the driver/entrant relationship is conducted on the international motor racing scene has changed dramatically over the past two decades. When Jonathan Williams drove Frank's Formula 2 Brabham to victory in the 1968 Monza Lottery race, he got a good meal for his pains. With Piers, he doesn't recall even having a written contract. Times change. Twenty years later, top drivers in the negotiating market criss-cross Europe in their private jets, visiting potential employers accompanied by a battery of managers and lawyers.

'Back in 1969 we paid Piers £2,500,' recalls Frank, 'and I think he got some bonus money, such as it was. The fact I couldn't pay him for six months would never have been tolerated in the 1970s or 1980s. But in his case it was "well, OK, but I need the money, chap . . . you've got to pay me sometime, chap." No heavy stuff at all.

'Yet that was the way in which he addressed life, reflecting the way he viewed people and his attitude towards money.'

Obviously, with Piers's death, the personal friendship element of the driver equation more or less vanished. At best, it changed considerably. Frank admits that from then on he was largely locked into a series of business arrangements with his employees. And it would be many years before he was negotiating from a position of strength at the front of the field. For the meantime, he found himself in a succession of deals with drivers who were grateful just to get their foot on the bottom rung of the F1 ladder which Frank's team represented in the early 1970s. Moreover, if they got a chance to move up and onwards, they would not worry about any on-going commitment to him, as Brazilian Carlos Pace would later demonstrate in 1973.

Pace, a debonair and popular rising star from São Paulo, had been a member of that first wave of Brazilian talent to surge on to the British scene in the wake of Emerson Fittipaldi's arrival in 1969. He drove a Formula 3 Lotus with some distinction during 1970, then moved up into F2 driving one of Frank's March 712s the following year.

Scoring Frank's sole F2 success of that troubled season at Imola, Pace was clearly ready for promotion to F1 the following season. He drove a second Williams March with great accomplishment for one so inexperienced, consolidating his reputation with a strong fifth place in the Spanish Grand Prix at Jarama. Yet just when Frank began to feel he had a real talent on his hand, Pace left him in the lurch and moved to Surtees.

'We had a verbal agreement with him for the second year, 1973, and everybody in his entourage knew that,' recalls Frank disappointedly. 'But he felt that he was wasting his time staying. He got an offer from what was effectively a works team (Surtees) and he went. It was a tough decision for us, but right for him at the time.

'Carlos Pace was very talented, oh yes; an absolute natural driver. He got a bit over-excited once in a while, but he was one tough, mean character in the car, a bit like Alan Jones. And, like Jones, he was never designed to take physical exercise. A bit overweight, perhaps, but one tough bastard in a car.'

Ironically, as things turned out, Pace would find no more success with Surtees and, after a disappointing start to the 1974 season, he transferred to Brabham in the middle of the year. He won the 1975 Brazilian Grand Prix at Interlagos, much to the delight of his countrymen, but died in a light aircraft accident near São Paulo just before the start of the 1977 European season.

After Pescarolo had used up his credibility crashing Frank's cars through 1971 and 1972, and Pace had jumped ship, Frank's team re-grouped yet again for 1973 when former BRM driver Howden Ganley was signed to lead the team. This mild-mannered New Zealander clearly wasn't going to be front-line F1 material, but Frank invested great optimism in his steady approach and his reputation for testing.

'Sadly, he was nothing like quick enough,' says Williams. 'He also had a reputation for testing cars which I felt was not accurate, but basically he just wasn't quick enough.'

Ganley hit the headlines in 1973 when his Williams-entered Iso Marlboro emerged from a prolonged period running behind the pace car in the lead of the Canadian Grand Prix at Mosport Park on a day when the official lap scoring system blew a fuse. By the end of the afternoon the lap chart published by the organisers was more akin to the read-out from an electro-cardiograph that had gone berserk.

In the immediate aftermath of the race, it seemed as though Ganley had actually won and there exists a touching clip of film as Frank disbelievingly runs his fingers through his thinning thatch, wondering whether he should go forward to collect the victor's spoils. It was just as well he did not, as things turned out, for a detailed post-mortem concluded that Peter Revson's McLaren was the winner – a view, incidentally, that the author has never shared on the basis of his own lap charting efforts.

At this stage in Frank's development as a team owner there was precious little time to worry about driver psychology, whether or not they felt comfortable within the team. Keeping the whole show afloat was a task which absorbed 110 per cent of his time, and worrying about an emotional life support system for his drivers was not a priority. Up until the end of the 1970s, F1 racing's reputation as a sink-or-swim, uncompromisingly committed environment, was absolute. Over-sensitive racing drivers were not something which Frank had encountered.

However, the charming and civilised qualities which Piers Courage had brought to bear on the F1 world were not totally lost and, to Frank's pleasure, in 1974 he would recruit one of his personal all-time favourites, Jacques Laffite. This wiry, thoroughly pleasant and gregarious Frenchman would share some hard times with Williams in 1974 and 1975, later returning for a couple of years (1982–3) when the good times had arrived for the team.

The fact that Laffite was very different from most F1 drivers in that he was easy-going, loved racing from the viewpoint of a purist, and was totally unmotivated by money, should not be allowed to obscure his very considerable talent behind the wheel. It was Jacques who nursed the uncompetitive Williams FW04 to second place in the 1975 German Grand Prix, thereby saving Frank's financial bacon at a time when it looked as though the team might genuinely come apart at the seams.

At the end of 1976 he would join the French Ligier team where he stayed until the end of 1981. Those two more years at Williams followed, after which, as a creature of habit, Jacques returned to Ligier. There he stayed until his front-line racing career ended when he sustained two broken legs in a multiple pile-up at Paddock Bend seconds after the start of the 1986 British Grand Prix at Brands Hatch.

Also driving for Frank in 1974–5 was the Italian Arturo Merzario, a real showman whose consistent penchant for over-revving the team's precious Cosworth DFV engines while changing down through the gears left Frank despairing that they would ever break him of the habit. For all that, Merzario did quite a good job for Williams, bagging third place on the grid for the 1974 South African Grand Prix, and finishing fourth at Monza the same year.

Financial expediency inevitably forced Frank into running a handful of no-hopers and promising rising stars in his second car during this period in exchange for sponsorship. History records that the brilliant young Englishman Tony Brise got his Grand Prix break with Frank in the 1975 Spanish Grand Prix at Barcelona. It was an inauspicious debut, Brise being eliminated in a collision with fellow aspirant Tom Pryce's Shadow. Less than a year later Brise was killed in the air crash that also claimed Graham Hill and four other members of the former World Champion's young team.

It would be wrong, however, to believe that Frank's cars were totally without merit at this time. The 1974 Williams, for example, may have been lacking in terms of detailed preparation, but it was a good handling machine. F3 graduate and Essex farmer Richard Robarts drove it in practice for the Swedish Grand Prix at Anderstorp and concluded that it was a nicer chassis than the much-touted Brabham BT44 which he had briefly driven in the first few races that year, confirming the form which Merzario underlined with his handful of finishes in the points.

At the end of 1973, Frank had briefly invited former Ferrari ace Jacky Ickx to drive his Iso Marlboro in the United States Grand Prix at Watkins Glen. He admits he was rather unimpressed when his guest performer turned up a day late, missing first practice, 'after some sort of cock-up with his air tickets' – and although Ickx finished seventh in the race, Frank doesn't recall it as a particularly fruitful weekend.

Ickx would cross the team's path again towards the end of 1975. Just when Frank was agreeing to sell a controlling interest to Walter Wolf, he found himself facing that situation where he was being offered Marlboro's very substantial shilling to take Ickx aboard again in 1976. In hindsight, it was absolutely the wrong thing to do, but financial pressures always dictated the expedient route in those days.

'Ickx was well past his best by then,' Frank remembers. 'He just could not come to terms with a bad car and, believe me, we gave him a bad car. In August, at Nürburgring, I said to him "Look, I'll give you some money, but you're not driving it again". He accepted that, but it was all very disappointing.'

At the other end of the scale, when Frank started up from scratch at the start of the 1977 European season, he was forced to take on a totally inexperienced young driver called Patrick Neve. A nice tidy driver, Neve had led the Silverstone F2 International Trophy meeting that year with the works March 772P in splendid style, being denied victory only when he was forced to make a pit stop to secure a slightly loose rear wheel. It was one of those days when the cards are poised to fall in favour of a driver or against him. For Neve, that afternoon, it all went wrong.

He would trundle along at the back of the F1 fields throughout the summer in Frank's private March, leaving pit lane eyebrows to rise. People were privately wondering for how long Williams would endure scurfing around among the also-rans, high on hope but low on finance as usual. But the sceptics had less than a year to wait before Frank started his serious, and long-overdue, assault on the bastions of the F1 establishment.

For 1978, Frank Williams signed up Alan Jones to drive his car and the eventual long-term results would considerably exceed the sum total of the partnership's constituent parts as they were perceived at the start of that season. The Jones/Williams relationship represented not only a crucial turning point in the fortunes of Frank's team, but also put into crystal clear focus the way in which the relationship between a team and its driver grows and develops over the years.

Nothing is cut and dried in F1. Grand Prix teams tend to operate on unpredictably shifting sands, dependent for their strength on the interaction of personnel, financial resources, inspired judgement and the priceless ability to do the right thing at the right time with the correct people. It is possible to marshal most of those elements, but if you don't have the last one – the luck, the timing, call it what you will – then creating something extra special, a cut above the average, will not be possible.

Jones and Williams would develop into one of Grand Prix racing's magical partnerships, a formidable alliance which would set the F1 pace across three World Championship seasons. But not even Frank himself could have anticipated just what a gem he had unearthed when the determined, 30-year-old Australian put pen to a contract at the end of October 1977.

It's probably fair to say that right then, the only person who truly believed that Alan Jones had World Championship potential was Jones himself. Many, with the benefit of hindsight, may claim the role of a seer in this respect, but most of them are being disingenuous.

His credentials were adequate, but hardly outstanding. The son of Australian racing hero Stan Jones, a rugged, popular and hard-drinking hedonist who used up his life at a break-neck speed in the fast lane, Alan inherited his father's toughness and resilience. He came to England at the turn of the 1970s, finished second in the 1972 British F3 Championship and had edged his way into F1 at the wheel of a private Hesketh at the start of 1975.

After briefly flirting with Graham Hill's team, for which he finished fifth in the 1975 German Grand Prix at Nürburgring, Jones switched to Team Surtees for 1976 and turned a few heads with some promising performances in the neat TS19. Although he achieved a handful of World Championship placings, it was in the non-title Race of Champions at Brands Hatch that Alan really made his mark, keeping ahead of James Hunt's McLaren M23 to lead through to half distance before the Englishman eventually went ahead.

This was good stuff, but not sufficient to keep Jones in play from the start of 1977. He fell out with John Surtees and turned his attention to the American racing scene where it was widely assumed that he would disappear into well-heeled obscurity. It would take somebody else's tragedy to re-open the gates of F1 opportunity for Alan Jones.

On lap 27 of the 1977 South African Grand Prix, a 19-year-old marshal at the Kyalami circuit near Johannesburg picked up a 40 lb fire extinguisher and ran across the circuit just beyond the flat-out brow on the startline straight. Jansen van Vuuren was a ticketing clerk with South African Airways at the city's Jan Smuts international airport during the week, but his weekend enthusiasm was motor racing, and the zeal with which he set out to quench a small engine fire on Renzo Zorzi's Shadow DN8, which had stopped on the other side of the track, reflected that interest.

Tragically, he never got to the other side. Van Vuuren was hit by Zorzi's team-mate Tom Pryce and both men were killed. Once the numbing effects of this tragedy had subsided, Arrows team manager Alan Rees found himself casting round for a replacement driver. Alan Jones was the man. Later in the summer, at the Osterreichring, Jones would be running second to James Hunt's McLaren when its engine failed. Victory in the Austrian Grand Prix fell into his lap. Of such convoluted and disjointed circumstances are World Championships fashioned.

Neve understandably had to be counted out of the 1978 equation. Frank appreciated his part in getting the revised Williams Grand Prix Engineering show on the road: 'He was a nice tidy driver, but not F1 material'.

Jones was one of three men whom Frank had been considering. The other two were Hans-Joachim Stuck, son of the pre-war Auto Union star, and Gunnar Nilsson who, as Mario Andretti's team-mate at Team Lotus, had won the rain-soaked 1977 Belgian Grand Prix at Zolder.

'Stuck, Jones and Nilsson were on the list,'' explains Frank, 'but by the time we were ready to make our choice, Gunnar had signed for Arrows and was ill anyway (the likeable Swede would in fact never race in 1978 and succumbed to cancer before the year was out). "Jonesey" became ours by defection of the others, if you like. In fact, if you work backwards over the years, you can see we've made all sorts of bum driver selections, but Jones was a great one. That said, it certainly wasn't premeditated in the sense that we recognised him as a great talent. We thought he would be nice and steady, get us some points and keep us in the Constructors' Association.'

Despite this cautious initial assessment of Jones's potential, Frank recalls being very impressed when they first met up to discuss business: 'He was a tough man mentally and knew just what he wanted. He had a clear idea of his own financial requirements – we paid him £40,000 that first season – but primarily he wanted a drive with Williams because he thought it was a team going places. A lot was happening during the second half of 1977 to form the bedrock of the company, with Patrick finding his feet on the design side and so on.'

Alan Jones had sniffed the air at Williams and correctly caught a whiff of its potential. He wasn't the only one. At last Frank had started with a fresh sheet of paper, with a designer he wanted, the driver he needed and, as important as any of those elements, the necessary sponsorship.

You will read elsewhere between these covers how Frank's relationship with the Saudi Arabian business community led to just the right sponsorship support at the right moment in the team's history. But now, in the closing months of 1977, one got the impression that the umbilical cord which still attached Frank Williams, distantly, to those dark days of Piers Courage's accident at Zandvoort had at last been severed.

The 1978 season saw Jones finding his feet, learning how to work with the team and quickly making a good impression. Within the F1 community everybody has their place and it only takes the slightest disruption to this perceived order for warning bells to jangle and opinions to become dramatically re-focused. It took only until the second race of 1978 before Jones tripped the F1 alarm system by planting Patrick's neat new Williams FW06 on the fourth row of the grid in Rio.

In the third race of the season, at Kyalami, he finished fourth to score the first Championship points for Williams GPE, and in the fourth, through the streets of Long Beach, he stood the F1 form book on its ear with a potentially winning performance.

Alan's drive at Long Beach was inspirational and awoke the team to the very real possibility of running at the front of the pack. Consequently, it is a race which deserved to be recalled here in some detail.

The 1978 season would come to be remembered as one in which Colin Chapman's superb ground effect Lotus 79s ruled the Championship roost in the hands of Mario Andretti and Ronnie Peterson. Even though the team was still relying on the previous year's type 78s, Andretti and Peterson arrived at Long Beach a point apart at the head of the Drivers' Championship points table. Jones was in equal eighth, with James Hunt, thanks to the three points he had collected in South Africa.

After qualifying through the streets of the Californian coastal city, the Michelin-shod Ferrari 312T3s of Carlos Reutemann and Gilles

Villeneuve buttoned up the front row with Niki Lauda's Brabham-Alfa BT46 and Andretti right behind them on the second rank. The third row contained John Watson's Brabham-Alfa and Peterson, the fourth Hunt's McLaren and Jones's Williams.

Ferrari fans remember this as the great day when Villeneuve led commandingly until he tripped over tail-ender Clay Regazzoni's Shadow and crashed into retirement. Williams fans recall it for that great moment when Jones stormed through to third place and began closing on Reutemann's second place Ferrari. After Gilles was written out of the equation, Alan ran second from lap 39 to lap 62, hardly slowed when the FW06's full-width nose wing collapsed to the point where its outer extremities were dragging on the circuit.

More seriously, a fuel pick-up problem slowed him dramatically over the last 18 laps, and he dropped progressively back through the field to finish seventh at the chequered flag. No matter, Frank Williams was delighted with what he had seen from the pit wall. 'I never dreamt we would be capable of running that high,' he enthused. 'It was a performance which convinced me we'd got absolutely the right man.' At one point when Alan was running second, Frank turned to Charlie Crichton-Stuart and told him: 'I really don't care if he doesn't finish this race – he's the most exciting driver I've seen since Ronnie Peterson appeared!'

Williams Grand Prix Engineering had to savour the taste of that Long Beach performance for many months in what turned out to be a predominantly barren season. Not until the French Grand Prix at Paul Ricard, three months later, would Jones score his second finish in the points, and although he ran impressively with the leading bunch at Brands Hatch, the British Grand Prix ended with another mechanical retirement. The team was still getting its act together and Patrick was finding his feet on the engineering side.

At Watkins Glen, in the penultimate race of the season, Jones finished a storming second to Reutemann's Ferrari after a performance which made a profound impact on Patrick Head and was extremely significant in more ways than were obvious. Jones's weekend had started on a precarious note when a front stub axle sheared going into a fast downhill right-hand corner.

It could have been a disastrous situation for the driver, but fortunately Alan managed to wrestle the car sideways before it ploughed off the road into the catch fencing, wrecking the chassis in the process. It was clear that Jones could not be allowed to drive the spare car until Patrick had identified and cured the problem with the hubs.

Fortunately, Charlie Crichton-Stuart's ability to charm the birds off the trees resulted in his persuading a local specialist engineering company in nearby Elmira to keep working through the night to heat-treat the remaining hubs. Taking Patrick's word that everything was now OK,

Jones qualified third behind Andretti and Reutemann before racing with commanding assurance to take second place on the rostrum.

'Perhaps working with Alan in 1978 on a car I had, in effect, almost completely designed on paper was the key to my interest in Formula 1 becoming completely serious and long-term,' reflected Patrick in 1990. 'I suppose I came through the transitional phase from thinking that it was all really a bit of fun, and that maybe I'll do something else this year, to realising that this was really quite good and, if we put out noses down, then we might seriously be able to achieve something, perhaps even win a Grand Prix.

'From then on I began to take things more seriously and the hub shaft failure on FW06 at Watkins Glen was really quite a sobering experience. We'd had something similar happen during practice for the Dutch Grand Prix at Zandvoort, where Alan also flew off the road, but I don't think I had analysed what happened in sufficient detail, nor taken sufficient steps to make certain it didn't happen again.' It was all part of the tortuous learning process in the making of a top-line F1 team.

For 1979, Frank had the resources available to expand into a two-car operation. He selected the highly respected Italian Swiss Clay Regazzoni as the ideal candidate for the second car, and the genial moustachioed former Ferrari driver played an admirable supporting role to Alan Jones. He would also go down in history as the winner of Frank's first World Championship victory, his FW07 inheriting the lead of the British Grand Prix at Silverstone after Jones's car suffered a cracked water pump casting and pulled in to retire amidst a cloud of smoke and steam.

Sheridan Thynne recalls how impressed he was at the team's fast burgeoning, somewhat dispassionate professionalism when Jones retired from that Silverstone race. Frank allowed himself barely a glance at Alan's stricken FW07 before turning back to the track where Regazzoni was leading.

'Frank had about half a second's glance at Jones, but instead of getting emotional about it, as I might have done, he looked straight back on to the track at Clay because Clay was still in business,' says Sherry. 'Frank had the self-discipline to pay zero attention to something that wasn't the absolute priority of the moment.'

'Clay was very similar to Laffite, an extremely easy-going guy,' recalls Frank with genuine pleasure. 'But he wasn't quite quick enough in qualifying, so he was obviously shown up by Alan.'

Jones really came into his own during 1979, armed with Patrick's splendid FW07 ground effect challenger which embodied the lessons the Williams designer had learned from Colin Chapman's Lotus 79 and polished with the results of his own technical development.

Jones and FW07 – memories of them are inextricably entwined within the pages of recent F1 history. While Fangio might be recalled in connection with Maserati or Mercedes-Benz, Stirling Moss with

Vanwall, and Jimmy Clark with Lotus, Jones's golden era of achievement wasn't just with Williams, it was with a specific Williams, the FW07. The car propelled him to a single World Championship for Williams, but almost won him three in a row.

Jonathan Williams, thoughtfully reviewing his own professional racing career, identified perfectly the challenge in bringing a car and a driver to their respective peaks at precisely the same time: 'One day you're hot, the next you're not.' Jones and the Williams FW07 were 'hot' from the start of the 1979 European season through to their final victory at Las Vegas before Alan's temporary retirement from the F1 business. The technical support, the ambience, the whole balance of the team was in perfect harmony from Jones's standpoint.

By the start of 1979, Jones had broken through that crucial barrier of self-belief which stands somewhere along every serious driver's career path. From thinking he might be able to get the job done in the right car, Alan entered 1979 knowing that he was a potential winner given the right circumstances. Enormously resilient and self-reliant, he was ideal for Williams at that time, just as Piers Courage had been back in 1969.

The one thing that Jones didn't need was an emotional life support system when he was out of the car. If you'd gone up to him and put a sympathetic arm round his shoulder, the chances are, at best, that you'd have been asked whether you were taking the piss. On a bad day, you might run the risk of getting thumped. He shrewdly assessed the characters and personalities of the people he met in the pit lane and divided them into two categories, the smaller of which contained those he had time for.

He was ideal to work with because Frank and Patrick almost always knew he was giving his best. Out of the cockpit his contribution to technical de-briefs was succinct and economical. With dry humour, he would often turn the responsibility for a deficient performance firmly round on to the designer's shoulders: 'I want you to know, Patrick, that you are in the shit' was a typical example of his straight talking. Then it was away to play tennis or have a beer with his mates. He wasn't neurotic, given to lying awake in bed all night wondering about ride heights and tyre compounds. To him, motor racing was something you got on and did, not agonised about.

Jones won the 1979 German, Austrian, Dutch and Canadian Grands Prix to finish third in the World Championship behind Ferrari men Jody Scheckter and Gilles Villeneuve. He also had the Belgian, British and, arguably, US Grands Prix in the bag when he retired. He would probably have won the Championship that year if the FW07 had been race ready a little earlier in the season. It's important to remember that the new Williams did not make its race debut until the Spanish Grand Prix at Jarama, the fifth round of the title chase by which time Ferrari had already won two races.

By the end of 1979, Williams Grand Prix Engineering had finally established itself as a team with World Championship winning credentials. Both Frank and Patrick agreed that it would be a good plan to replace Regazzoni with a faster driver for 1980, one who would have a very realistic chance of winning if Jones didn't last the distance. The man they focused their attention on was Carlos Reutemann, possibly the only driver in contemporary F1 history to display the same introspective and cerebral approach to the business of motor racing as Ayrton Senna.

Reutemann was 37 years old when he signed up for Williams at the start of 1980. Behind him lay a fine record of achievement, some nine Grand Prix victories, with Brabham and Ferrari between 1974 and 1978, but his 1979 season with Team Lotus had been an unmitigated disaster which sapped his credibility in the pit lane. He joined Williams as number two to Jones on a two-year contract.

'In his day Carlos was every bit as quick as Jones,' says Frank firmly. 'He is a lovely man; I could talk about the Jones/Reutemann angle all day. With hindsight, we, the team, should have let him know more often how highly we regarded him. That would have helped the relationship, I'm sure. But I was seriously influenced by Jones.

'I took a very masculine attitude towards drivers and assumed that they should behave – or should be treated – like Alan. Carlos had terrific talent, an utterly charming man.'

The friendship has endured. If Frank meets up with Reutemann at a race, they immediately start a lengthy debate about the merits of one Cosworth engine over another at some specific race back in 1981, or begin an argument over which tyre choice they made.

Early in 1990, Frank had yet another example of the man's honest simplicity. The telephone rang at the Williams factory and the call was put through to Frank's office. It was Carlos, in a telephone box at Didcot station. He'd come on a chance visit to see his old employer. A few days earlier, Argentina's President Mennem had invited him to join a group of celebrities on the first scheduled Aerolineas Argentinas Boeing 747 flight to Heathrow since the end of the Falklands crisis in 1982. On arrival, Carlos took a cab to Paddington station, a train to Didcot . . . and here he was.

'I think in 1979, when FW07 started to race, every driver was extremely impressed, particularly at Silverstone,' recalls Carlos, 'and everybody suddenly wanted to drive for Frank. That season I had about 11 or 12 mechanical failures in the Lotus. I had to buy myself out of my contract with Chapman, but it was the best thing I did. I was an old guy by F1 standards and there wasn't much time left.'

Did he mind signing as number two to Alan? 'No, no,' he says with a grin, 'because I was in the middle of the shit with Lotus . . . when you're a starving man, you eat rabbit food, if necessary. You are thankful for anything you can get.'

Reutemann was restored to the winner's rostrum at Monaco in 1980, but that was the sole victory he scored during his first season with Williams. Jones, by contrast, reeled off confident wins in Argentina, France, Britain, Canada and the USA to clinch the Championship. Moreover, between Montreal in 1980 and Brazil in 1981, the Williams team would notch up four successive 1–2 results. Three were in the order Jones–Reutemann and the fourth, which would cause considerable aggravation, saw Carlos finishing ahead.

'The first year with Frank was tough from the driving point of view,' Reutemann confesses. 'I was completely out of shape. At the end of 1978 I changed from Ferrari to Lotus, who had ground effect with their type 79. But although it had been competitive in 1978, it was no good the following year, so I did not have serious ground effect experience until I got into the FW07B at the start of 1980.

'It took me quite a time to find out the best technique with these cars, to establish the limit.'

'It is difficult to explain what happened in 1981,' he continues reflectively. 'When I signed my contract with Frank there was a "seven second" clause in it. If I was leading the race by seven seconds, then I could win the race; if Jones was closer behind than seven seconds, then I had to let Alan past.

'The first race in 1981 was Long Beach. Patrese was leading from the start and I was second, pulling away from Jones, I remember. I had about four or five seconds in hand after Patrese made a pit stop with a misfire, but he rejoined right in front of me and lost me a lot of time, allowing Jones to catch up again.

'Then I screwed up lapping Marc Surer's Ensign and Jones took the lead, so from that moment the race was over for me. I eased up and drove steadily home to finish second. I think I was 20, 30 seconds behind Jones.'

At Rio's Jacarepagua circuit the Brazilian Grand Prix was held in treacherously wet conditions. Reutemann immediately grabbed the initiative, Jones falling dutifully into line behind, believing that Carlos would play the decent man and abide by the terms of his contract.

Reutemann recalls: 'We started the race in Brazil, in the rain, and to be honest I never drove particularly hard. Frank just showed me pit signals to the third place man and believe me, I never thought Jones was running so close behind. About three or four laps from the end, Frank put out a sign signalling me that we would reverse the order. I was obviously very upset.

'I couldn't relinquish the lead. I would have rather parked the car at the back of the circuit and walked away, never gone back to the paddock. Obviously, from then on the situation was impossible. Jones was very upset, with good reason.'

Frank says: 'With about four laps to go, Alan realised he was going to get screwed and for sure he tried like hell, but the gap didn't close. I think

Carlos had the measure of him on the track, on that day, in those conditions.'

Needless to say, there was a furore in the Williams garage after this particular race was over. 'Alan threw a wobbly in the garage, even though we tried desperately to calm him down,' recalls Williams. 'I think we told Carlos that he'd broken his contract. We didn't pay him any money at all for that win . . . and he never mentioned the subject. I recall that very clearly.'

Sheridan Thynne comments: 'The fact that Reutemann never queried the absence of payment was an indication of how exceptionally clever he was. Very clever people never fight battles they are going to lose.'

Needless to say, any personal relationship between the two men was finished from that point onwards. 'After that episode at Rio, there's no doubt that they were poles apart,' says Frank honestly, 'and while they treated each other professionally, pooling technical information, they did not like each other. From Jones, it was a definite animosity, underlined by the famous remark he made in the motorhome at Las Vegas a couple of hours after his final win for us at the end of the season, just as he was about to retire.

'Carlos said "OK, Alan, well, goodbye . . . shall we bury the hatchet?" And Jones replied, "Yeah, in your . . . g back mate" and walked away. But for all that, it was nowhere near the situation which developed at McLaren between Senna and Prost in 1988 and 1989. Jones and Reutemann were clever enough to know that they had crossover technical contributions to make and, to a large extent, needed each other.'

Throughout the summer of 1981, Jones looked well capable of retaining his Championship title. He was consistently quick, and his overwhelming determination had in no way become blunted as a result of winning that first title crown. Had it not been for fuel feed problems at Monaco and Hockenheim he would have scored two additional, very impressive, victories to add to his successes at Long Beach and Las Vegas. On the debit side, he demonstrated an uncharacteristic slice of emotion by flying off the road at Zolder during the Belgian Grand Prix as he tried to teach Carlos who was boss in the Williams line-up – his frustration that day compounded by the fact that Reutemann survived to win the race.

Carlos had a steady and consistent year, yet there was something unnerving about his mental approach to the business of tackling the Championship contest. After the British Grand Prix at Silverstone, where his second place finish to John Watson's McLaren gave him a 17-point lead in the points table, he shook the author by making a personal bet that he would not win the Championship. Whether or not this was a psychological ploy designed to avoid raising his hopes too high was something I never fathomed out.

The 1981 season was admittedly difficult for Williams in particular and F1 as a whole. Grand Prix racing had almost been torn apart by the destructive dispute between the sport's governing body FISA and the Formula One Constructors' Association over the prohibition, from the start of 1981, of the sliding aerodynamic side skirts which were an essential element behind the competitive efficiency of the contemporary breed of ground effect racers.

This polarized into a battle between the British-based specialist constructors who pioneered and developed ground effect and the two key major manufacturers, Renault and Ferrari, who the Brits reckoned were operating hand-in-glove with the sport's governing body in an attempt to further the performance of their new turbocharged engines.

One by-product of this situation was Goodyear's decision to withdraw from F1 at the start of the season. That meant that Michelin had to service the entire field, and when Goodyear came back in time for the 1981 French Grand Prix it was to service only Williams and Brabham.

Reutemann says: 'The change from Michelin to Goodyear was very bad for Frank. After we went to Dijon I knew the Brabham was quicker on Goodyear, and Patrick took two or three races to make the FW07B fully competitive. I was very lucky to finish second at Silverstone, but the car was competitive at Hockenheim, and better again at Zandvoort and Monza.'

Gradually Reutemann's advantage was whittled away. He eventually went into the final race of the season with a single point in hand over Piquet. The title clincher took place in the unlikely setting of Las Vegas, the Nevada gambling city in which a track had been laid out round the parking lot of the Caesars Palace casino. Reutemann blitzed the opposition to take pole position on the grid, then faded unaccountably to seventh place and lost the title to Piquet. By one point.

'Las Vegas was the only race where I wasn't fully in control,' he reflects. 'At every race I knew what wheel diameter, tyre stagger, ride heights and so-on that I needed. I chose the spare car from first practice, with a normal Cosworth V8 – number 304 – in chassis FW07B/12 which is now in the Williams collection at Didcot.'

Carlos has a computer-like capacity to recall specific and minute details relating to the chassis set-up and performance of an individual car at an individual race. Unsurprisingly, the fine detail of this Las Vegas outing are seared into his sub-conscious for all time:

'I used 2,500 lb front springs, 3,500 lb springs at the rear. The set-up was very stiff, but very quick. I think Jones chose 1,500 lb front springs and 2,000 lb in the rear. I was very happy with my car. I wanted to race it and told Patrick not to touch it; the engine, handling and gearchange was perfect. I said "Leave it as it is," but I don't think Patrick was very happy about that.

'Then on Saturday morning I touched the right rear wheel of Piquet's

Brabham with my left front suspension. The impact bent a wishbone. It was replaced, but the car never handled properly again. No chance to drive it again, no way. No question, it was the most disappointing day of my career.'

For the second day of qualifying he switched to FW07B/17. He never felt comfortable in it: 'Different engine, different power band, different feel to the gearchange, different seating position. I think I am half a second slower.

'Sunday morning, we have a problem with the brakes. Then I never had the chance to choose a matched set of tyres, something I always liked to do. So when I start the race I have a problem with the gearchange and the tyres are not fast. There was no way . . .'

Ironically, Carlos's phenomenal powers of recall credit his qualifying performance in FW07B/17 at Monza that very same year as the best single lap of his career. 'It was fantastic,' he grins. 'No downforce, qualifying tyres . . . I hit the rev limiter before I got to the Lesmo right-handers and went through without lifting the throttle. Fantastic! I think that was the best-handling car I ever drove.'

This performance earned him second place on the starting grid. Yet in the race he became psyched out by a few rain spots and slipped to seventh before recovering to finish third behind Alain Prost's Renault and Jones in the other Williams. 'If that had been a sunny day, my life might have been totally different,' he muses.

This Italian Grand Prix was one of Jones's most remarkable races. In London the previous week Alan had been involved in a territorial dispute over the same piece of the Chiswick High Road with a Transit van. Fisticuffs had ensued, with the result that Jones drove the Italian Grand Prix with a broken finger.

He was also on the receiving end of a bawling-out from his employer, but not for his impromptu antics in a London street. Jones told Frank that he was quitting at the end of the season. Williams told him that this was, not to put too fine a point on it, bloody inconsiderate.

'We had no bright ideas at all,' Frank recalls. 'We were by then a team accustomed to winning with number one style drivers. Villeneuve was with Ferrari, Pironi had just resigned, Piquet was staying with Brabham, and Laffite was with Ligier. Then we had Mansour Ojjeh wasting our time at the next race, bending our ear about how we ought to have Eddie Cheever, when in fact Patrick and I should have been working out the best tyre choice for the following day's race. It was a very difficult time.'

Inwardly, Williams knew enough about drivers to understand that Jones wasn't being deliberately contrary. Yet he tried enormously hard to persuade the Australian to review his decision. Alan's resolve wavered. After Las Vegas, he back tracked to England where he tried Patrick Head's new secret weapon, the Williams FW07D six wheeler – with four small driven wheels at the rear. He was impressed, but it wasn't sufficient to make him change his mind.

As if this wasn't enough, a month or so after the end of the season, Carlos Reutemann announced that he too was calling it a day. In the event, Reutemann changed his mind, ran the first two races of 1982 – and then abruptly quit for good.

'When I crossed the line in Las Vegas, I felt something funny in my body,' says Reutemann. 'So when I started 1982 I was very tired. We went to South Africa for the first race and the drivers got involved in an enormous row with FISA over the licences. I raced in South Africa and went on to the second race in Brazil which was usually a good barometer for me.

'We started the first day's practice and I felt no spark. I really didn't know what lap times I was doing. And I didn't much care. I drove badly, doing everything wrong. I didn't know whether I was driving ten-tenths or not. So I took the decision to stop, but two years later I think I could have come back. At the end of 1981 I think I should have left Frank after losing the Championship by such a narrow margin.'

Within three months, the team which had won the 1981 Constructors' World Championship suddenly found itself deprived of two top drivers. It was a set of circumstances which threw into graphic relief the complexities of the entrant/driver relationship, underlining the fact that if the competitive spark flickers out, no worthwhile purpose is served in pressuring a driver to continue racing.

It would be all too easy to reach the conclusion that Jones and Reutemann had let Williams down, Certainly Carlos's behaviour in quitting, then changing his mind, then quitting again seemed extraordinary at the time. By the time he retired for good, of course, the team had signed Keke Rosberg as a nominal replacement for Jones, as will be recounted in the next chapter.

'I never really understood why Carlos left for that second time after Rio in 1982,' Frank reflects. 'He may have thought "Oh no, with Rosberg, I've got another Jones on my hands. Is it all worth it?" '

One tantalising thought is that Reutemann might have been forewarned by the Argentine government that the Falklands crisis was likely to break in the months that followed. That would have made his position as *de facto* number one driver for a British F1 team untenable. Frank concedes it has crossed his mind, but tends to reject the notion.

Sheridan Thynne believes otherwise: 'I think he did know. We must not lose sight of the fact that international sportsmen are part of the PR system for countries like Argentina, and he was among their two or three best sporting personalities.

'I always imagined they did tell him, as a member of the world-wide Argentinian establishment.'

Rosberg, Mansell and Piquet

When it became clear that Alan Jones really was going to retire at the end of 1981, Frank Williams and his colleagues began casting round carefully to find somebody who would effectively take over the role of number two to Carlos Reutemann. With the established front runners all committed to other teams by the time Jones sprang his decision on the team at Monza, there was a great deal of consideration to be done. Williams had become accustomed to having a pair of potential winners in its line-up, but where was the new star coming from?

Towards the end of the 1981 season, former twice World Champion Niki Lauda signalled he was ready for a comeback after just over two seasons away from the cockpit. The Austrian star was being courted heavily by McLaren chief Ron Dennis who had been trying to cajole him into such a decision for some time. But Lauda also spoke with Williams.

'We talked to Niki at the end of 1981 when he was preparing for his comeback,' Frank admits. 'Several telephone calls took place, but I think, having tested a McLaren, Niki felt morally committed to Ron. Anyway, we could never have offered him the sort of money that Ron had put on the table.

'There was also some contact with John Watson. We were very close indeed to doing a deal with him for 1982, making a substantial and competitive offer for his services. I'm sure he considered it closely, but eventually he opted to stay with McLaren.'

The answer to this dilemma eventually turned out to be one of Grand Prix racing's less immediately obvious talents, a 33-year-old Finn with the near-unpronounceable name of Keijo Rosberg. 'Keke', as he was popularly known, was the son of a vet and amateur rally driver who had agonized over his boy's racing ambitions ever since he began racing karts in the mid-1960s. Although Lars Rosberg would have liked his son to have pursued a career in dentistry or computer programming, he supported Keke with warmth and enthusiasm during his kart racing years. In turn, Keke acknowledges that this did a great deal to cement a personal bond with his father throughout his adolescence. After he eventually clinched the World Championship at Las Vegas at the end of 1982, one of his first telephone calls from the Williams' motorhome was to his parents.

Keke wrestled his way to international motor racing prominence through Formula Super Vee, Formula 2 and Atlantic. In 1978 he made the leap into F1 at the wheel of the Ron Tauranac-designed Theodore owned by Hong Kong-based wheeler-dealer Teddy Yip, winning a rain-soaked International Trophy race at Silverstone from ex-Champion Emerson Fittipaldi. Yet it was not until James Hunt abruptly retired from the Wolf team over 12 months later that the Finn got a regular Grand Prix ride.

At the end of 1979, Walter Wolf pulled out of the sponsorship business after three years of financing his own team, leaving what was left of his organisation to merge with Fittipaldi Automotive. Rosberg was offered a two-year contract, for 1980 and 1981, with the newly reconstituted team. He accepted it – and almost sank without trace.

Drastically short on sponsorship, the Fittipaldi team's form spiralled downwards to the point where Keke left them in the middle of 1981. He was getting nowhere, damaging his professional reputation and hadn't been paid. The future looked bleak. Yet an invitation to a Williams test session at Paul Ricard later than autumn was to provide not only the way back into the F1 milieu, but a direct route to the top of the tree.

Also being tested that day was Frenchman Jean-Pierre Jarier, but it was Rosberg who really excited Charlie Crichton-Stuart and the team's aerodynamicist Frank Dernie.

'It was obvious he was tremendously quick and determined from the outset,' recalls Charlie. 'On our first night in the hotel down at Ricard he was up until one o'clock drinking with us, then the next morning Frank Dernie suggested "Let's put this guy on qualifiers and tell him to go for it, without even a lap to warm up". So Keke appeared, bleary-eyed, drinking endless black coffees and smoking about half a dozen Marlboros at once. Into the car and snap! He was instantly quick. A blind one-eyed monkey could see his potential.'

Keke was undeniably flash, brash and extrovert. He could have been absolutely insufferable were it not for his delightfully dry, self-deprecating sense of humour. In his mansion in the Berkshire countryside he had a stained glass window made depicting his helmet. 'A bit vulgar, isn't it?' he would laugh when he saw the nervous reaction of doubtful visitors. Everybody agreed that it was.

Reutemann greeted his arrival with a perhaps unconscious dose of dry humour. Faced with the team's boss enthusiastically canvassing his opinion, Carlos said thoughtfully: 'I tell you Frank, long blond hair, the Rolex, the gold identity bracelet, the Gucci briefcase . . . I think he is very quick, Frank!'

Williams admits that, while not sceptical about Keke's potential, 'I just thought we wouldn't get another Jones in the car and, to be fair, he wasn't another Jones. He was as quick as Alan, for sure, but he wasn't as mentally complete as Alan when he joined us. He needed to be bolstered up and we had serious communication difficulties. He was also seriously short on experience, as witness the 1982 Belgian Grand Prix at Zolder which he had in the bag before he locked up his brakes on the penultimate lap and handed the race to John Watson.'

Keke arrived on the scene at the start of 1982 when the Williams team was switching from its trusted FW07s to the newer FW08, effectively an uprated version of the previous car built round a stiffer aluminium honeycomb chassis and incorporating a lighter pull-rod front suspension system which also produced aerodynamic and weight-saving benefits. It was a difficult time for F1 design technology since the cars were using non-flexible mountings for their aerodynamic side skirts and it was necessary to run with extremely stiff suspension in order to produce consistent handling qualities.

Add to that the fact that Williams were among the last front line teams to go into battle using naturally aspirated Cosworth V8 engines at a time when it seemed that the new generation of turbos were set to sweep the board, and Keke clearly faced quite a task. He buckled down to it with an outward disdain for the classical niceties of F1 driving style which tended to make Patrick Head wince.

For Keke, everything seemed to be in black and white, with no shades of grey. 'During that first season in particular, in terms of communication with the team's engineers, he was given to making erratic, nonsensical, sweeping statements,' explains Williams. 'He would say things like "The car is impossible to handle . . . impossible to drive . . . got no brakes". Whereas, if he had considered things carefully, he would have said something like "The brakes were a bit difficult, I think we need more bias to the front".

'There really was a major communications problem between him and Patrick throughout our first season together, although Keke worked mostly with Frank Dernie because Patrick spent a lot of time on the Metro 6R4 rally car programme which we were doing for British Leyland.'

Either way, Keke proved he was a real racer and, for one with such a wild image, he looked after the machinery with remarkable consistency. The record books tell of few spins or accidents, a fact about which he preens himself. On his way to his sole victory of the 1982 season, in the Swiss Grand Prix at Dijon-Prenois, he did admit to the ostensibly suicidal move of banging his left front wheel against the right-hand side pod of Andrea de Cesaris's Ligier attempting to move the obstructive Italian from his path. 'But that was when I was lapping him,' he explained innocently, as if that fact made the technique instantly valid and acceptable.

Off-track, his chain smoking drove the super fit Frank Williams to distraction. Moreover, Keke's chubby demeanour suggested he was overweight, which at a compact 10 stone he clearly wasn't. At one point Frank made the tactical error of suggesting that Keke could lose weight if he took more exercise. Rosberg immediately responded by observing that in fact he did train and work out, 'but not as much as Frank, because I don't have so much spare time as he does.'

'Keke, for me, was an absolutely mercurial driver,' observes Charlie Crichton-Stuart. 'I don't believe that there was anybody better equipped to win that 1982 Championship, battling against the turbo odds with a Cosworth DFV, driving every single lap of every single race absolutely flat-out.'

In 1983, now armed with a flat-bottomed version of the FW08, Rosberg triumphed brilliantly at Monaco, then when the team switched to Honda turbo power for the following year, he scored a similarly impressive triumph in the one and only Dallas Grand Prix, emerging from the cockpit as cool as a cucumber in torrid conditions which saw half his colleagues collapsing with fatigue. In 1985, as the Williams-Honda bandwagon began to pick up serious momentum, he scored excellent victories in the Detroit and Australian Grands Prix.

Rosberg freely acknowledges that, in 1983, he was taking every risk he could to try and keep the naturally aspirated, Cosworth-engined Williams up with the much more powerful turbos.

'Having won the Championship in 1982, I was at the point where I was probably the fastest in my career,' he states firmly. 'I just wasn't prepared to accept that anybody could beat me and was prepared to take massive risks to stay with the turbos. I absolutely loved every minute of it!'

At the end of 1985, Keke left Williams to join Alain Prost in the McLaren international line-up. He had made up his mind to make the switch early in the season, troubled that Frank Williams had chosen to sign up Nigel Mansell as his partner to replace the outgoing Jacques Laffite. But Rosberg had paid too much attention to pit lane tittle-tattle which signalled that Mansell was an awkward customer to be avoided. Indeed, on the winners' rostrum at Dallas, the Finn had delivered a stinging rebuke to Mansell over what he regarded as his unacceptable driving tactics in the early stages of the race.

Many of his colleagues might have kept quiet, but Rosberg was always one to call a spade a spade in fairly uncompromising terms. He also realised that he had a communications problem with Patrick in 1984.

'I felt very much at home at Williams, with the exception of the 1984 season when I found Patrick impossible to deal with,' he says with brazen candour. 'He had been on a diet and lost about 30lb and, frankly, was like a bear that had been shot in the backside. It got to the point at Zandvoort where I said to Frank "Look, I don't mind not being friends with Patrick, but if I can't work with him, then I'm just wasting my time here".

'So Patrick switched to Jacques's car and I said, "well, that's a good way of side-stepping the issue, I don't think". I ask you; moving the guy who was one of the best engineers in the F1 business, if not the very best in the business, to the team's other car . . .'

Keke went down to Didcot, thumped Frank Williams's table and said 'I'm going'. Frank said 'You're not' and, mercifully for Keke's career prospects, they managed to solve the problem. Had Keke walked out and accepted Renault's offer for 1985, his Grand Prix career would probably have finished there and then. The French national team was on the skids and 1985 would be its final year of operation.

For the new season, thankfully, Patrick and Keke got on well again and Rosberg admits to having thoroughly enjoyed himself, although by then he had determined to finish his F1 career with McLaren in 1986. On the Mansell front, he found that the Englishman's alleged awkwardness had been considerably exaggerated. With characteristic generosity of spirit , he acknowledged he had been wrong. He got on well with Mansell and grew to like the man who, statistically, would go on to become the most successful F1 driver yet employed by Williams Grand Prix Engineering.

By the end of his four-year spell with Williams, Keke had matured considerably and, in the team's estimation, become a more technically able performer.

'He realised that he had to think a lot more about the business of being a Grand Prix driver,' Frank remembers, 'and he really began to flourish as he did more testing and accumulated more experience. He was unquestionably very intelligent, but I always felt to some extent he short-changed himself because he never spent anywhere near long enough in our de-briefs. Twenty minutes, and he was off. He could also be very impatient, particularly with Honda, although I doubt he'd agree with me there.

'One thing, though – he always had great judgement on tyres. He invariably managed to select the best compounds, just by feel. He had brilliant car control, not in a rock-ape manner – he was too clever for that – and, again, like Reutemann, if Patrick and I had given him more personal attention, I think he would have liked that.'

Keke makes no bones about the fact that he loved his time as a Williams driver and still feels an enormous affection for Frank and his team. 'I had a tremendous time there and will always be very grateful for the break they gave me,' he insists. 'Not only the management, but the mechanics under Alan Challis were a very special bunch of people. Even now, I still feel more at home with Williams than I ever did at McLaren because that was Alain Prost's team and I never quite integrated with them in the same way I did with the guys at Didcot. At Williams, I knew everybody.'

Viewed from the touchlines, not all the Williams team driver selections during the early 1980s looked particularly astute. But such choices, made by any team, should be considered in the context of the circumstances prevailing at the time. For example, at the start of 1982, having successfully got Rosberg aboard as Reutemann's team-mate, when Carlos abruptly retired following the Brazilian Grand Prix, the range of available replacements was not particularly broad.

The driver chosen to fill the breach was genial Irishman Derek Daly. By no means short on confidence, he just wasn't quite quick enough, particularly during qualifying, added to which the bravado which Rosberg applied to the role of team leader was inevitably going to make the Williams number two role a particularly difficult challenge.

Did Frank believe, in retrospect, that he was a bit too cautious when it came to driver selection? 'Yes, on occasions, I do,' he admits. 'We chose Daly because we wanted to be conservative. But we should have been braver. The same applies to Jacques Laffite, second time around.'

Daly's contract was not renewed for 1983 and Laffite, then one of F1's most experienced campaigners, was signed on to partner Keke on a two-year arrangement. It wasn't the answer.

'There wasn't really anybody else available on the market of appropriate status,' muses Williams, 'and you have to remember that Jacques by then had won six Grands Prix for Ligier. But he was never quicker than the car. While Keke could lift a car to a level beyond its immediate potential, selecting Jacques was perhaps an error of judgement, with hindsight.' Frank reduced his retainer for the second year (1984) and Jacques meekly accepted, perhaps in tacit acknowledgement that he hadn't really delivered the goods.

However, at a time when professional racing drivers were generally becoming more ascetic personalities, Laffite's breezy informality made him tremendously popular on a personal level. Even when Frank wanted to be cross with him, he found it an extremely difficult task.

Sheridan Thynne remembers one incident which perfectly encapsulated Laffite's disarmingly sunny, outwardly innocent demeanour; 'During the Belgian Grand Prix at Spa in 1983, on the Thursday prior to the race, there was a meeting scheduled involving Frank, Patrick, the team's engineers, Goodyear technicians and the drivers. Four o'clock for four o'clock was everybody's strict deadline.

'No Jacques. Five past four, no Jacques. Ten past four, no Jacques. Quarter past four, no Jacques. Finally, at about twenty past four, Jacques was to be seen sauntering cheerfully across the paddock on the balls of his feet, looking relaxed, not ostentatiously hurrying, not looking as if he was going to say "Dammit, I'm late" . . .

'Frank saw him out of the motorhome window and said to the assembled company "I'm going to give him a bollocking" because a number of not-unimportant people, and even more people who thought they were important, had been sitting doing nothing for 20 minutes.

'Jacques breezily opened the motorhome door and said "Allo, everybody . . . this week I watched old films on the video to improve my English, so" – turning to Frank – "what's new pussycat?" And he gave him a kiss on the cheek. Everybody dissolved into laughter. He admitted afterwards that he realised he had to do something in order to defuse the situation. That was very typical of Jacques!'

Such endearingly light-hearted qualities certainly made Laffite a well-loved member of the team. But with the pace of F1 picking up dramatically in the mid-1980s, and particularly with the need to maximize the potential offered by the partnership with Honda, it was clear that the genial Frenchman would have to be dropped from the line-up at the end of 1984. It was around this time that Frank, by his own admission, 'kinda screwed things up' when an opportunity presented itself to recruit a young Brazilian rising star. His name was Ayrton Senna.

This ascetic, serious-minded young man had first crossed Frank's path during the summer of 1983 when he was fighting wheel-to-wheel with Martin Brundle for victory in the national British Formula 3 championship. Even at this stage of his career it was quite obvious that he had a remarkable talent and Williams invited him to have a try behind the wheel of an FW08C during a test session at Donington Park.

'I don't think I came back to the factory thinking I'd seen a revelation,' Frank confesses. 'But he was very quick indeed – like a second faster than our regular test driver Jonathan Palmer after only 15 laps. I knew we ought to keep an eye on him, but I didn't believe he was on today's agenda, so to speak.'

Senna signed for the Toleman team at the start of 1984, served a glittering F1 apprenticeship, and his name popped up again at the end of that season. Williams made him an offer but, on balance, the Brazilian preferred the look of the Lotus-Renault package for 1985 in preference to the fledgeling Williams-Honda. As a result, Frank turned his attention to Nigel Mansell.

Looking back over the Englishman's 16 career Grand Prix victories, it is sometimes easy to forget his perceived status within the F1 community at the end of 1984. Four-and-a-bit seasons with Team Lotus had earned the man from Birmingham a reputation as a determined trier who, more often than not, over-drove his machinery in his anxiety to achieve results. He could be a prickly customer to deal with and, many people believed, had a temperament intermittently fuelled by paranoia. All this masked the fact that he was blindingly, overwhelmingly, quick. Yet he was not the obvious choice for Williams, and Frank agrees that he was hardly overwhelmed by a sense of burning conviction when he finally got Mansell's signature on the bottom of a contract.

'Sure for 1984 we knew we would switch Jacques,' he recalls, 'and Ayrton was our original choice, but he went to Lotus as early as August.

Nigel was next on the list, but I have to confess that I was rather dickering around on the matter, blowing hot one day and cold the next. Eventually, at Zandvoort, Patrick said to me "For goodness sake Frank, make a decision and we'll live with it". So I went straight out of the motorhome and told Nige "Put it there".'

Mansell had his first test run in a Williams FW09B at Donington Park during the autumn of 1984. He arrived at Williams with something of a reputation as a moaner, always nit-picking and complaining about something with the car. But Frank never saw a trace of that from the outset of their relationship.

'Absolutely not,' he insists. 'If anything, it was the opposite. He had a very positive attitude to that first test run – sort of, "well, I know the FW09B isn't supposed to be the best car but, really, it seems a bit of all right to me".'

Inevitably, the rest of the F1 fraternity began to poke fun at Frank's decision, especially as, the day before Mansell's recruitment was made public, television screens all over the world had been filled with the image of the Englishman's Lotus 94T bogged down in a sand trap at Monza, spinning its rear wheels in a furious and futile effort to get underway again.

With some malicious glee, the end-of-season McLaren team party featured a 10-minute clip of all Nigel's incidents. It was a real case of 'oh Frank, what the hell have you done?'

Williams says: 'I well recall James Hunt, at that Ron Dennis World Championship celebration, making some really snide remarks about Mansell, but everybody tended to overlook all the very positive aspects about his driving capabilities.

'What we already knew was that he was exceptionally quick. On tight circuits, and in the rain, he was magic. That was pure car control, so there were a lot of obvious plus points to consider.

'To be honest, I though he would produce what I had expected from Alan Jones in 1978, that he would be a good number two, always in there at the end, always getting in or near the points. No way could I ever have been said to think "Wow, we've got a potential World Champion" but by the second half of 1985, I began to realise that we'd got something a bit special on our hands.'

For the 1985 season, Rosberg and Mansell were armed with the totally new Williams FW10, the first of Patrick Head's designs to be manufactured round a moulded carbon-fibre monocoque. It represented a quantum leap forward from the FW09, the track behaviour of which caused more than a passing degree of tension between Rosberg and Head during the course of the previous season. Mansell took some time to get into his stride, but once Honda uprated its V6 turbo engine to dramatic effect in the middle of the season, he started to fly.

However, Rosberg's avowed intention to leave Williams at the end of the year left Frank understandably anxious to sign up a replacement of similar calibre in good time. Mindful of the situation into which the team found itself squeezed at the end of 1981 when Jones sprang his decision to quit at Monza, Williams started to make overtures to Brabham team leader Nelson Piquet, knowing that the Brazilian was unhappy about the way in which negotiations with team chief Bernie Ecclestone were progressing with regard to his 1986 contract.

Piquet had won the World Championship for Brabham in 1981 and 1983 and had come to be regarded almost as a fixture within the team environment. He admitted that he felt comfortable in a team which had, effectively, been developed around him. Bernie knew that, and gambled that he would prefer to stay, while at the same time offering what Nelson believed was less than the going rate. It wasn't enough and so, in the car park at the Osterreichring, on the day prior to the Austrian Grand Prix, he did a deal to join Williams.

However, although Nelson was obviously widely perceived as de facto number one driver, by the time Mansell first climbed into the new Williams-Honda FW11 to start the 1986 season, he had successfully tucked his first two F1 victories under his belt. His first such success had been an emotional triumph in the 1985 Grand Prix of Europe at Brands Hatch, followed up by an even more commanding victory in the South African Grand Prix at Kyalami. Inadvertently, the seeds of discord for 1986 had been sown in the closing stages of the previous year, for Nigel could no longer be considered a dutiful number two driver, even less the push-over that Piquet had privately predicted to his friends he would be.

Nelson kicked off his Williams career on a high note, winning the Brazilian Grand Prix at Rio after Mansell had been helped off the road by Ayrton Senna mid-way round the opening lap, More seriously, though, Frank Williams would not be present at the pit wall during this potentially explosive season. A couple of weeks prior to the first race, he had been involved in the car crash which would so dramatically change his life for ever.

Mansell went on to win the Belgian Grand Prix at Spa after Nelson retired with engine trouble, then erupted into a spell of domination with commanding victories in the Canadian, French and British Grands Prix where he out-ran the Brazilian fair and square. By the middle of the season, Mansell was fast becoming Piquet's nemesis. 'I didn't join Williams to have my team-mate use the knowledge that I contributed in order to beat me,' he was to grumble increasingly.

Quite clearly, Piquet and Williams Grand Prix Engineering were at odds over the terms of the contract which had been entered into during the summer of 1985. It was to prove an area which would require considerable tact to keep under any semblance of control, reflecting just how difficult it is for a Grand Prix team to balance the conflicting egos of the individuals they employ to drive their cars.

Piquet, quite genuinely, believed that guaranteed unconditional number one status was implicit in the arrangement he had reached with Frank. Williams rejects this contention as nonsense. Mansell, meanwhile, was quite happy to make hay while the sun shone, dramatically enhancing his own reputation while making a very serious bid for the 1986 Drivers' World Championship.

Frank Williams recalls: 'What Nelson thought he was being guaranteed was a repeat of the Reutemann fiasco of 1981, when we controlled – or tried to control – the second driver. What in fact was discussed in the Osterreichring car park was that, in a classic case of one driver leading the championship and needing every bit of support, then we would obviously control his team-mate. But he was not given unconditional priority over the second driver. We took the view that they were both running for the Championship and would have to fight it out between them.'

What made this problem worse was that it was allowed to fester. Both drivers talked to their own private cliques, the rumours and gossip spread along the pit lane with osmotic relentlessness. Moreover, Piquet picked up on subtleties within the way Williams operated during 1986 which merely fuelled his conviction that he was somehow being discriminated against.

As an example of how a committed professional sportsman can get things wildly out of focus, Piquet found himself somehow irked that Patrick Head took over the engineering responsibilities for Mansell's car after the first couple of races. This was a perfectly innocent and logical change in staffing within the race team. Sergio Rinland, who had engineered Nigel's car at the start of the year, left the company and Patrick moved in to fill his position. This left aerodynamicist Frank Dernie tending to Nelson.

'Nelson took this very seriously indeed,' recalls Frank Williams. 'He felt that he was being short-changed. Maybe, with hindsight, we should have taken Frank Dernie off Nelson's car and switched them round. Either way, Nelson was upset about the way in which things had developed. He had made his deal with me and, quite properly, looked to me to take care of him and sort out any subsequent problems.

'In fairness to him, while he diligently came to see me in hospital after every race, he never complained about it until I was back at work. Then he came to the factory in August 1986 and I remember him sitting here, eyes moist, saying he was desperately concerned, feeling that he was not getting a fair crack of the whip, that Nigel was getting preferential treatment. I tried very hard to disabuse him of that notion.'

The problem, as Sheridan Thynne saw it, was that Nelson had some close friends who were saying quite openly to him that since they knew Nelson was obviously quicker than Nigel, if Nigel turned out to be quicker than him in any practice session, then it must be because Nigel was getting superior equipment.

'Whether they actually believed that notion, I don't know,' reflected Sheridan. 'But the fact remains that he did actually have put into his mind the idea that we were actually somehow favouring Mansell. But that would have been a clear breach of our contract, of commonsense and long established Williams practice.

'It was something of a shame that he didn't have a real friend who could assess the situation and say "Look, you're not being screwed by Williams, but you're clearly not happy about the situation, so why don't you arrange a meeting with Patrick Head on the Tuesday after a race and get it sorted out?" Unfortunately, no such friend seemed to exist and, in that respect, I don't believe he was well served by the people around him.'

Notwithstanding the personal problems that Piquet seemed to have found in his relationship with the Williams team, Patrick Head admits that he was impressed by the Brazilian's whole approach to the business of motor racing, seeing him as a self-contained individual with a well-organised set of priorities within his own mind. At the same time, he could also see the attraction of Mansell's flat-out-at-all-times philosophy.

He explained it thus: 'The fact of the matter is that with highly competitive racing drivers, you are dealing with proud, aggressive people. The sort of person who will push himself to the absolute limit in order to win a race is not the sort of person who is going to say "After you Claude; my team has told me to finish second, so that's what I'm going to do."

'They are not that type of person. There was never any conscious attempt to be anti-Piquet or overtly pro-Mansell. But when you got to a test and one driver goes round a given circuit for two days in the 1min 21sec bracket, then the other arrives and, on his third lap, does a 1min 19.9sec, slowly the team starts to think that this guy is more serious than the other.

'In Nelson's case, I never had any doubt about his ability; he knows exactly the level he's running at on 1min 21sec, he knows he can pull out another second if need be, but that's the level he's going to test at. He knows what the car is going to do when it goes a second quicker. He's a very up-together, very confident driver, confident in his own ability, and rightly so. That's the way he wants to test.

'But you get a bloke like Mansell, who only knows one speed, and you have a problem getting the mechanics not to sub-consciously fall in line with the guy who's always giving 100 per cent. Nelson doesn't really have an ego problem in terms of lap times at a test. He'll run all day with a full fuel load and not worry about absolute fast times, because he knows, when it comes to the race, when that green light comes on he'll be in good shape. He's doing his homework and knows that the race is the only thing that counts. He's a kid in some ways, off the track, but as far as racing is concerned, he knows that he's doing. In that respect he is very mature.'

At the end of 1986, Mansell's unfortunate and spectacular tyre failure in the Australian Grand Prix not only wiped out his chance of taking the Drivers' World Championship, but also effectively destroyed Nelson's as well. Suspecting that there might be a general tyre problem, Nelson was brought in for fresh rubber, thereby relinquishing the lead, and the title, to the McLaren-mounted Alain Prost. In the disappointment surrounding the failure of his title challenge, Nelson's annoyance with what he took to be the situation at Williams became aggravated.

The specific facts surrounding this unfortunate sequence of events have been attributed in some quarters to poor strategy on the part of the Williams team pit wall management. Yet detailed examination of the sequence of events leading up to Mansell's tyre failure revealed that Prost was extraordinarily fortunate to arrive in a position where he could emerge from the race with his second successive world crown.

One of the key elements of success in contemporary F1 racing is to make the best use of the tyres available and, to this end, the teams are in continual collaboration with their tyre suppliers throughout a Grand Prix weekend. In the case of the tyres being used on the Williams-Honda FW11s in Adelaide, Goodyear advised that a non-stop run would not be possible, so routine tyre stops were scheduled for both Mansell and Piquet during the course of the race.

However, while lapping Gerhard Berger's Benetton-BMW, Prost accidently bumped one of his McLaren's front wheels against the rear of the slower car, picked up a slow puncture as a result and, on lap 32 of the 82-lap race, came into the pits for a change.

The Goodyear technicians immediately examined the discarded tyres which had been removed from the McLaren and concluded that, on the basis of the apparent wear rate, a non-stop run would be quite feasible after all. This information was speedily communicated to Williams and assimilated by chief designer Patrick Head.

By lap 63, Piquet and Mansell were running second and third behind Keke Rosberg when the leading McLaren suddenly suffered a major rear tyre failure and stopped on the circuit. In situations like this there is an understandable tendency to fail safe. The apparent facts of the Rosberg situation were assessed as quickly as possible and Patrick Head was advising the Williams drivers over the radio link that they should prepare for precautionary tyre stops when Mansell's failure occurred. Bringing in Piquet immediately afterwards was simply prudent logic, even though it conspired to lose him the Drivers' Championship. Yet the stark fact was that this was preferable to risking possible injury, or worse.

Yet, when looking back over the 1986 season, Piquet rationalised things differently in his own mind. All he could see was a succession of failures to control his own team-mate in the manner he had expected when he entered into the contract. When the apparent trend continued in

1987, with Mansell still proving the man who set the pace, the final straw for Nelson came in the British Grand Prix at Silverstone where the Englishman drove an absolutely inspired race, making up over 25 seconds after an unscheduled tyre stop, to snatch the lead from him with just over two laps go with a heart-stopping manoeuvre going into Stowe corner. Anybody who saw Piquet's shell-shocked expression at the post-race press conference could read the signs that his relationship with the Williams team was well and truly over.

Within weeks, before the end of August 1987, Piquet had done a deal to drive a Lotus-Honda for the following season. He would finish the season with his third Drivers' World Championship, clinched in his favour when Mansell crashed his Williams-Honda FW11B during practice for the inaugural Japanese Grand Prix at Suzuka and injured his back. During this particular season, Mansell had again won six races, Piquet three.

In fact, Piquet had been feeling very much below par from a physical standpoint throughout the 1987 season. During qualifying for the San Marino Grand Prix at Imola his FW11B crashed heavily, almost certainly due to a tyre failure, and he sustained delayed concussion which was sufficiently serious for FISA Medical Delegate Professor Syd Watkins to forbid him to take part in the race.

He was back in the cockpit at Monaco, where he finished second to Senna's Lotus-Honda, but the after-effects lingered. Nelson, who could almost list sleeping as one of his hobbies, now found deep relaxation enormously difficult. Frank Dernie, his engineer through that season, stated his belief that the shunt took the edge off Nelson's ability. Two years later, after a similarly large pre-season testing shunt at Rio with the Williams-Renault FW12C, Thierry Boutsen would also feel physically off the boil for several races.

'I think he was struggling a bit from the physical viewpoint in the next few races,' says Dernie. 'Clearly, he was not ultra-fit. But he won the 1987 World Championship by driving with his brains.' Yet Nelson retained his belief in and commitment towards test and development work, delighting in honing a performance advantage which would offer him a leg-up even before he went out on to the starting grid.

The Williams active-ride suspension system offered him one such advantage. Although Patrick Head believes he could quite well have won the 1987 Italian Grand Prix at Monza with a regular 'passive' suspension system on the FW11B, in Nelson's mind the advantage of the system had been confirmed in a pre-race test at Imola. There he completed a race distance in a 'reactive' car almost a minute inside Mansell's San Marino Grand Prix winning time. He went to the grid at Monza with a smile on his face.

The Piquet/Mansell relationship had developed into an unhappy situation which put into sharp perspective the problems involved in balancing contrasting driver temperaments. More than that, it also emphasised the challenge facing every top team which seeks to employ two potential winning drivers.

One can significantly reduce the problem by employing a number two driver who is demonstrably not in the same class as the number one and, ironically, when Nigel Mansell agreed to return to Williams for 1991 after a two season sojourn with Ferrari, it was under precisely such terms that he did so. His absolute number one status was complemented by the presence of Riccardo Patrese as the team's second driver.

It would also be foolish to underestimate the problems faced by any team willingly entering a Piquet/Mansell situation. After the Jones/Reutemann fiasco of 1981, it seemed scarcely possible that tensions could rise any higher between team-mates, yet they did at Williams during 1986 and 1987. Yet even this would be small beer compared with the venomous acrimony that accompanied Ron Dennis's attempts to pair Ayrton Senna and Alain Prost in the McLaren line-up in 1988 and 1989. Top racing drivers, like any professional sportsmen of excellence, have such towering self-confidence that it is always likely to get out of control.

Of course, Sheridan Thynne rightly points out, any number one driver at Williams has his position protected by only two things; his guaranteed access to the spare car, and his own driving ability. The Piquet contract went back and forth between lawyers acting for Williams and the Brazilian before it was signed in 1985, with both parties apparently understanding its terms. Only later did the problems begin on Nelson's side.

Since that time Sheridan has become largely responsible for the detail drafting of Williams driver contracts, the format of which, once established, has changed very little. Outsiders believe that F1 driver contracts are incredibly complex documents, but the fact of the matter is that they are somewhat more straightforward than generally imagined.

The contracts basically set out the driver's obligations to the team from the driving, testing and promotional standpoint, the team's financial commitment to the driver, including taxation considerations, and the insurance aspect. Once a driver has agreed a contract with Williams, he is guaranteed his money even if he were to be killed during the course of the year. That stark, however remote, possibility is covered by the provision of an insurance policy, the cost of which is born jointly by the team and driver. It is a matter of some quiet satisfaction to the team that neither Williams Grand Prix Engineering nor any of its drivers has ever felt the need to go to law to resolve any arguments arising from the contact between them.

During the course of 1986, Mansell would also be wooed by Ferrari, and the Englishman briefly found himself entangled in an agreement for 1987 from which he later withdrew, signing a further two-year agreement with Frank for 1987 and 1988. Yet Nigel was burdened with what

Sheridan regards as 'an over-romantic view' of the Italian team and clearly believed a stint at Maranello was something 'one had to do ' as a self-respecting F1 driver at some time in one's career.

For 1989, the opportunity again presented itself for Mansell to switch to Ferrari. At this point the Englishman, fed up after half a season spent struggling with the Judd-engined Williams FW12 after the team lost its supply of Honda turbo engines at the end of 1987, was only too happy to make the switch.

Frank Williams has no hesitation in describing Nigel as a great racing driver.

'By the end of his time with us in 1988, he had also developed to the point where he was much better equipped from a personal viewpoint to handle the disappointments which inevitably crop up from time to time in this business,' Frank explains.

'Considering that he had signed with us for 1987 and 1988 sincerely believing that he had two years of Honda engines ahead of him, he was obviously thoroughly brassed off, but his contract did not say that, in the event of not having Honda engines, he could go. The point was that he didn't even try to go. He was vocal in his disappointment about the way in which the Judd engine performed, and the reactive suspension system, but then it was a bad year for all of us.'

Throughout the 1988 season, Mansell had been partnered by Riccardo Patrese and the willing Italian stayed on for the following two years when he was joined by Belgian driver Thierry Boutsen. Stylish and smooth, Boutsen just wasn't quite out of the top drawer in terms of speed, yet his victories with the Renault-engined car in the rain-soaked 1989 Canadian and Australian Grands Prix were masterly demonstrations of a delicate and sure-footed touch.

In 1990, Williams would go on to win two more Grands Prix. Riccardo triumphed in the San Marino race at Imola and Thierry never put a wheel wrong to hold Ayrton Senna's McLaren-Honda back in second place during the Hungarian event at Budapest. Yet somehow the relationship between the Williams team and the Belgian driver never quite gelled. However unconsciously, the feeling at Didcot that Thierry wasn't quite up to the front-running mark communicated itself to the driver who began to feel unloved and unwanted during the first half of 1990.

Grand Prix racing is a brutally competitive business and if Williams was to do justice to its potential winning status in its third season in partnership with Renault, it had become quite clear that one of the established and active 'top three' drivers of the decade had somehow to be recruited. During the summers of 1989 and 1990, Frank Williams therefore made approaches to, as well as other lesser lights, Alain Prost, Ayrton Senna and Nigel Mansell.

Serious contact with Prost was established shortly after the controversial 1989 San Marino Grand Prix at Imola where, in the Frenchman's view, Senna had reneged on a 'no passing' agreement going into the first corner. When this was added to the tension that had built up between the two men at McLaren in 1988, it was easy to see that Alain was getting very disenchanted with his lot. At Monaco, Frank asked if they could talk seriously about a contract for 1990. Alain agreed.

'Negotiations ran step by step,' explains Williams, 'first in general terms, later getting down to more specific matters. He came to Didcot after the 1989 British Grand Prix and spent three hours talking with Patrick Head and me in the conference centre.'

Frank felt that negotiations looked promising, although Patrick had some private reservations. He had no doubts as to Prost's qualities as a driver, but wondered about his mental state. 'He seemed consumed by his dislike for Senna in a way that rather took me aback,' says Head. 'It was as if he couldn't talk about anything else.'

However, come the German Grand Prix and Marlboro really brought out the big guns. If Prost wasn't going to drive for McLaren, then they wanted him to switch to Ferrari. A lot of pressure was clearly applied, inducements offered. Frank suddenly found him difficult to reach by telephone. It always seemed a case of 'We'll talk next week . . .'

'To be honest, I think Alain strung us out a bit unfairly,' says Frank. 'It wasn't until the Monday before the Italian Grand Prix that he told me he was going to Ferrari. We'd been out-manoeuvred. In retrospect, we should have gone straight back into the market with a bigger offer. But he'd been a personally sponsored Marlboro driver for many years, and had the prospect of retaining that link even after he retires from the cockpit. I'm sure that was a factor.'

As far as Senna was concerned, Williams had got into the habit of chatting socially to him on the telephone ever since 1984. The opportunity for Ayrton to join the team in 1988 had even been discussed, but the Brazilian was wary about the chief's personal lack of mobility.

Frank says 'When he was here in 1987 discussing the possibility of joining us, he eventually admitted that one of the reasons he decided against us was that he wanted a team boss rushing about overseeing everything like the good old days. For certain those sort of words reflected the Honda view, but we had a board meeting and decided we were prepared to invest the sort of money he wanted. He took the offer seriously, but McLaren were ahead.'

By the middle of 1990, the Williams management was still trying to meet the pressing need to sign up an absolute front-line superstar. Initially, they decided to sign French rising star Jean Alesi who had demonstrated such promising form driving for the Tyrrell team, getting the Frenchman's signature on a conditional contract very early in the year. Moreover, US Indy racing star Al Unser Junior firmly believed his name to be on Frank's shopping list, notwithstanding his lack of F1 experience. Matters began to get confused.

Tantalisingly, the prospect of finally signing Ayrton Senna for 1991 also arose to complicate the situation further. The Brazilian's three-year deal with McLaren was nearing its end and, shrewdly, he was keen to examine every option.

'When we talked this time round, my lack of mobility wasn't a problem with him,' Frank noted, 'because he'd had a couple of years seeing me round the place, knowing that I was in touch with what was going on. I think he had a better appreciation of our management structure.'

Senna's negotiations for an extension of his McLaren contract appeared deadlocked, and he talked to Frank with an apparently increasing intensity and commitment, even though some observers believed that he was doing nothing more than using Williams GPF as a bargaining counter in his dialogue with Ron Dennis. There was also the possibility that Nigel Mansell, by now disenchanted with Ferrari, would come back into the fold.

The complexities of these closely enmeshed dealings, and the inevitable egos of the drivers concerned, conspired to lay a diplomatic minefield in the path of the Williams management during the height of these dealings. Alesi took umbrage when word got out that Frank was also talking to Senna.

At the end of August, a fortnight after Thierry Boutsen had notched up a faultless flag-to-flag victory for Williams-Renault in the Hungarian Grand Prix, beating Senna by less than a second, Ayrton finally announced he would be staying with McLaren for 1991. Mansell, meanwhile had announced that he would retire from racing at the end of the 1990 season after his Ferrari retired with mechanical problems when he had been dominating the British Grand Prix at Silverstone.

Yet Frank suspected that 'Nigel may have made an emotional judgement after Silverstone.' The two men talked again at the Belgian Grand Prix. But the chat was more about aeroplanes than motor racing.

Williams could offer the one thing Nigel craved – absolute, exclusive number one status in a top Grand Prix team. Riccardo Patrese, delighted winner of the 1990 San Marino Grand Prix, was happy to continue in the number two role alongside the English star.

On the evening of the Spanish Grand Prix at Jerez, Sheridan Thynne flew to Nigel Mansell's home on the Isle of Man in Mansell's Learjet. By lunchtime, a formal statement was issued to the press. For 1991, Nigel was returning to the team for which he had won 13 Grand Prix victories.

He had finally put away his own personal uncertainties after a few months wracked by confusion. Williams had offered him the dream deal he had always craved – the number one status and, more crucially, a technical package which just might enable him to nail down that elusive World Championship title.

In his first test for Williams in Portugal at the end of the season, the team members present were suddenly reminded of that minuscule difference between a fine driver and a front-line ace. Mansell's presence took the team's whole operation up one gear. He requested minuscule changes to the cockpit set-up, to the adjustment of the brake pedal. He carried the team with him, suffusing them with optimism and confidence. On his 22nd lap, he took the Williams-Renault round Estoril on control tyres faster than it had ever been done before.

Whatever lay ahead, in that one day he had rekindled a spark within the team that, whether consciously or not, had been missing for the past two seasons.

The new Williams-Renault FW14, powered by the significantly revised Renault RS3 67-degree V10 cylinder engine, was finally readied for preliminary testing just over a fortnight before the first race of the 1991 season. The venue for this first run was the newly established South Circuit at Silverstone, created as part of the massive rebuilding programme carried out over the winter of 1990/91. Despite the weather being inhospitably wet, chilly and depressing, the media interest attaching to Nigel Mansell's first sortie in the new car was understandably enormous.

The car, equipped from the outset with the Williams team's own electro-hydraulic change mechanism activating its six-speed transverse gearbox, looked attractive enough to the casual eye. Inevitably, though, the proof of the pudding would be in the eating, namely the first round of the title chase which took place through the streets of Phoenix, Arizona, on March 10.

Mansell appreciated how much engineering effort and attention to detail had been expended on the new car, both by the Williams design team under Patrick Head and Adrian Newey, and Renault Sport with the new engine, and was suitably optimistic.

'We have one heck of a good chance of winning the world championship in 1991,' he affirmed before the first race. 'I have more zest than ever before. I have done my apprenticeship and I've had my share of the heartache. Now I want to win the championship. I have to compliment Frank Williams, Sheridan Thynne and Patrick Head and the team's sponsors for the fantastic job they have done in convincing me that we have a real prospect of winning the title this year.'

At Phoenix, the Williams FW14s proved strong from the outset, Riccardo Patrese and Nigel Mansell qualifying third and fourth behind the new McLaren MP4/6 of reigning world champion Ayrton Senna and Alain Prost's Ferrari 642. Nigel ran third in the opening stages of the race, troubled only by a slightly soft brake pedal movement. Riccardo fell in close behind and, on lap 21, tried to outbrake his team-mate only to take a time-consuming trip up an escape road and drop back to sixth.

Nigel was still lying third on lap 25 when a gearbox malfunction led to his retirement. 'My problem began about 10 laps before the gearchange broke,' he reported. 'It started to miss gears and then packed up. It's obviously very disappointing, but what we have achieved today is pretty encouraging.'

A similar problem befell Patrese who lasted a further 15 laps, by which time he was in second place after Prost dropped back following a slow routine tyre stop. The gearchange abruptly selected second, spinning him to a halt broadside across the circuit, whence he was hit by Roberto Moreno's Benetton. Both drivers escaped unhurt and the new Williams sustained only superficial damage from the impact.

The second round of the championship battle took place at São Paulo's Interlagos circuit, effectively Ayrton Senna's backyard. But although the Brazilian finished the race day celebrating victory for the first time on home soil, the talk of the paddock was of Mansell's superb challenge for victory which only ended with more gearchange problems after 59 of the race's 70 laps.

The root of the problems at Phoenix had been identified as being associated with the change from fifth to sixth gear, so for the Brazilian race the FW14s ran with five speeds only, Riccardo and Nigel qualified second and third on the grid, and while Senna led from the start, Mansell immediately took up second place in his wake. By lap nine, Ayrton was 2.8s ahead, but then the gap began to diminish. However, by lap 20, having rattled off a succession of very quick consecutive laps, Mansell had closed to within a second of the leading McLaren which was now very definitely under pressure from his challenge.

At the end of lap 25, Nigel came in for fresh tyres. The mechanics performed a slick change, but the Williams proved reluctant to select first gear. Mansell was stationary for an agonising 14.59s. On the next lap Senna capitalised on his unexpectedly extended advantage by making a quick 6.93s stop, so as the chase settled down again the gap separating the two cars was 7.6s. Had Mansell's stop been of similar duration, he would almost certainly have squeezed ahead of Senna after the McLaren's stop for tyres.

With Senna now troubled by gearbox problems of his own, Mansell again scythed into his advantage, closing to within 4s when, on lap 50, a cut tyre sent him back into the pits for fresh rubber. But still he didn't give up, slashing a 34.2s deficit back to just over 20s before the FW14's electro-hydraulic gearchange selected second instead of fourth and he pirouetted to a halt in a plume of tyre smoke.

Nigel tried to rejoin, but the gearbox was now apparently jammed in first, so there was no choice but to abandon the FW14 and walk back to the pits, leaving Patrese to chase the troubled Senna home to the finish, failing by just over 2s to catch the ailing McLaren.

Five weeks now ensued before the championship battle resumed for the main rump of the European season; five weeks in which to mould and channel the undisguised potential demonstrated by the Williams FW14 in those first two races. It had been a promising start, certainly, but a lot of work remained to be done if Williams was to sustain the world championship challenge it so clearly offered.

Disappointingly, the San Marino Grand Prix at Imola produced two more retirements, but there was a positive indication of further progress as Riccardo Patrese, who had qualified second on the front row, went ahead from the start on a soaking track surface to become the first driver apart from Senna to lead a 1991 World Championship Grand Prix. He later retired with electrical problems and Nigel's frustrations were further compounded with another non-finish when he spun into retirement with a broken wheel rim and punctured tyre after receiving a nudge from Martin Brundle's Brabham-Yamaha as they completed the opening lap of the race.

Monaco was next on the agenda. Superficially, Nigel had a difficult time in qualifying and Riccardo outqualified the Englishman. Nigel did not feel confident with the chassis set-up of the car during qualifying, but a morale-boosting run to second place in the race, after a hard fight, at last got his Championship points tally off the ground.

Finally, in the fifth round of the Championship at Montreal, all the elusive technical and human elements came together to confirm that those early hopes for the Williams-Renault FW14 had not been misplaced. Although Riccardo started from pole position, Nigel was alongside him on the front row and took the lead from the start. He controlled the race superbly all the way until the last lap. Just as the official at the finish line was preparing to unfurl the chequered flag, his Williams rolled to a halt on the exit of the hairpin, barely half a mile from victory.

The instant assumption was that Mansell had run out of fuel, but this was not the case. Inadvertently, he had allowed the engine revs to drop too low when the electro-hydraulic gearbox baulked between ratios at the hairpin. As the engine died, there was insufficient electrical charge to activate the hydraulic system to engage the next gear.

A fortnight later Riccardo stormed to the team's first victory of the year in the Mexican Grand Prix, beating his team-mate by just over a second after a mysterious loss of power in the middle of the race cost Mansell a lot of time. Six rounds of the Championship battle had been completed and, although Williams clearly had Senna and McLaren on the run, the Brazilian's sequence of four successive victories at the beginning of the year left him with a commanding advantage.

Going into the French Grand Prix at the new Magny-Cours circuit, Senna had 44 points with Patrese second on 20, Mansell's old team-mate Nelson Piquet third on 16, with Nigel himself fourth on 13. It looked a long shot, but then everything clicked and Mansell surged to three consecutive victories at Magny-Cours, Silverstone and Hockenheim.

The McLaren bandwagon had by this time not only lost its early season momentum, but virtually ground to a halt. In fact, that was precisely what happened to Senna in the British and German races. Comprehensively outclassed by the Williams, he suffered the indignation of running out of fuel on the last lap in both events.

With eight races gone Williams had edged ahead of McLaren to take the lead of the Constructors' Championship by a single point while Mansell had Senna firmly in his sights in the battle for the drivers' title, the Englishman now only eight points adrift. Then Senna bounced back to beat Nigel in Hungary and score a lucky victory at Spa when Mansell, again dominating the race, fell victim to an electrical malfunction while comfortably in command.

In the complex game of Grand Prix snakes and ladders, Nigel was almost back where he started, going into the Italian Grand Prix 22 points adrift of Senna. A brilliant win at Monza was compromised by Ayrton Senna finishing runner-up, so Nigel only hauled back four points – the difference between first (10) and second (6) – as the Championship battle went into its final phase.

Then came the most bitter blow of the season, possibly of Nigel Mansell's entire career. While dominating the Portuguese Grand Prix at Estoril, the Williams pit crew fumbled a crucial tyre stop. Owing to a misunderstanding, Mansell was waved back into the fray before the wheel securing nut was in place. Under maximum acceleration, wheel and Williams parted company and Nigel was left stranded in the pit lane on three wheels. In the panic that followed, the wheel was re-attached in the acceleration lane of the pits, a point where work on the car is strictly forbidden. Although Mansell resumed, the stewards convened a meeting and he was black flagged 20 laps later after a dynamic charge through from 17th to sixth position.

From the viewpoint of Mansell's continued stake in the World Championship battle, Riccardo Patrese's victory over Ayrton Senna at least meant that the McLaren driver was seven points short of being absolutely certain about the title with three races still left to run. Now Nigel faced the task of steering the Williams FW14 to victory in the last three races on the calendar and at Barcelona, the following weekend, he cleared the first of these three hurdles by achieving a superbly judged win in the first Spanish Grand Prix to be held at the new Circuit de Catalunya.

Riccardo stormed home in third place behind Alain Prost's Ferrari with Senna trailing home a subdued fifth, having made an incorrect tyre choice and paid for it with an uncharacteristic spin. Thus not only had Mansell ensured that the battle for the drivers' title would continue at least to the penultimate race of the year, but Williams had again moved ahead of McLaren by a single point in the battle for the equally prestigious Constructors' Championship.

APPENDIX 1
Race results 1969-1991

The accompanying results table includes all the Formula 1 race results achieved by Williams-entered Grand Prix cars from Piers Courage's debut at the wheel of the ex-works Brabham in the 1969 Race of Champions through to the second round of the 1991 season.

Key to abbreviations: Rtd – retired; DNS – did not start; NC – non classified; DNQ – did not qualify; NS – non starter.

1969

16 March	Race of Champions, Brands Hatch		
	Piers Courage	Brabham-Cosworth BT26	Rtd
30 April	International Trophy, Silverstone		
	Piers Courage	Brabham-Cosworth BT26	5th
5 May	SPANISH GRAND PRIX, Montjuich Park, Barcelona		
	Piers Courage	Brabham-Cosworth BT26	Rtd
18 May	MONACO GRAND PRIX, Monte Carlo		
	Piers Courage	Brabham-Cosworth BT26	2nd
21 June	DUTCH GRAND PRIX, Zandvoort		
	Piers Courage	Brabham-Cosworth BT26	Rtd
6 July	FRENCH GRAND PRIX, Clermont-Ferrand		
	Piers Courage	Brabham-Cosworth BT26	Rtd
19 July	BRITISH GRAND PRIX, Silverstone		
	Piers Courage	Brabham-Cosworth BT26	5th
3 Aug	GERMAN GRAND PRIX, Hockenheim		
	Piers Courage	Brabham-Cosworth BT26	Rtd
7 Sept	ITALIAN GRAND PRIX, Monza		
	Piers Courage	Brabham-Cosworth BT26	5th

20 Sept	CANADIAN GRAND PRIX, Mosport Park, nr Toronto		
	Piers Courage	Brabham-Cosworth BT26	Rtd
5 Oct	UNITED STATES GRAND PRIX, Watkins Glen, NY		
	Piers Courage	Brabham-Cosworth BT26	2nd
19 Oct	MEXICAN GRAND PRIX, Mexico City		
	Piers Courage	Brabham-Cosworth BT26	10th

1970

7 March	SOUTH AFRICAN GRAND PRIX, Kyalami, nr Johannesburg		
	Piers Courage	de Tomaso-Cosworth 505	Rtd
19 April	SPANISH GRAND PRIX, Jarama, nr Madrid		
	Piers Courage	de Tomaso-Cosworth 505	DNS
26 April	International Trophy, Silverstone		
	Piers Courage	de Tomaso-Cosworth 505	3rd
10 May	MONACO GRAND PRIX, Monte Carlo		
	Piers Courage	de Tomaso-Cosworth 505	NC
7 June	BELGIAN GRAND PRIX, Spa-Francorchamps, nr Malmedy		
	Piers Courage	de Tomaso-Cosworth 505	Rtd
21 June	DUTCH GRAND PRIX, Zandvoort		
	Piers Courage	de Tomaso-Cosworth 505	fatal acci- dent
19 July	BRITISH GRAND PRIX, Brands Hatch		
	Brian Redman	de Tomaso-Cosworth 505	NS
2 Aug	GERMAN GRAND PRIX, Hockenheim, nr Heidelberg		
	Brian Redman	de Tomaso-Cosworth 505	DNQ
16 Aug	AUSTRIAN GRAND PRIX, Osterreichring, nr Knittelfeld		
	Tim Schenken	de Tomaso-Cosworth 505	Rtd
6 Sept	ITALIAN GRAND PRIX, Monza		
	Tim Schenken	de Tomaso-Cosworth 505	Rtd
20 Sept	CANADIAN GRAND PRIX, St. Jovite, nr Montreal		
	Tim Schenken	de Tomaso-Cosworth 505	NC
4 Oct	UNITED STATES GRAND PRIX, Watkins Glen, NY		
	Tim Schenken	de Tomaso-Cosworth 505	Rtd

1971

24 Jan	Argentine Grand Prix, Buenos Aires		
	Henri Pescarolo	March-Cosworth 701	2nd
6 March	SOUTH AFRICAN GRAND PRIX, Kyalami, nr Johannesburg		
	Henri Pescarolo	March-Cosworth 701	11th
21 March	Race of Champions, Brands Hatch		
	Ronnie Peterson	March-Cosworth 711	Rtd
	Ray Allen	March-Cosworth 701	6th
28 March	Questor Grand Prix, Ontario Motor Speedway, California		
	Henri Pescarolo	March-Cosworth 711	20th
	Derek Bell	March-Cosworth 701	15th
9 April	International Trophy, Oulton Park, Cheshire		
	Cyd Williams	March-Cosworth 701	DNS
18 April	SPANISH GRAND PRIX, Montjuich Park, Barcelona		
	Henri Pescarolo	March-Cosworth 711	Rtd
23 May	MONACO GRAND PRIX, Monte Carlo		
	Henri Pescarolo	March-Cosworth 711	8th
13 June	Rindt Memorial Trophy, Hockenheim, nr Heidelberg		
	Ray Allen	March-Cosworth 701	Rtd
20 June	DUTCH GRAND PRIX, Zandvoort		
	Henri Pescarolo	March-Cosworth 711	13th
4 July	FRENCH GRAND PRIX, Circuit Paul Ricard, nr Bandol		
	Henri Pescarolo	March-Cosworth 711	Rtd
17 July	BRITISH GRAND PRIX, Silverstone		
	Henri Pescarolo	March-Cosworth 711	4th
1 Aug	GERMAN GRAND PRIX, Nürburgring		
	Henri Pescarolo	March-Cosworth 711	Rtd
15 Aug	AUSTRIAN GRAND PRIX, Osterreichring, nr Knittelfeld		
	Henri Pescarolo	March-Cosworth 711	6th
21 Aug	Gold Cup, Oulton Park, Cheshire		
	Henri Pescarolo	March-Cosworth 711	Rtd
5 Sept	ITALIAN GRAND PRIX, Monza		
	Henri Pescarolo	March-Cosworth 711	Rtd
19 Sept	CANADIAN GRAND PRIX, Mosport Park, nr Toronto		
	Henri Pescarolo	March-Cosworth 711	DNS

3 Oct	UNITED STATES GRAND PRIX, Watkins Glen, NY		
	Henri Pescarolo	March-Cosworth 711	Rtd
24 Oct	Victory Race, Brands Hatch		
	Henri Pescarolo	March-Cosworth 711	Rtd

1972

23 Jan	ARGENTINE GRAND PRIX, Buenos Aires		
	Henri Pescarolo	March-Cosworth 721	8th
4 March	SOUTH AFRICAN GRAND PRIX, Kyalami, nr Johannesburg		
	Henri Pescarolo	March-Cosworth 721	11th
	Carlos Pace	March-Cosworth 711	17th
30 March	Brazilian Grand Prix, Interlagos, São Paulo		
	Henri Pescarolo	March-Cosworth 721	Rtd
	Carlos Pace	March-Cosworth 711	Rtd
23 April	International Trophy, Silverstone		
	Henri Pescarolo	March-Cosworth 721	Rtd
1 May	SPANISH GRAND PRIX, Jarama nr Madrid		
	Henri Pescarolo	March-Cosworth 721	11th
	Carlos Pace	March-Cosworth 711	6th
14 May	MONACO GRAND PRIX, Monte Carlo		
	Henri Pescarolo	March-Cosworth 721	Rtd
	Carlos Pace	March-Cosworth 711	17th
4 June	BELGIAN GRAND PRIX, Nivelles, nr Brussels		
	Henri Pescarolo	March-Cosworth 721	NC
	Carlos Pace	March-Cosworth 711	5th
18 June	Republica Grand Prix, Vallelunga, nr Rome		
	Henri Pescarolo	March-Cosworth 711	Rtd
2 July	FRENCH GRAND PRIX, Clermont-Ferrand		
	Henri Pescarolo	March-Cosworth 721	DNS
	Carlos Pace	March-Cosworth 711	Rtd
15 July	BRITISH GRAND PRIX, Brands Hatch		
	Henri Pescarolo	Politoys-Cosworth FX3	Rtd
	Carlos Pace	March-Cosworth 711	Rtd
30 July	GERMAN GRAND PRIX, Nürburgring		
	Henri Pescarolo	March-Cosworth 721	Rtd
	Carlos Pace	March-Cosworth 711	NC

13 Aug	AUSTRIAN GRAND PRIX, Osterreichring nr Knittelfeld		
	Henri Pescarolo	March-Cosworth 721	DNS
	Carlos Pace	March-Cosworth 711	NC
28 Aug	Rothmans 50,000 Formule Libre race, Brands Hatch		
	Henri Pescarolo	March-Cosworth 721	3rd
10 Sept	ITALIAN GRAND PRIX, Monza		
	Henri Pescarolo	March-Cosworth 721	Rtd
	Carlos Pace	March-Cosworth 711	Rtd
24 Sept	CANADIAN GRAND PRIX, Mosport Park, nr Toronto		
	Henri Pescarolo	March-Cosworth 721	13th
	Carlos Pace	March-Cosworth 711	9th
8 Oct	UNITED STATES GRAND PRIX, Watkins Glen, NY		
	Henri Pescarolo	March-Cosworth 721	14th
	Carlos Pace	March-Cosworth 711	Rtd
22 Oct	Challenge Trophy race, Brands Hatch		
	Henri Pescarolo	March-Cosworth 721	Rtd
	Chris Amon	Politoys-Cosworth FX3	DNS

1973

28 Jan	ARGENTINE GRAND PRIX, Buenos Aires		
	Howden Ganley	Iso-Marlboro-Cosworth FX3	NC
	Giovanni Galli	Iso-Marlboro-Cosworth FX3	Rtd
11 Feb	BRAZILIAN GRAND PRIX, Interlagos, São Paulo		
	Howden Ganley	Iso-Marlboro-Cosworth FX3B	7th
	Giovanni Galli	Iso-Marlboro-Cosworth FX3B	9th
3 March	SOUTH AFRICAN GRAND PRIX, Kyalami, nr Johannesburg		
	Howden Ganley	Iso-Marlboro-Cosworth FX3B	10th
	Jackie Pretorius	Iso-Marlboro-Cosworth FX3B	Rtd
18 March	Race of Champions, Brands Hatch		
	Howden Ganley	Iso-Marlboro-Cosworth FX3B	Rtd
	Tony Trimmer	Iso-Marlboro-Cosworth FX3B	4th

7 April	International Trophy, Silverstone		
	Howden Ganley	Iso-Marlboro-Cosworth FX3B	Rtd
29 April	SPANISH GRAND PRIX, Montjuich, Barcelona		
	Howden Ganley	Iso-Marlboro-Cosworth IR	Rtd
	Giovanni Galli	Iso-Marlboro-Cosworth IR	11th
20 May	BELGIAN GRAND PRIX, Zolder, nr Hasselt		
	Howden Ganley	Iso-Marlboro-Cosworth IR	Rtd
	Giovanni Galli	Iso-Marlboro-Cosworth IR	Rtd
3 June	MONACO GRAND PRIX, Monte Carlo		
	Howden Ganley	Iso-Marlboro-Cosworth IR	Rtd
	Giovanni Galli	Iso-Marlboro-Cosworth IR	Rtd
17 June	SWEDISH GRAND PRIX, Anderstorp		
	Howden Ganley	Iso-Marlboro-Cosworth IR	11th
	Tom Belso	Iso-Marlboro-Cosworth IR	DNS
July 1	FRENCH GRAND PRIX, Circuit Paul Ricard, nr Bandol		
	Howden Ganley	Iso-Marlboro-Cosworth IR	14th
	Henri Pescarolo	Iso-Marlboro-Cosworth IR	Rtd
14 July	BRITISH GRAND PRIX, Silverstone		
	Howden Ganley	Iso-Marlboro-Cosworth IR	9th
	Graham McRae	Iso-Marlboro-Cosworth IR	Rtd
29 July	DUTCH GRAND PRIX, Zandvoort		
	Howden Ganley	Iso-Marlboro-Cosworth IR	9th
	Gijs van Lennep	Iso-Marlboro-Cosworth IR	6th
5 Aug	GERMAN GRAND PRIX, Nürburgring		
	Howden Ganley	Iso-Marlboro-Cosworth IR	DNS
	Henri Pescarolo	Iso-Marlboro-Cosworth IR	10th
19 Aug	AUSTRIAN GRAND PRIX, Osterreichring, nr Knittelfeld		
	Howden Ganley	Iso-Marlboro-Cosworth IR	NC
	Gijs van Lennep	Iso-Marlboro-Cosworth IR	9th
9 Sept	ITALIAN GRAND PRIX, Monza		
	Howden Ganley	Iso-Marlboro-Cosworth IR	NC
	Gijs van Lennep	Iso-Marlboro-Cosworth IR	6th
23 Sept	CANADIAN GRAND PRIX, Mosport Park, nr Toronto		
	Howden Ganley	Iso-Marlboro-Cosworth IR	6th
	Tim Schenken	Iso-Marlboro-Cosworth IR	14th

7 Oct	UNITED STATES GRAND PRIX, Watkins Glen NY		
	Howden Ganley	Iso-Marlboro-Cosworth IR	12th
	Jacky Ickx	Iso-Marlboro-Cosworth IR	7th

1974

13 Jan	ARGENTINE GRAND PRIX, Buenos Aires		
	Arturo Merzario	Iso-Marlboro-Cosworth FW	Rtd
27 Jan	BRAZILIAN GRAND PRIX, Interlagos, São Paulo		
	Arturo Merzario	Iso-Marlboro-Cosworth FW	Rtd
3 Feb	Presidente Medici GP, Brasilia, Brazil		
	Arturo Merzario	Iso-Marlboro-Cosworth FW	3rd
30 Mar	SOUTH AFRICAN GRAND PRIX, Kyalami, nr Johannesburg		
	Arturo Merzario	Iso-Marlboro-Cosworth FW	6th
	Tom Belso	Iso-Marlboro-Cosworth FW	Rtd
28 April	SPANISH GRAND PRIX, Jarama, nr Madrid		
	Arturo Merzario	Iso-Marlboro-Cosworth FW	Rtd
	Tom Belso	Iso-Marlboro-Cosworth FW	DNQ
12 May	BELGIAN GRAND PRIX, Nivelles, nr Brussels		
	Arturo Merzario	Iso-Marlboro-Cosworth FW	Rtd
	Gijs van Lennep	Iso-Marlboro-Cosworth FW	14th
26 May	MONACO GRAND PRIX, Monte Carlo		
	Arturo Merzario	Iso-Marlboro-Cosworth FW	Rtd
9 June	SWEDISH GRAND PRIX, Anderstorp		
	Tom Belso	Iso-Marlboro-Cosworth FW	8th
	Richard Robarts	Iso-Marlboro-Cosworth FW	DNS
23 June	DUTCH GRAND PRIX, Zandvoort		
	Arturo Merzario	Iso-Marlboro-Cosworth FW	Rtd
	Gijs van Lennep	Iso-Marlboro-Cosworth FW	DNQ
7 July	FRENCH GRAND PRIX, Dijon-Prenois		
	Arturo Merzario	Iso-Marlboro-Cosworth FW	9th
	Jean-Pierre Jabouille	Iso-Marlboro-Cosworth FW	DNQ
20 July	BRITISH GRAND PRIX, Brands Hatch		
	Arturo Merzario	Iso-Marlboro-Cosworth FW	Rtd
	Tom Belso	Iso-Marlboro-Cosworth FW	DNQ
4 Aug	GERMAN GRAND PRIX, Nürburgring		
	Arturo Merzario	Iso-Marlboro-Cosworth FW	Rtd
	Jacques Laffite	Iso-Marlboro-Cosworth FW	Rtd

18 Aug	AUSTRIAN GRAND PRIX, Osterreichring, nr Knittelfeld		
	Arturo Merzario	Iso-Marlboro-Cosworth FW	Rtd
	Jacques Laffite	Iso-Marlboro-Cosworth FW	NC
8 Sept	ITALIAN GRAND PRIX, Monza		
	Arturo Merzario	Iso-Marlboro-Cosworth FW	4th
	Jacques Laffite	Iso-Marlboro-Cosworth FW	Rtd
22 Sept	CANADIAN GRAND PRIX, Mosport Park, nr Toronto		
	Arturo Merzario	Iso-Marlboro-Cosworth FW	Rtd
	Jacques Laffite	Iso-Marlboro-Cosworth FW	NC
6 Oct	UNITED STATES GRAND PRIX, Watkins Glen, NY		
	Arturo Merzario	Iso-Marlboro-Cosworth FW	Rtd
	Jacques Laffite	Iso-Marlboro-Cosworth FW	Rtd

1975

12 Jan	ARGENTINE GRAND PRIX, Buenos Aires		
	Arturo Merzario	Williams-Cosworth FW	NC
	Jacques Laffite	Williams-Cosworth FW	Rtd
26 Jan	BRAZILIAN GRAND PRIX, Interlagos, São Paulo		
	Arturo Merzario	Williams-Cosworth FW	Rtd
	Jacques Laffite	Williams-Cosworth FW	11th
3 March	SOUTH AFRICAN GRAND PRIX, Kyalami, nr Johannesburg		
	Arturo Merzario	Williams-Cosworth FW	Rtd
	Jacques Laffite	Williams-Cosworth FW	NC
16 March	Race of Champions, Brands Hatch		
	Arturo Merzario	Williams-Cosworth FW	7th
	Maurizio Flammini	Williams-Cosworth FW	DNS
12 April	International Trophy, Silverstone		
	Arturo Merzario	Williams-Cosworth FW	DNS
27 April	SPANISH GRAND PRIX, Montjuich Park, Barcelona		
	Arturo Merzario	Williams-Cosworth FW	Rtd
	Tony Brise	Williams-Cosworth FW	7th
11 May	MONACO GRAND PRIX, Monte Carlo		
	Arturo Merzario	Williams-Cosworth FW	DNQ
	Jacques Laffite	Williams-Cosworth FW	DNQ

25 May	BELGIAN GRAND PRIX, Zolder, nr Hasselt		
	Arturo Merzario	Williams-Cosworth FW	Rtd
	Jacques Laffite	Williams-Cosworth FW	Rtd
8 June	SWEDISH GRAND PRIX, Anderstorp		
	Damien Magee	Williams-Cosworth FW	14th
	Ian Scheckter	Williams-Cosworth FW	Rtd
22 June	DUTCH GRAND PRIX, Zandvoort		
	Jacques Laffite	Williams-Cosworth FW	Rtd
	Ian Scheckter	Williams-Cosworth FW	12th
6 July	FRENCH GRAND PRIX, Circuit Paul Ricard, nr Bandol		
	Francois Migault	Williams-Cosworth FW	DNS
	Jacques Laffite	Williams-Cosworth FW	11th
19 July	BRITISH GRAND PRIX, Silverstone		
	Jacques Laffite	Williams-Cosworth FW	Rtd
3 Aug	GERMAN GRAND PRIX, Nürburgring		
	Jacques Laffite	Williams-Cosworth FW	2nd
	Ian Ashley	Williams-Cosworth FW	DNS
17 Aug	AUSTRIAN GRAND PRIX, Osterreichring, nr Knittelfeld		
	Jacques Laffite	Williams-Cosworth FW	Rtd
	Jo Vonlanthen	Williams-Cosworth FW	Rtd
24 Aug	SWISS GRAND PRIX, Dijon-Prenois		
	Jacques Laffite	Williams-Cosworth FW	10th
	Jo Vonlanthen	Williams-Cosworth FW	14th
7 Sept	ITALIAN GRAND PRIX, Monza		
	Jacques Laffite	Williams-Cosworth FW	Rtd
	Renzo Zorzi	Williams-Cosworth FW	14th
5 Oct	UNITED STATES GRAND PRIX, Watkins Glen, NY		
	Jacques Laffite	Williams-Cosworth FW	DNS
	Lella Lombardi	Williams-Cosworth FW	DNS

1976

25 Jan	BRAZILIAN GRAND PRIX, Interlagos, São Paulo		
	Jacky Ickx	Wolf-Williams-Cosworth FW05	8th
	Renzo Zorzi	Wolf-Williams-Cosworth FW04	9th

6 March	SOUTH AFRICAN GRAND PRIX, Kyalami, nr Johannesburg		
	Jacky Ickx	Wolf-Williams-Cosworth FW05	16th
	Michel Leclere	Wolf-Williams-Cosworth FW05	13th
14 March	Race of Champions, Brands Hatch		
	Jacky Ickx	Wolf-Williams-Cosworth FW05	3rd
28 March	UNITED STATES GRAND PRIX WEST, Long Beach, California		
	Jacky Ickx	Wolf-Williams-Cosworth FW05	DNQ
	Michel Leclere	Wolf-Williams-Cosworth FW05	DNQ
11 April	International Trophy, Silverstone		
	Jacky Ickx	Wolf-Williams-Cosworth FW05	Rtd
	Mario Andretti	Wolf-Williams-Cosworth FW05	7th
2 May	SPANISH GRAND PRIX, Jarama, nr Madrid		
	Jacky Ickx	Wolf-Williams-Cosworth FW05	7th
	Michel Leclere	Wolf-Williams-Cosworth FW05	10th
16 May	BELGIAN GRAND PRIX, Zolder, nr Hasselt		
	Jacky Ickx	Wolf-Williams-Cosworth FW05	DNQ
	Michel Leclere	Wolf-Williams-Cosworth FW05	11th
30 May	MONACO GRAND PRIX, Monte Carlo		
	Jacky Ickx	Wolf-Williams-Cosworth FW05	DNQ
	Michel Leclere	Wolf-Williams-Cosworth FW05	11th
13 June	SWEDISH GRAND PRIX, Anderstorp		
	Jacky Ickx	Wolf-Williams-Cosworth FW05	Rtd
	Michel Leclere	Wolf-Williams-Cosworth FW05	10th

4 July	FRENCH GRAND PRIX, Circuit Paul Ricard, nr Bandol		
	Jacky Ickx	Wolf-Williams-Cosworth FW05	10th
	Michel Leclere	Wolf-Williams-Cosworth FW05	13th
18 July	BRITISH GRAND PRIX, Brands Hatch		
	Jacky Ickx	Wolf-Williams-Cosworth FW05	DNQ
1 Aug	GERMAN GRAND PRIX, Nürburgring		
	Arturo Merzario	Wolf-Williams-Cosworth FW05	Rtd
15 Aug	AUSTRIAN GRAND PRIX, Osterreichring, nr Knittelfeld		
	Arturo Merzario	Wolf-Williams-Cosworth FW05	Rtd
29 Aug	DUTCH GRAND PRIX, Zandvoort		
	Arturo Merzario	Wolf-Williams-Cosworth FW05	Rtd
12 Sept	ITALIAN GRAND PRIX, Monza		
	Arturo Merzario	Wolf-Williams-Cosworth FW05	DNS
3 Oct	CANADIAN GRAND PRIX, Mosport Park, nr. Toronto		
	Arturo Merzario	Wolf-Williams-Cosworth FW05	Rtd
	Chris Amon	Wolf-Williams-Cosworth FW05	DNS
10 Oct	UNITED STATES GRAND PRIX, Watkins Glen, NY		
	Arturo Merzario	Wolf-Williams-Cosworth FW05	Rtd
	Warwick Brown	Wolf-Williams-Cosworth FW05	14th
24 Oct	JAPANESE GRAND PRIX, Mount Fuji		
	Arturo Merzario	Wolf-Williams-Cosworth FW05	Rtd
	Hans Binder	Wolf-Williams-Cosworth FW05	Rtd

1977

8 May	SPANISH GRAND PRIX, Jarama, nr Madrid		
	Patrick Neve	March-Cosworth 761	12th

5 June	BELGIAN GRAND PRIX, Zolder, nr Hasselt		
	Patrick Neve	March-Cosworth 761	10th
19 June	SWEDISH GRAND PRIX, Anderstorp		
	Patrick Neve	March-Cosworth 761	15th
7 July	FRENCH GRAND PRIX, Dijon-Prenois		
	Patrick Neve	March-Cosworth 761	DNQ
16 July	BRITISH GRAND PRIX, Silverstone		
	Patrick Neve	March-Cosworth 761	10th
31 July	GERMAN GRAND PRIX, Hockenheim, nr Heidelberg		
	Patrick Neve	March-Cosworth 761	DNQ
14 Aug	AUSTRIAN GRAND PRIX, Osterreichring, nr Knittelfeld		
	Patrick Neve	March-Cosworth 761	9th
28 Aug	DUTCH GRAND PRIX, Zandvoort		
	Patrick Neve	March-Cosworth 761	DNQ
11 Sept	ITALIAN GRAND PRIX, Monza		
	Patrick Neve	March-Cosworth 761	7th
2 Oct	UNITED STATES GRAND PRIX, Watkins Glen NY		
	Patrick Neve	March-Cosworth 761	18th
9 Oct	CANADIAN GRAND PRIX, Mosport Park, nr Toronto		
	Patrick Neve	March-Cosworth 761	Rtd

1978

15 Jan	ARGENTINE GRAND PRIX, Buenos Aires		
	Alan Jones	Williams-Cosworth FW06	Rtd
29 Jan	BRAZILIAN GRAND PRIX, Rio de Janeiro		
	Alan Jones	Williams-Cosworth FW06	11th
4 March	SOUTH AFRICAN GRAND PRIX, Kyalami		
	Alan Jones	Williams-Cosworth FW06	4th
2 April	UNITED STATES GRAND PRIX WEST, Long Beach, California		
	Alan Jones	Williams-Cosworth FW06	7th
7 May	MONACO GRAND PRIX, Monte Carlo		
	Alan Jones	Williams-Cosworth FW06	Rtd
21 May	BELGIAN GRAND PRIX, Zolder, nr Hasselt		
	Alan Jones	Williams-Cosworth FW06	10th
4 June	SPANISH GRAND PRIX, Jarama, nr Madrid		
	Alan Jones	Williams-Cosworth FW06	8th

17 June	SWEDISH GRAND PRIX, Anderstorp		
Alan Jones	Williams-Cosworth FW06	Rtd
2 July	FRENCH GRAND PRIX, Circuit Paul Ricard, nr Bandol		
Alan Jones	Williams-Cosworth FW06	5th
16 July	BRITISH GRAND PRIX, Brands Hatch		
Alan Jones	Williams-Cosworth FW06	Rtd
30 July	GERMAN GRAND PRIX, Hockenheim, nr Heidelberg		
Alan Jones	Williams-Cosworth FW06	Rtd
13 Aug	AUSTRIAN GRAND PRIX, Osterreichring, nr Knittelfeld		
Alan Jones	Williams-Cosworth FW06	Rtd
27 Aug	DUTCH GRAND PRIX, Zandvoort		
Alan Jones	Williams-Cosworth FW06	Rtd
10 Sept	ITALIAN GRAND PRIX, Monza		
Alan Jones	Williams-Cosworth FW06	13th
1 Oct	UNITED STATES GRAND PRIX, Watkins Glen, NY		
Alan Jones	Williams-Cosworth FW06	2nd
8 Oct	CANADIAN GRAND PRIX, Montreal		
Alan Jones	Williams-Cosworth FW06	9th

1979

21 Jan	ARGENTINE GRAND PRIX, Buenos Aires		
Alan Jones	Williams-Cosworth FW06	9th
Clay Regazzoni	Williams-Cosworth FW06	10th
4 Feb	BRAZILIAN GRAND PRIX, Interlagos, São Paulo		
Alan Jones	Williams-Cosworth FW06	Rtd
Clay Regazzoni	Williams-Cosworth FW06	15th
3 March	SOUTH AFRICAN GRAND PRIX, Kyalami, nr Johannesburg		
Alan Jones	Williams-Cosworth FW06	Rtd
Clay Regazzoni	Williams-Cosworth FW06	9th
8 April	UNITED STATES GRAND PRIX WEST, Long Beach, California		
Alan Jones	Williams-Cosworth FW06	3rd
Clay Regazzoni	Williams-Cosworth FW06	Rtd
29 April	SPANISH GRAND PRIX, Jarama, nr Madrid		
Alan Jones	Williams-Cosworth FW07	Rtd
Clay Regazzoni	Williams-Cosworth FW07	Rtd

13 May	BELGIAN GRAND PRIX, Zolder, nr Hasselt		
	Alan Jones	Williams-Cosworth FW07	Rtd
	Clay Regazzoni	Williams-Cosworth FW07	Rtd
27 May	MONACO GRAND PRIX, Monte Carlo		
	Alan Jones	Williams-Cosworth FW07	Rtd
	Clay Regazzoni	Williams-Cosworth FW07	2nd
1 July	FRENCH GRAND PRIX, Dijon-Prenois		
	Alan Jones	Williams-Cosworth FW07	4th
	Clay Regazzoni	Williams-Cosworth FW07	6th
14 July	BRITISH GRAND PRIX, Silverstone		
	Alan Jones	Williams-Cosworth FW07	Rtd
	Clay Regazzoni	Williams-Cosworth FW07	1st
29 July	GERMAN GRAND PRIX, Hockenheim, nr Heidelberg		
	Alan Jones	Williams-Cosworth FW07	1st
	Clay Regazzoni	Williams-Cosworth FW07	2nd
12 Aug	AUSTRIAN GRAND PRIX, Osterreichring, nr Knittelfeld		
	Alan Jones	Williams-Cosworth FW07	1st
	Clay Regazzoni	Williams-Cosworth FW07	5th
26 Aug	DUTCH GRAND PRIX, Zandvoort		
	Alan Jones	Williams-Cosworth FW07	1st
	Clay Regazzoni	Williams-Cosworth FW07	Rtd
9 Sept	ITALIAN GRAND PRIX, Monza		
	Alan Jones	Williams-Cosworth FW07	9th
	Clay Regazzoni	Williams-Cosworth FW07	3rd
30 Sept	CANADIAN GRAND PRIX, Montreal		
	Alan Jones	Williams-Cosworth FW07	1st
	Clay Regazzoni	Williams-Cosworth FW07	3rd
7 Oct	UNITED STATES GRAND PRIX, Watkins Glen, NY		
	Alan Jones	Williams-Cosworth FW07	Rtd
	Clay Regazzoni	Williams-Cosworth FW07	Rtd

1980

13 Jan	ARGENTINE GRAND PRIX, Buenos Aires		
	Alan Jones	Williams-Cosworth FW07	1st
	Carlos Reutemann	Williams-Cosworth FW07B	Rtd

27 Jan	BRAZILIAN GRAND PRIX, Interlagos, São Paulo		
	Alan Jones	Williams-Cosworth FW07B	3rd
	Carlos Reutemann	Williams-Cosworth FW07B	Rtd
2 March	SOUTH AFRICAN GRAND PRIX, Kyalami, nr Johannesburg		
	Alan Jones	Williams-Cosworth FW07	Rtd
	Carlos Reutemann	Williams-Cosworth FW07B	5th
30 March	UNITED STATES GRAND PRIX WEST, Long Beach, California		
	Alan Jones	Williams-Cosworth FW07B	Rtd
	Carlos Reutemann	Williams-Cosworth FW07B	Rtd
4 May	BELGIAN GRAND PRIX, Zolder, nr Hasselt		
	Alan Jones	Williams-Cosworth FW07B	2nd
	Carlos Reutemann	Williams-Cosworth FW07B	3rd
18 May	MONACO GRAND PRIX, Monte Carlo		
	Alan Jones	Williams-Cosworth FW07B	Rtd
	Carlos Reutemann	Williams-Cosworth FW07B	1st
1 June	SPANISH GRAND PRIX, Jarama		
	Alan Jones	Williams-Cosworth FW07B	1st
	Carlos Reutemann	Williams-Cosworth FW07B	Rtd
29 June	FRENCH GRAND PRIX, Circuit Paul Ricard, nr Bandol		
	Alan Jones	Williams-Cosworth FW07B	1st
	Carlos Reutemann	Williams-Cosworth FW07B	6th
13 July	BRITISH GRAND PRIX, Brands Hatch		
	Alan Jones	Williams-Cosworth FW07B	1st
	Carlos Reutemann	Williams-Cosworth FW07B	3rd
10 Aug	GERMAN GRAND PRIX, Hockenheim, nr Heidelberg		
	Alan Jones	Williams-Cosworth FW07B	3rd
	Carlos Reutemann	Williams-Cosworth FW07B	2nd
17 Aug	AUSTRIAN GRAND PRIX, Osterreichring, nr Knittelfeld		
	Alan Jones	Williams-Cosworth FW07B	2nd
	Carlos Reutemann	Williams-Cosworth FW07B	3rd
31 Aug	DUTCH GRAND PRIX, Zandvoort		
	Alan Jones	Williams-Cosworth FW07B	11th
	Carlos Reutemann	Williams-Cosworth FW07B	4th
14 Sept	ITALIAN GRAND PRIX, Imola, nr Bologna		
	Alan Jones	Williams-Cosworth FW07B	2nd
	Carlos Reutemann	Williams-Cosworth FW07B	3rd

29 Sept	CANADIAN GRAND PRIX, Montreal		
	Alan Jones	Williams-Cosworth FW07B	1st
	Carlos Reutemann	Williams-Cosworth FW07B	2nd
5 Oct	UNITED STATES GRAND PRIX, Watkins Glen, NY		
	Alan Jones	Williams-Cosworth FW07B	1st
	Carlos Reutemann	Williams-Cosworth FW07B	2nd

1981

7 Feb	SOUTH AFRICAN GRAND PRIX, Kyalami, nr Johannesburg		
	Alan Jones	Williams-Cosworth FW07B	Rtd
	Carlos Reutemann	Williams-Cosworth FW07B	1st
15 March	UNITED STATES GRAND PRIX WEST, Long Beach, California		
	Alan Jones	Williams-Cosworth FW07C	1st
	Carlos Reutemann	Williams-Cosworth FW07C	2nd
29 March	BRAZILIAN GRAND PRIX, Rio de Janeiro		
	Alan Jones	Williams-Cosworth FW07C	2nd
	Carlos Reutemann	Williams-Cosworth FW07C	1st
12 April	ARGENTINE GRAND PRIX, Buenos Aires		
	Alan Jones	Williams-Cosworth FW07C	4th
	Carlos Reutemann	Williams-Cosworth FW07C	2nd
3 May	SAN MARINO GRAND PRIX, Imola, nr Bologna		
	Alan Jones	Williams-Cosworth FW07C	12th
	Carlos Reutemann	Williams-Cosworth FW07C	3rd
17 May	BELGIAN GRAND PRIX, Zolder, nr Hasselt		
	Alan Jones	Williams-Cosworth FW07C	Rtd
	Carlos Reutemann	Williams-Cosworth FW07C	1st
31 May	MONACO GRAND PRIX, Monte Carlo		
	Alan Jones	Williams-Cosworth FW07C	2nd
	Carlos Reutemann	Williams-Cosworth FW07C	Rtd
21 June	SPANISH GRAND PRIX, Jarama, nr Madrid		
	Alan Jones	Williams-Cosworth FW07C	7th
	Carlos Reutemann	Williams-Cosworth FW07C	4th
5 July	FRENCH GRAND PRIX, Dijon Prenois		
	Alan Jones	Williams-Cosworth FW07C	17th
	Carlos Reutemann	Williams-Cosworth FW07C	10th

18 July	BRITISH GRAND PRIX, Silverstone		
	Alan Jones	Williams-Cosworth FW07C	Rtd
	Carlos Reutemann	Williams-Cosworth FW07C	2nd
2 Aug	GERMAN GRAND PRIX, Hockenheim, nr Heidelberg		
	Alan Jones	Williams-Cosworth FW07C	11th
	Carlos Reutemann	Williams-Cosworth FW07C	2nd
16 Aug	AUSTRIAN GRAND PRIX, Osterreichring, nr Knittelfeld		
	Alan Jones	Williams-Cosworth FW07C	4th
	Carlos Reutemann	Williams-Cosworth FW07C	5th
30 Aug	DUTCH GRAND PRIX, Zandvoort		
	Alan Jones	Williams-Cosworth FW07C	3rd
	Carlos Reutemann	Williams-Cosworth FW07C	Rtd
13 Sept	ITALIAN GRAND PRIX, Monza		
	Alan Jones	Williams-Cosworth FW07C	2nd
	Carlos Reutemann	Williams-Cosworth FW07C	3rd
27 Sept	CANADIAN GRAND PRIX, Montreal		
	Alan Jones	Williams-Cosworth FW07C	Rtd
	Carlos Reutemann	Williams-Cosworth FW07C	10th
17 Oct	CAESARS PALACE GRAND PRIX, Las Vegas, Nevada		
	Alan Jones	Williams-Cosworth FW07C	1st
	Carlos Reutemann	Williams-Cosworth FW07C	8th

1982

23 Jan	SOUTH AFRICAN GRAND PRIX, Kyalami, nr Johannesburg		
	Carlos Reutemann	Williams-Cosworth FW07C	2nd
	Keke Rosberg	Williams-Cosworth FW07C	5th
21 March	BRAZILIAN GRAND PRIX, Rio de Janeiro		
	Carlos Reutemann	Williams-Cosworth FW07C	Rtd
	*Keke Rosberg	Williams-Cosworth FW07C	2nd
4 April	UNITED STATES GRAND PRIX WEST, Long Beach, California		
	Keke Rosberg	Williams-Cosworth FW07C	2nd
	Mario Andretti	Williams-Cosworth FW07C	Rtd
10 April	Race of Champions, Brands Hatch		
	Keke Rosberg	Williams-Cosworth FW08C	1st

9 May	BELGIAN GRAND PRIX, Zolder, nr Hasselt		
	Keke Rosberg	Williams-Cosworth FW08	2nd
	Derek Daly	Williams-Cosworth FW08	Rtd
23 May	MONACO GRAND PRIX, Monte Carlo		
	Keke Rosberg	Williams-Cosworth FW08	Rtd
	Derek Daly	Williams-Cosworth FW08	6th
6 June	UNITED STATES GRAND PRIX, Detroit, Michigan		
	Keke Rosberg	Williams-Cosworth FW08	4th
	Derek Daly	Williams-Cosworth FW08	5th
13 June	CANADIAN GRAND PRIX, Montreal		
	Keke Rosberg	Williams-Cosworth FW08	Rtd
	Derek Daly	Williams-Cosworth FW08	7th
3 July	DUTCH GRAND PRIX, Zandvoort		
	Keke Rosberg	Williams-Cosworth FW08	3rd
	Derek Daly	Williams-Cosworth FW08	5th
18 July	BRITISH GRAND PRIX, Brands Hatch		
	Keke Rosberg	Williams-Cosworth FW08	Rtd
	Derek Daly	Williams-Cosworth FW08	5th
25 July	FRENCH GRAND PRIX, Circuit Paul Ricard, nr Bandol		
	Keke Rosberg	Williams-Cosworth FW08	5th
	Derek Daly	Williams-Cosworth FW08	7th
8 Aug	GERMAN GRAND PRIX, Hockenheim, nr Heidelberg		
	Keke Rosberg	Williams-Cosworth FW08	3rd
	Derek Daly	Williams-Cosworth FW08	Rtd
15 Aug	AUSTRIAN GRAND PRIX, Osterreichring, nr Knittelfeld		
	Keke Rosberg	Williams-Cosworth FW08	2nd
	Derek Daly	Williams-Cosworth FW08	Rtd
29 Aug	SWISS GRAND PRIX, Dijon-Prenois, France		
	Keke Rosberg	Williams-Cosworth FW08	1st
	Derek Daly	Williams-Cosworth FW08	9th
12 Sept	ITALIAN GRAND PRIX, Monza		
	Keke Rosberg	Williams-Cosworth FW08	8th
	Derek Daly	Williams-Cosworth FW08	Rtd
25 Sept	CAESARS PALACE GRAND PRIX, Las Vegas, Nevada		
	Keke Rosberg	Williams-Cosworth FW08	4th
	Derek Daly	Williams-Cosworth FW08	5th

*later excluded

1983

13 March	BRAZILIAN GRAND PRIX, Rio de Janeiro		
	*Keke Rosberg	Williams-Cosworth FW08C	2nd
	Jacques Laffite	Williams-Cosworth FW08C	4th
27 March	UNITED STATES GRAND PRIX WEST, Long Beach, California		
	Keke Rosberg	Williams-Cosworth FW08C	Rtd
	Jacques Laffite	Williams-Cosworth FW08C	4th
17 April	FRENCH GRAND PRIX, Circuit Paul Ricard, nr Bandol		
	Keke Rosberg	Williams-Cosworth FW08C	5th
	Jacques Laffite	Williams-Cosworth FW08C	6th
1 May	SAN MARINO GRAND PRIX, Imola, nr Bologna		
	Keke Rosberg	Williams-Cosworth FW08C	4th
	Jacques Laffite	Williams-Cosworth FW08C	7th
15 May	MONACO GRAND PRIX, Monte Carlo		
	Keke Rosberg	Williams-Cosworth FW08C	1st
	Jacques Laffite	Williams-Cosworth FW08C	Rtd
22 May	BELGIAN GRAND PRIX, Spa Francorchamps, nr Malmedy		
	Keke Rosberg	Williams-Cosworth FW08C	5th
	Jacques Laffite	Williams-Cosworth FW08C	6th
5 June	UNITED STATES GRAND PRIX, Detroit, Michigan		
	Keke Rosberg	Williams-Cosworth FW08C	2nd
	Jacques Laffite	Williams-Cosworth FW08C	5th
12 June	CANADIAN GRAND PRIX, Montreal		
	Keke Rosberg	Williams-Cosworth FW08C	4th
	Jacques Laffite	Williams-Cosworth FW08C	Rtd
16 July	BRITISH GRAND PRIX, Silverstone		
	Keke Rosberg	Williams-Cosworth FW08C	11th
	Jacques Laffite	Williams-Cosworth FW08C	12th
7 Aug	GERMAN GRAND PRIX, Hockenheim, nr Heidelberg		
	Keke Rosberg	Williams-Cosworth FW08C	10th
	Jacques Laffite	Williams-Cosworth FW08C	6th
14 Aug	AUSTRIAN GRAND PRIX, Osterreichring, nr Knittelfeld		
	Keke Rosberg	Williams-Cosworth FW08C	8th
	Jacques Laffite	Williams-Cosworth FW08C	Rtd

28 Aug	DUTCH GRAND PRIX, Zandvoort		
	Keke Rosberg	Williams-Cosworth FW08C	Rtd
	Jacques Laffite	Williams-Cosworth FW08C	Rtd
11 Sept	ITALIAN GRAND PRIX, Monza		
	*Keke Rosberg	Williams-Cosworth FW08C	11th
	Jacques Laffite	Williams-Cosworth FW08C	DNQ
25 Sept	GRAND PRIX OF EUROPE, Brands Hatch		
	Keke Rosberg	Williams-Cosworth FW08C	Rtd
	Jacques Laffite	Williams-Cosworth FW08C	DNQ
	Jonathan Palmer	Williams-Cosworth FW08C	13th
15 Oct	SOUTH AFRICAN GRAND PRIX, Kyalami, nr Johannesburg		
	Keke Rosberg	Williams-Honda FW09	5th
	Jacques Laffite	Williams-Honda FW09	Rtd

*later excluded

1984

25 March	BRAZILIAN GRAND PRIX, Rio de Janeiro		
	Keke Rosberg	Williams-Honda FW09	2nd
	Jacques Laffite	Williams-Honda FW09	Rtd
7 April	SOUTH AFRICAN GRAND PRIX, Kyalami, nr Johannesburg		
	Keke Rosberg	Williams-Honda FW09	Rtd
	Jacques Laffite	Williams-Honda FW09	Rtd
29 April	BELGIAN GRAND PRIX, Zolder, nr Hasselt		
	Keke Rosberg	Williams-Honda FW09	4th
	Jacques Laffite	Williams-Honda FW09	Rtd
6 May	SAN MARINO GRAND PRIX, Imola, nr Bologna		
	Keke Rosberg	Williams-Honda FW09	Rtd
	Jacques Laffite	Williams-Honda FW09	Rtd
20 May	FRENCH GRAND PRIX, Dijon-Prenois		
	Keke Rosberg	Williams-Honda FW09	6th
	Jacques Laffite	Williams-Honda FW09	8th
3 June	MONACO GRAND PRIX, Monte Carlo		
	Keke Rosberg	Williams-Honda FW09	5th
	Jacques Laffite	Williams-Honda FW09	9th

17 June	CANADIAN GRAND PRIX, Montreal		
	Keke Rosberg	Williams-Honda FW09	Rtd
	Jacques Laffite	Williams-Honda FW09	Rtd
24 June	UNITED STATES GRAND PRIX, Detroit, Michigan		
	Keke Rosberg	Williams-Honda FW09	Rtd
	Jacques Laffite	Williams-Honda FW09	6th
8 July	UNITED STATES GRAND PRIX, Dallas, Texas		
	Keke Rosberg	Williams-Honda FW09	1st
	Jacques Laffite	Williams-Honda FW09	4th
22 July	BRITISH GRAND PRIX, Brands Hatch		
	Keke Rosberg	Williams-Honda FW09B	Rtd
	Jacques Laffite	Williams-Honda FW09B	Rtd
5 Aug	GERMAN GRAND PRIX, Hockenheim, nr Heidelberg		
	Keke Rosberg	Williams-Honda FW09B	Rtd
	Jacques Laffite	Williams-Honda FW09B	Rtd
19 Aug	AUSTRIAN GRAND PRIX, Osterreichring, nr Knittelfeld		
	Keke Rosberg	Williams-Honda FW09B	Rtd
	Jacques Laffite	Williams-Honda FW09B	Rtd
26 Aug	DUTCH GRAND PRIX, Zandvoort		
	Keke Rosberg	Williams-Honda FW09B	10th
	Jacques Laffite	Williams-Honda FW09B	Rtd
9 Sept	ITALIAN GRAND PRIX, Monza		
	Keke Rosberg	Williams-Honda FW09B	Rtd
	Jacques Laffite	Williams-Honda FW09B	Rtd
7 Oct	GRAND PRIX OF EUROPE, new Nürburgring, nr Koblenz		
	Keke Rosberg	Williams-Honda FW09B	Rtd
	Jacques Laffite	Williams-Honda FW09B	Rtd
21 Oct	PORTUGUESE GRAND PRIX, Estoril		
	Keke Rosberg	Williams-Honda FW09B	Rtd
	Jacques Laffite	Williams-Honda FW09B	14th

1985

7 April	BRAZILIAN GRAND PRIX, Rio de Janeiro		
	Keke Rosberg	Williams-Honda FW10	Rtd
	Nigel Mansell	Williams-Honda FW10	Rtd

21 April	PORTUGUESE GRAND PRIX, Estoril		
	Keke Rosberg	Williams-Honda FW10	Rtd
	Nigel Mansell	Williams-Honda FW10	5th
5 May	SAN MARINO GRAND PRIX, Imola, nr Bologna		
	Keke Rosberg	Williams-Honda FW10	Rtd
	Nigel Mansell	Williams-Honda FW10	5th
19 May	MONACO GRAND PRIX, Monte Carlo		
	Keke Rosberg	Williams-Honda FW10	8th
	Nigel Mansell	Williams-Honda FW10	7th
16 June	CANADIAN GRAND PRIX, Montreal		
	Keke Rosberg	Williams-Honda FW10	4th
	Nigel Mansell	Williams-Honda FW10	6th
23 June	UNITED STATES GRAND PRIX, Detroit, Michigan		
	Keke Rosberg	Williams-Honda FW10	1st
	Nigel Mansell	Williams-Honda FW10	Rtd
7 July	FRENCH GRAND PRIX, Circuit Paul Ricard, nr Bandol		
	Keke Rosberg	Williams-Honda FW10	2nd
	Nigel Mansell	Williams-Honda FW10	DNS
21 July	BRITISH GRAND PRIX, Silverstone		
	Keke Rosberg	Williams-Honda FW10	Rtd
	Nigel Mansell	Williams-Honda FW10	Rtd
4 Aug	GERMAN GRAND PRIX, new Nürburgring, nr Koblenz		
	Keke Rosberg	Williams-Honda FW10	12th
	Nigel Mansell	Williams-Honda FW10	6th
18 Aug	AUSTRIAN GRAND PRIX, Osterreichring, nr Knittelfeld		
	Keke Rosberg	Williams-Honda FW10	Rtd
	Nigel Mansell	Williams-Honda FW10	Rtd
25 Aug	DUTCH GRAND PRIX, Zandvoort		
	Keke Rosberg	Williams-Honda FW10	Rtd
	Nigel Mansell	Williams-Honda FW10	6th
8 Sept	ITALIAN GRAND PRIX, Monza		
	Keke Rosberg	Williams-Honda FW10	Rtd
	Nigel Mansell	Williams-Honda FW10	11th
15 Sept	BELGIAN GRAND PRIX, Spa Francorchamps, nr Malmedy		
	Keke Rosberg	Williams-Honda FW10	4th
	Nigel Mansell	Williams-Honda FW10	2nd

6 Oct	GRAND PRIX OF EUROPE, Brands Hatch		
	Keke Rosberg	Williams-Honda FW10	3rd
	Nigel Mansell	Williams-Honda FW10	1st
19 Oct	SOUTH AFRICAN GRAND PRIX, Kyalami, nr Johannesburg		
	Keke Rosberg	Williams-Honda FW10	2nd
	Nigel Mansell	Williams-Honda FW10	1st
3 Nov	AUSTRALIAN GRAND PRIX, Adelaide		
	Keke Rosberg	Williams-Honda FW10	1st
	Nigel Mansell	Williams-Honda FW10	Rtd

1986

23 Mar	BRAZILIAN GRAND PRIX, Rio de Janeiro		
	Nigel Mansell	Williams-Honda FW11	Rtd
	Nelson Piquet	Williams-Honda FW11	1st
13 Apr	SPANISH GRAND PRIX, Jerez		
	Nigel Mansell	Williams-Honda FW11	2nd
	Nelson Piquet	Williams-Honda FW11	Rtd
27 April	SAN MARINO GRAND PRIX, Imola, nr Bologna		
	Nigel Mansell	Williams-Honda FW11	Rtd
	Nelson Piquet	Williams-Honda FW11	2nd
11 May	MONACO GRAND PRIX, Monte Carlo		
	Nigel Mansell	Williams-Honda FW11	4th
	Nelson Piquet	Williams-Honda FW11	7th
25 May	BELGIAN GRAND PRIX, Spa Francorchamps, nr Malmedy		
	Nigel Mansell	Williams-Honda FW11	1st
	Nelson Piquet	Williams-Honda FW11	Rtd
15 June	CANADIAN GRAND PRIX, Montreal		
	Nigel Mansell	Williams-Honda FW11	1st
	Nelson Piquet	Williams-Honda FW11	3rd
22 June	UNITED STATES GRAND PRIX, Detroit, Michigan		
	Nigel Mansell	Williams-Honda FW11	5th
	Nelson Piquet	Williams-Honda FW11	Rtd
6 July	FRENCH GRAND PRIX, Circuit Paul Ricard, nr Bandol		
	Nigel Mansell	Williams-Honda FW11	1st
	Nelson Piquet	Williams-Honda FW11	3rd

13 July	BRITISH GRAND PRIX, Brands Hatch		
	Nigel Mansell	Williams-Honda FW11	1st
	Nelson Piquet	Williams-Honda FW11	2nd
27 July	GERMAN GRAND PRIX, Hockenheim, nr Heidelberg		
	Nigel Mansell	Williams-Honda FW11	3rd
	Nelson Piquet	Williams-Honda FW11	1st
10 Aug	HUNGARIAN GRAND PRIX, Hungaroring, nr Budapest		
	Nigel Mansell	Williams-Honda FW11	3rd
	Nelson Piquet	Williams-Honda FW11	1st
17 Aug	AUSTRIAN GRAND PRIX, Osterreichring, nr Knittelfeld		
	Nigel Mansell	Williams-Honda FW11	Rtd
	Nelson Piquet	Williams-Honda FW11	Rtd
7 Sept	ITALIAN GRAND PRIX, Monza		
	Nigel Mansell	Williams-Honda FW11	2nd
	Nelson Piquet	Williams-Honda FW11	1st
21 Sept	PORTUGUESE GRAND PRIX, Estoril		
	Nigel Mansell	Williams-Honda FW11	1st
	Nelson Piquet	Williams-Honda FW11	3rd
12 Oct	MEXICAN GRAND PRIX, Mexico City		
	Nigel Mansell	Williams-Honda FW11	5th
	Nelson Piquet	Williams-Honda FW11	4th
26 Oct	AUSTRALIAN GRAND PRIX, Adelaide		
	Nigel Mansell	Williams-Honda FW11	Rtd
	Nelson Piquet	Williams-Honda FW11	2nd

1987

12 April	BRAZILIAN GRAND PRIX, Rio de Janeiro		
	Nigel Mansell	Williams-Honda FW11B	6th
	Nelson Piquet	Williams-Honda FW11B	2nd
3 May	SAN MARINO GRAND PRIX, Imola, nr Bologna		
	Nigel Mansell	Williams-Honda FW11B	1st
	Nelson Piquet	Williams-Honda FW11B	DNS
17 May	BELGIAN GRAND PRIX, Spa Francorchamps, nr Malmedy		
	Nigel Mansell	Williams-Honda FW11B	Rtd
	Nelson Piquet	Williams-Honda FW11B	Rtd

31 May	MONACO GRAND PRIX, Monte Carlo		
	Nigel Mansell	Williams-Honda FW11B	Rtd
	Nelson Piquet	Williams-Honda FW11B	2nd
21 June	UNITED STATES GRAND PRIX, Detroit, Michigan		
	Nigel Mansell	Williams-Honda FW11B	5th
	Nelson Piquet	Williams-Honda FW11B	2nd
5 July	FRENCH GRAND PRIX, Circuit Paul Ricard, nr Bandol		
	Nigel Mansell	Williams-Honda FW11B	1st
	Nelson Piquet	Williams-Honda FW11B	2nd
12 July	BRITISH GRAND PRIX, Silverstone		
	Nigel Mansell	Williams-Honda FW11B	1st
	Nelson Piquet	Williams-Honda FW11B	2nd
26 July	GERMAN GRAND PRIX, Hockenheim, nr Heidelberg		
	Nigel Mansell	Williams-Honda FW11B	Rtd
	Nelson Piquet	Williams-Honda FW11B	1st
9 Aug	HUNGARIAN GRAND PRIX, Hungaroring, nr Budapest		
	Nigel Mansell	Williams-Honda FW11B	14th
	Nelson Piquet	Williams-Honda FW11B	1st
16 Aug	AUSTRIAN GRAND PRIX, Osterreichring, nr Knittelfeld		
	Nigel Mansell	Williams-Honda FW11B	1st
	Nelson Piquet	Williams-Honda FW11B	2nd
6 Sept	ITALIAN GRAND PRIX, Monza		
	Nigel Mansell	Williams-Honda FW11B	3rd
	Nelson Piquet	Williams-Honda FW11B	1st
21 Sept	PORTUGUESE GRAND PRIX, Estoril		
	Nigel Mansell	Williams-Honda FW11B	Rtd
	Nelson Piquet	Williams-Honda FW11B	3rd
27 Sept	SPANISH GRAND PRIX, Jerez		
	Nigel Mansell	Williams-Honda FW11B	1st
	Nelson Piquet	Williams-Honda FW11B	4th
18 Oct	MEXICAN GRAND PRIX, Mexico City		
	Nigel Mansell	Williams-Honda FW11B	1st
	Nelson Piquet	Williams-Honda FW11B	2nd
1 Nov	JAPANESE GRAND PRIX, Suzuka, nr Nagoya		
	Nigel Mansell	Williams-Honda FW11B	DNS
	Nelson Piquet	Williams-Honda FW11B	Rtd

15 Nov	AUSTRALIAN GRAND PRIX, Adelaide		
	Riccardo Patrese	Williams-Honda FW11B	Rtd
	Nelson Piquet	Williams-Honda FW11B	Rtd

1988

3 April	BRAZILIAN GRAND PRIX, Rio de Janeiro		
	Nigel Mansell	Williams-Judd FW12	Rtd
	Riccardo Patrese	Williams-Judd FW12	Rtd
1 May	SAN MARINO GRAND PRIX, Imola, nr Bologna		
	Nigel Mansell	Williams-Judd FW12	Rtd
	Riccardo Patrese	Williams-Judd FW12	13th
15 May	MONACO GRAND PRIX, Monte Carlo		
	Nigel Mansell	Williams-Judd FW12	Rtd
	Riccardo Patrese	Williams-Judd FW12	6th
29 May	MEXICAN GRAND PRIX, Mexico City		
	Nigel Mansell	Williams-Judd FW12	Rtd
	Riccardo Patrese	Williams-Judd FW12	Rtd
12 June	CANADIAN GRAND PRIX, Montreal		
	Nigel Mansell	Williams-Judd FW12	Rtd
	Riccardo Patrese	Williams-Judd FW12	Rtd
19 June	UNITED STATES GRAND PRIX, Detroit		
	Nigel Mansell	Williams-Judd FW12	Rtd
	Riccardo Patrese	Williams-Judd FW12	Rtd
3 July	FRENCH GRAND PRIX, Circuit Paul Ricard, nr Bandol		
	Nigel Mansell	Williams-Judd FW12	Rtd
	Riccardo Patrese	Williams-Judd FW12	Rtd
10 July	BRITISH GRAND PRIX, Silverstone		
	Nigel Mansell	Williams-Judd FW12	2nd
	Riccardo Patrese	Williams-Judd FW12	8th
24 July	GERMAN GRAND PRIX, Hockenheim, nr Heidelberg		
	Nigel Mansell	Williams-Judd FW12	Rtd
	Riccardo Patrese	Williams-Judd FW12	Rtd
7 Aug	HUNGARIAN GRAND PRIX, Hungaroring, nr Budapest		
	Nigel Mansell	Williams-Judd FW12	Rtd
	Riccardo Patrese	Williams-Judd FW12	6th

28 Aug	BELGIAN GRAND PRIX, Spa Francorchamps, nr Malmédy		
	Martin Brundle	Williams-Judd FW12	7th
	Riccardo Patrese	Williams-Judd FW12	Rtd
11 Sept	ITALIAN GRAND PRIX, Monza		
	Jean-Louis Schlesser	Williams-Judd FW12	11th
	Riccardo Patrese	Williams-Judd FW12	7th
25 Sept	PORTUGUESE GRAND PRIX, Estoril		
	Nigel Mansell	Williams-Judd FW12	Rtd
	Riccardo Patrese	Williams-Judd FW12	Rtd
2 Oct	SPANISH GRAND PRIX, Jerez		
	Nigel Mansell	Williams-Judd FW12	2nd
	Riccardo Patrese	Williams-Judd FW12	5th
30 Oct	JAPANESE GRAND PRIX, Suzuka, nr Osaka		
	Nigel Mansell	Williams-Judd FW12	Rtd
	Riccardo Patrese	Williams-Judd FW12	6th
13 Nov	AUSTRALIAN GRAND PRIX, Adelaide		
	Nigel Mansell	Williams-Judd FW12	Rtd
	Riccardo Patrese	Williams-Judd FW12	4th

1989

26 March	BRAZILIAN GRAND PRIX, Rio de Janeiro		
	Thierry Boutsen	Williams-Renault FW12C	Rtd
	Riccardo Patrese	Williams-Renault FW12C	Rtd
23 Apr	SAN MARINO GRAND PRIX, Imola, nr Bologna		
	Thierry Boutsen	Williams-Renault FW12C	4th
	Riccardo Patrese	Williams-Renault FW12C	Rtd
7 May	MONACO GRAND PRIX, Monte Carlo		
	Thierry Boutsen	Williams-Renault FW12C	10th
	Riccardo Patrese	Williams-Renault FW12C	15th
26 May	MEXICAN GRAND PRIX, Mexico City		
	Thierry Boutsen	Williams-Renault FW12C	Rtd
	Riccardo Patrese	Williams-Renault FW12C	2nd
4 June	UNITED STATES GRAND PRIX, Phoenix, Arizona		
	Thierry Boutsen	Williams-Renault FW12C	6th
	Riccardo Patrese	Williams-Renault FW12C	2nd

18 June	CANADIAN GRAND PRIX, Montreal		
	Thierry Boutsen	Williams-Renault FW12C	1st
	Riccardo Patrese	Williams-Renault FW12C	2nd
9 July	FRENCH GRAND PRIX, Circuit Paul Ricard, nr Bandol		
	Thierry Boutsen	Williams-Renault FW12C	Rtd
	Riccardo Patrese	Williams-Renault FW12C	3rd
16 July	BRITISH GRAND PRIX, Silverstone		
	Thierry Boutsen	Williams-Renault FW12C	10th
	Riccardo Patrese	Williams-Renault FW12C	Rtd
30 July	GERMAN GRAND PRIX, Hockenheim, nr Heidelberg		
	Thierry Boutsen	Williams-Renault FW12C	Rtd
	Riccardo Patrese	Williams-Renault FW12C	4th
13 Aug	HUNGARIAN GRAND PRIX, Hungaroring, nr Budapest		
	Thierry Boutsen	Williams-Renault FW12C	3rd
	Riccardo Patrese	Williams-Renault FW12C	Rtd
27 Aug	BELGIAN GRAND PRIX, Spa Francorchamps, nr Malmedy		
	Thierry Boutsen	Williams-Renault FW12C	4th
	Riccardo Patrese	Williams-Renault FW12C	Rtd
10 Sept	ITALIAN GRAND PRIX, Monza		
	Thierry Boutsen	Williams-Renault FW12C	3rd
	Riccardo Patrese	Williams-Renault FW12C	4th
24 Sept	PORTUGUESE GRAND PRIX, Estoril		
	Thierry Boutsen	Williams-Renault FW13	Rtd
	Riccardo Patrese	Williams-Renault FW13	Rtd
1 Oct	SPANISH GRAND PRIX, Jerez		
	Thierry Boutsen	Williams-Renault FW13	Rtd
	Riccardo Patrese	Williams-Renault FW12C	5th
22 Oct	JAPANESE GRAND PRIX, Suzuka, nr Osaka		
	Thierry Boutsen	Williams-Renault FW13	3rd
	Riccardo Patrese	Williams-Renault FW13	2nd
5 Nov	AUSTRALIAN GRAND PRIX, Adelaide		
	Thierry Boutsen	Williams-Renault FW13	1st
	Riccardo Patrese	Williams-Renault FW13	2nd

1990

11 Mar	UNITED STATES GRAND PRIX, Phoenix, Arizona		
	Thierry Boutsen	Williams-Renault FW13B	3rd
	Riccardo Patrese	Williams-Renault FW13B	9th
25 March	BRAZILIAN GRAND PRIX, Interlagos, São Paulo		
	Thierry Boutsen	Williams-Renault FW13B	5th
	Riccardo Patrese	Williams-Renault FW13B	13th
13 May	SAN MARINO GRAND PRIX, Imola, nr Bologna		
	Thierry Boutsen	Williams-Renault FW13B	Rtd
	Riccardo Patrese	Williams-Renault FW13B	1st
27 May	MONACO GRAND PRIX, Monte Carlo		
	Thierry Boutsen	Williams-Renault FW13B	4th
	Riccardo Patrese	Williams-Renault FW13B	Rtd
10 June	CANADIAN GRAND PRIX, Montreal		
	Thierry Boutsen	Williams-Renault FW13B	Rtd
	Riccardo Patrese	Williams-Renault FW13B	Rtd
24 June	MEXICAN GRAND PRIX, Mexico City		
	Thierry Boutsen	Williams-Renault FW13B	5th
	Riccardo Patrese	Williams-Renault FW13B	9th
8 July	FRENCH GRAND PRIX, Circuit Paul Ricard, nr Bandol		
	Thierry Boutsen	Williams-Renault FW13B	Rtd
	Riccardo Patrese	Williams-Renault FW13B	6th
15 July	BRITISH GRAND PRIX, Silverstone		
	Thierry Boutsen	Williams-Renault FW13B	2nd
	Riccardo Patrese	Williams-Renault FW13B	Rtd
29 July	GERMAN GRAND PRIX, Hockenheim, nr Heidelberg		
	Thierry Boutsen	Williams-Renault FW13B	6th
	Riccardo Patrese	Williams-Renault FW13B	5th
12 Aug	HUNGARIAN GRAND PRIX, Hungaroring, nr Budapest		
	Thierry Boutsen	Williams-Renault FW13B	1st
	Riccardo Patrese	Williams-Renault FW13B	4th
25 Aug	BELGIAN GRAND PRIX, Spa Francorchamps, nr Malmedy		
	Thierry Boutsen	Williams-Renault FW13B	Rtd
	Riccardo Patrese	Williams-Renault FW13B	Rtd

9 Sept	ITALIAN GRAND PRIX, Monza		
	Thierry Boutsen	Williams-Renault FW13B	Rtd
	Riccardo Patrese	Williams-Renault FW13B	5th
23 Sept	PORTUGUESE GRAND PRIX, Estoril		
	Thierry Boutsen	Williams-Renault FW13B	Rtd
	Riccardo Patrese	Williams-Renault FW13B	7th
30 Sept	SPANISH GRAND PRIX, Jerez		
	Thierry Boutsen	Williams-Renault FW13B	4th
	Riccardo Patrese	Williams-Renault FW13B	5th
21 Oct	JAPANESE GRAND PRIX, Suzuka, nr Osaka		
	Thierry Boutsen	Williams-Renault FW13B	5th
	Riccardo Patrese	Williams-Renault FW13B	4th
4 Nov	AUSTRALIAN GRAND PRIX, Adelaide		
	Thierry Boutsen	Williams-Renault FW13B	5th
	Riccardo Patrese	Williams-Renault FW13B	6th

1991

10 Mar	UNITED STATES GRAND PRIX, Phoenix		
	Nigel Mansell	Williams-Renault FW14	Rtd
	Riccardo Patrese	Williams-Renault FW14	Rtd
24 Mar	BRAZILIAN GRAND PRIX, Interlagos, São Paulo		
	Nigel Mansell	Williams-Renault FW14	Rtd
	Riccardo Patrese	Williams-Renault FW14	2nd

STOP PRESS

Since this book was first published, further Williams' race performances have been as follows: SAN MARINO GRAND PRIX, Nigel Mansell retired, Riccardo Patrese retired; MONACO GRAND PRIX, Nigel Mansell 2nd, Riccardo Patrese retired; CANADIAN GRAND PRIX, Nigel Mansell 6th, Riccardo Patrese 2nd; MEXICAN GRAND PRIX, Nigel Mansell 2nd, Riccardo Patrese 1st; FRENCH GRAND PRIX, Nigel Mansell 1st, Riccardo Patrese 5th; BRITISH GRAND PRIX, Nigel Mansell 1st, Riccardo Patrese retired; GERMAN GRAND PRIX, Nigel Mansell 1st, Riccardo Patrese 2nd; HUNGARIAN GRAND PRIX, Nigel Mansell 2nd, Riccardo Patrese 3rd; BELGIAN GRAND PRIX, Nigel Mansell retired, Riccardo Patrese 5th; ITALIAN GRAND PRIX, Nigel Mansell 1st, Riccardo Patrese retired; PORTUGUESE GRAND PRIX, Nigel Mansell disqualified, Riccardo Patrese 1st; SPANISH GRAND PRIX, Nigel Mansell 1st, Riccardo Patrese 3rd.

APPENDIX 2

Williams F1 car specifications

1969 BRABHAM-COSWORTH BT26
Chassis: Tubular frame covered with stressed skin. **Suspension:** Double wishbones/outboard springs, front and rear. **Tyres:** Dunlop. **Engine:** Cosworth DFV V8, 2995 cc, developing 430 bhp at 10,000 rpm. **Gearbox:** Hewland DG300.

1970 DE TOMASO-COSWORTH 505
Chassis: aluminium alloy monocoque with magnesium internal bulkheads. **Suspension:** Double wishbones/outboard springs, front and rear. **Tyres:** Dunlop. **Engine:** Cosworth DFV V8, 2995 cc, developing 430 bhp at 10,000 rpm. **Gearbox:** Hewland DG300.

1971 MARCH-COSWORTH 711
Chassis: aluminium alloy monocoque. **Suspension:** Double wishbones and rocker arms with inboard springs at front. Double wishbones/outboard springs at rear. **Tyres:** Firestone. **Engine:** Cosworth DFV V8, 2993 cc, developing 440 bhp at 10,000 rpm. **Gearbox:** Hewland FG400.

1972 MARCH-COSWORTH 721
Chassis: aluminium alloy monocoque. **Suspension:** Double wishbones and rocker arms with inboard springs at front. Double wishbones/outboard springs at rear. **Tyres:** Firestone. **Engine:** Cosworth DFV V8, 2993 cc, developing 450 bhp at 10,000 rpm. **Gearbox:** Hewland FG400.

1972 POLITOYS-COSWORTH FX3
Chassis: aluminium alloy monocoque. **Suspension:** Double wishbones/outboard springs at front. Single top link, parallel lower links, twin radius rods and outboard springs at rear. **Tyres:** Firestone. **Engine:** Cosworth DFV V8, 2993 cc, developing 450 bhp at 10,000 rpm. **Gearbox:** Hewland FG400.

1973 ISO-MARLBORO-COSWORTH IR
Chassis: aluminium alloy monocoque. **Suspension:** Double wishbones/outboard springs at front. Single top link, parallel lower links, twin radius rods and outboard springs at rear. **Tyres:** Firestone. **Engine:** Cosworth DFV V8, 2992 cc, developing 460 bhp at 10,250 rpm. **Gearbox:** Hewland FG400.

1974 ISO-MARLBORO-COSWORTH FW
Chassis: aluminium alloy monocoque. **Suspension:** Double wishbones/outboard springs at front. Single top link, parallel lower links, twin radius rods and outboard springs at rear. **Tyres:** Firestone. **Engine:** Cosworth DFV V8, 2993 cc, developing 460 bhp at 10,250 rpm. **Gearbox:** Hewland FG400.

1975 WILLIAMS-COSWORTH FW
Chassis: aluminium alloy monocoque. **Suspension:** Double wishbones/outboard springs at front. Single top link, parallel lower links, twin radius rods and outboard springs at rear. **Tyres:** Goodyear. **Engine:** Cosworth DFV V8, 2992 cc, developing 465 bhp at 10,500 rpm. **Gearbox:** Hewland FG400.

1976 WOLF-WILLIAMS-COSWORTH FW05
Chassis: aluminium alloy monocoque. **Suspension:** Double wishbones with inboard springs activated by rocker arms at front. Single top link, parallel lower links, twin radius rods and outboard springs at rear. **Tyres:** Goodyear. **Engine:** Cosworth DFV V8, 2993 cc, developing 465 bhp at 10,500 rpm. **Gearbox:** Hewland FGA400.

1977 MARCH-COSWORTH 761
Chassis: aluminium alloy monocoque. **Suspension:** Double wishbones with outboard springs at front. Single top link, parallel lower links, twin radius rods and outboard springs at rear. **Tyres:** Goodyear. **Engine:** Cosworth DFV V8, 2993 cc, developing 465 bhp at 10,500 rpm. **Gearbox:** Hewland FGA400.

1978 WILLIAMS-COSWORTH FW06
Chassis: aluminium alloy monocoque. **Suspension:** Bottom wishbones with top rocker arm activating inboard springs/dampers at front. Single top link, single radius rods, lower wishbones and outboard springs at rear. **Tyres:** Goodyear. **Engine:** Cosworth DFV V8, 2993 cc, developing 475 bhp at 10,750 rpm. **Gearbox:** Hewland FGA400.

1979 WILLIAMS-COSWORTH FW07
Chassis: aluminium alloy monocoque. **Suspension:** Lower wishbones and inboard springs activated by top rocker arm at front and rear. **Tyres:** Goodyear. **Engine:** Cosworth DFV V8, 2993 cc, developing 480 bhp at 10,800 rpm. **Gearbox:** Hewland FGB.

1980 WILLIAMS-COSWORTH FW07B
Chassis: aluminium alloy monocoque. **Suspension:** Lower wishbones and inboard springs activated by top rocker arm at front and rear. **Tyres:** Goodyear. **Engine:** Cosworth DFV V8, 2993 cc, developing 485 bhp at 10,800 rpm. **Gearbox:** Hewland FGB.

1981 WILLIAMS-COSWORTH FW07C
Chassis: aluminium alloy monocoque. **Suspension:** Lower wishbones and inboard springs activated by top rocker arm at front and rear. **Tyres:** Goodyear. **Engine:** Cosworth DFV V8, 2993 cc, developing 490 bhp at 11,100 rpm. **Gearbox:** Williams/Hewland FGB.

1982 WILLIAMS-COSWORTH FW07D
Chassis: aluminium alloy monocoque. **Suspension:** Lower wishbones and inboard springs activated by top rocker arm at front and rear. **Tyres:** Goodyear. **Engine:** Cosworth DFV V8, 2993 cc, developing 505 bhp at 11,100 rpm. **Gearbox:** Williams/Hewland FGB.

1982 WILLIAMS-COSWORTH FW08
Chassis: aluminium alloy honeycomb monocoque. **Suspension:** Upper and lower wishbones with inboard springs activated by pull-rod at front. Upper and lower wishbones with inboard springs activated by rocker arm at rear. **Tyres:** Goodyear. **Engine:** Cosworth DFV V8, 2993 cc, developing 515 bhp at 11,300 rpm. **Gearbox:** Williams/Hewland FGB.

1983 WILLIAMS-COSWORTH FW08C
Chassis: aluminium alloy honeycomb monocoque. **Suspension:** Upper and lower wishbones with inboard springs activated by pull-rod at front. Upper and lower wishbones with inboard springs activated by rocker arm at rear. **Tyres:** Goodyear. **Engine:** Cosworth DFV V8, 2993 cc, developing 535 bhp at 11,300 rpm. **Gearbox:** Williams/Hewland FGB.

1983/84 WILLIAMS-HONDA FW09/FW09B
Chassis: aluminium alloy honeycomb monocoque with some non-stressed carbon-fibre internal panels. **Suspension:** Upper and lower wishbones with inboard springs activated by pull-rod at front. Upper and lower wishbones with inboard springs activated by rocker arm at rear. **Tyres:** Goodyear. **Engine:** Honda RA163-E, 1.5-litre twin turbo, developing 650 bhp at 12,000 rpm. **Gearbox:** Williams/Hewland.

1985 WILLIAMS-HONDA FW10/FW10B
Chassis: moulded carbon-fibre composite monocoque with aluminium internal bulkheads. **Suspension:** Upper and lower wishbones with inboard springs activated by push-rod at front. Upper and lower wishbones with inboard springs activated by rocker arm (FW10) or inboard springs activated by pull-rod at rear (FW10B). **Tyres:** Goodyear. **Engine:** Honda RA163-E, 1.5-litre twin turbo, developing 800 bhp (race boost) at 11,000 rpm. **Gearbox:** Williams/Hewland.

1986 WILLIAMS-HONDA FW11
Chassis: moulded carbon-fibre and Kevlar honeycomb monocoque with carbon-Kevlar internal bulkheads. **Suspension:** Upper and lower wishbones with inboard springs activated by push-rods front and rear. **Tyres:** Goodyear. **Engine:** Honda RA166-E, 1.5-litre twin turbo V6 developing 900 bhp (race boost) at over 11,000 rpm. **Gearbox:** Williams/Hewland.

1987 WILLIAMS-HONDA FW11B
Chassis: moulded carbon-fibre and Kevlar honeycomb monocoque with carbon-Kevlar internal bulkheads. **Suspension:** Upper and lower wishbones with inboard springs activated by push-rods front and rear. Reactive system used by winning car in Italian Grand Prix. **Tyres:** Goodyear. **Engine:** Honda RA166-E and RA167-G 1.5-litre twin turbo V6 developing 900 bhp at over 11,000 rpm. **Gearbox:** Williams/Hewland.

1988 WILLIAMS-JUDD FW12
Chassis: moulded carbon-fibre and Kevlar honeycomb monocoque with carbon-Kevlar internal bulkheads. **Suspension:** Computer controlled reactive system from start of season to British Grand Prix, thereafter double wishbones/push-rod activation of inboard springs. **Tyres:** Goodyear. **Engine:** Judd CV, 90-degree 3498 cc V8 developing 600 bhp at 11,200 rpm. **Gearbox:** Williams transverse.

1989 WILLIAMS-RENAULT FW12C
Chassis: moulded carbon-fibre and Kevlar honeycomb monocoque with carbon-Kevlar internal bulkheads. **Suspension:** Upper and lower wishbones with inboard springs activated by push-rods at front and by pull-rods at rear. **Tyres:** Goodyear. **Engine:** Renault RS01 67-degree 3500 cc V10, developing 650 bhp at over 11,000 rpm. **Gearbox:** Williams transverse.

1989/90 WILLIAMS-RENAULT FW13/FW13B

Chassis: moulded carbon-fibre and Kevlar honeycomb monocoque with carbon-Kevlar internal bulkheads. **Suspension:** Upper and lower wishbones with inboard springs activated by push-rods at front and by pull-rods at rear. **Tyres:** Goodyear. **Engine:** Renault RS01 67-degree 3500 cc V10, developing 630 bhp at over 11,000 rpm and RS2 developing 660 bhp at 12,800 rpm from mid season 1990. **Gearbox:** Williams transverse.

1991 WILLIAMS-RENAULT FW14

Chassis: Carbon Aramid epoxy composite, manufactured by Williams using Fiberite products. **Suspension:** Double wishbones activated by push-rods at front and rear. **Engine:** Renault RS3, 67-degree V10 developing 695bhp at 13,000rpm. **Tyres:** Goodyear. **Gearbox:** Six-speed Williams transverse, semi-automatic with electro-hydraulic gearchange activation.

INDEX